Empires of Entertainment

Empires of Entertainment

Media Industries and the Politics of Deregulation, 1980–1996

JENNIFER HOLT

RUTGERS UNIVERSITY PRESS

NEW BRUNSWICK, NEW JERSEY, AND LONDON

LIBRARY OF CONGRESS CATALOGING-IN-PUBLICATION DATA

Holt, Jennifer.
  Empires of entertainment : media industries and the politics of deregulation,
1980–1996 / Jennifer Holt.
      p.   cm.
  Includes bibliographical references and index.
  ISBN 978–0–8135–5052–7 (hardcover : alk. paper) — ISBN 978–0–8135–5053–4
(pbk. : alk. paper)
  1. Mass media—Ownership—United States. 2. Mass media—Economic aspects—
United States. 3. Broadcasting—Law and legislation—United States. 4. Telecom-
munication—Deregulation—United States. 5. Telecommunication policy—United
States. I. Title.
P96.E252U6345 2011
338.4'7302230973—dc22

                                                                            2010040705
                                                                                    CIP

A British Cataloging-in-Publication record for this book is available
from the British Library.

Visit our Web site: http://rutgerspress.rutgers.edu

Manufactured in the United States of America

CONTENTS

ACKNOWLEDGMENTS

I have had a great deal of help over the years to bring this across the finish line, and I owe many thanks for all of the contributions that have made this a better book. This project began at UCLA, where fellow grad students Marc Seigel, Jerry Mosher, Tim Halloran, Cecilia Hastings, Vincent Brook, Ruth Haldimann-Steinberg, and Rebecca Epstein offered valuable critiques in the early phase of this research. The UCLA faculty were especially supportive of my work throughout my time in Los Angeles. I remain grateful for the guidance and counsel of my committee, Steve Mamber, John Caldwell, Chon Noriega, and Douglas Kellner. I found a wonderful mentor and friend in Vivian Sobchack, lasting support from Janet Bergstrom, and pure generosity and continued inspiration from John Caldwell.

I was advised and influenced by many other outstanding scholars who took an interest in my work and helped to shape the form and substance of this manuscript. John Wiley, Jonathan Kuntz, Justin Wyatt, Denise Mann, Lisa Kernan, Robert Vianello, and Douglas Gomery all contributed their time, energy, and expertise while I was at UCLA. Thomas Schatz has been in my corner since my time at UT-Austin, and has always found time to work with me on this project. Tom has taught me all I know about conducting archival and industrial research, and has been the world's greatest mentor over many years. His many readings and detailed critiques of this manuscript in all forms have made me a better writer. I am also quite thankful to fellow UT grads Alisa Perren, Cynthia Meyers, and Megan Mullen. Alisa and Cynthia have been fantastic sounding boards for my work for many years, and Megan offered early drafts of her book chapters that were very helpful for perspective on cable history.

At UCSB, I won the lottery in supportive and brilliant colleagues. Every single person in the Film and Media Studies department has helped me with this project in their own unique way. I am so lucky to have landed here, with Edward Branigan, Chuck Wolfe, Constance Penley, Dick Hebdige, Janet Walker (mentor supreme), Anna Everett, Bhaskar Sarkar, Peter Bloom, Greg Siegel, Michael Curtin, Cristina Venegas, and Lisa Parks. Special thanks go to Greg for his editing, and to Lisa and Cristina for their true friendship and guidance that went well beyond the research and writing. Department guru Dana Welch helped me with scans and all things technological, Ethan Tussey provided outstanding research assistance, and Emily Carman was a great help when preparing the manuscript.

While writing, I received valuable awards from the Interdisciplinary Humanities Center and the Regents Junior Faculty Fellowship at UCSB. The Hellman Family Fellowship for untenured faculty also provided critical research funding at an important time. I am truly fortunate that these generous organizations chose to support my work.

The Antitrust Division at the Department of Justice in Washington, D.C., gave me all I needed (and more) to start this project; Janie Ingalls, Leona Johnson, and Attorney Bernard Hollander helped me identify, access, and process primary sources that were critical to the formulation of my argument. I am eternally grateful for their help in navigating the bureaucracy and government files that provided the backbone for this history. I am also very appreciative of the staff at the Ronald Reagan Presidential Library, where I received expert assistance finding archival materials.

I am sincerely grateful to Leslie Mitchner at Rutgers for believing in this project and shepherding the book through the publishing process with extraordinary focus and efficiency, and to Katie Keeran for administrative assistance. Rick Delaney made this book a better one with his masterful copyediting. Anonymous readers at Rutgers offered thoughtful comments on an early draft, as did Stephen Prince. Stephen's suggestions were especially helpful and improved the structure and quality of the book. Editors Ann Martin, Mark Jancovich, and Ron Rice worked with me on published articles about this topic, and this book has benefited from their expertise. I am also thankful to Matt Caldwell for the cover design.

There is no way I could have finished this project without the love and support of amazing friends. Rebecca Epstein, Miranda Banks, David Meyer, Kelly Goldberg, Jack Jason, Ryan Rayston, Chris Davies, Lana Saffrin, Amy Stein, Lisa Parks, Cristina Venegas, Lisa Hajjar, Winddance Twine, Alisa Perren, and Jacalyn Gross are all responsible in some way for this book getting done. I cannot thank them enough.

Lastly, I feel very lucky for my sturdy Chicago roots, my Southern connection, and lots of big love from little people in Portland. My family's constant belief in me has always helped me to believe in myself. My deepest gratitude goes to Denyse, Barry, Wava, Meredith, Matt, Mia, and Gracie. I dedicate this book to them.

JH
Santa Barbara, California
August 2010

Portions of chapter 4 were previously published as "In Deregulation We Trust: The Synergy of Politics and Industry in Reagan-Era Hollywood," *Film Quarterly* 55, no. 2 (Winter 2001–02): 22–29. The manuscript also contains portions of "The Age of the Conglomerate or How Six Companies Ate the New Hollywood," in *Media Ownership: Research and Regulation,* ed. Ronald Rice (Hampton Press, 2008) and *"It's Not Film, It's TV: Rethinking Industrial Identity,"* in *Jump Cut* no. 52 (Summer 2010).

Empires of Entertainment

Introduction

The Foundation of Empires

When discussing the perils of doing business in the modern media landscape, industry mogul Ted Turner once remarked, "You need to control everything. . . . The game's over when they break you up. But in the meantime, you play to win. And you know you've won when the government stops you."[1] "Winning," according to Turner's vision, is achieving a significant measure of market control and exploiting that to strategic advantage before forcing the hand of government regulators and enacting the inevitable corporate restructuring. Judging by the current political economy of entertainment, the game for the modern media industries is far from over. Just six conglomerates now dominate the global media marketplace, sharing the common traits of convergence, consolidation, and a major international presence along with the apparent drive to "control everything," and there are no signs that these companies will be reined in anytime soon.[2]

During the 1980s, Turner was one of the first in the industry to bring film, broadcast, and cable properties together under common ownership. He engineered his success with risky, aggressive acquisitions of content to enhance his growing roster of cable networks. He was able to do this in part because of widespread deregulation in the media industries; these policies worked in Turner's favor once he was part of a large corporation and, by his own admission, the success he found as an "independent" in the late 1960s and early 1970s could never be replicated by smaller players today.[3] That is because the rules of engagement—between media industries and government regulators—have been redefined since he started amassing television properties and building his own empire. The climate during the 1980s became one favoring consolidation within and across media, and paved the way for Turner's own path from running a billboard business and buying his first UHF station in Atlanta to becoming vice chairman of the largest media conglomerate in the world.

Turner's story is at the heart of the history of entertainment empires and their construction. It was at the outset of the Reagan era and shortly after Turner inaugurated his own storied rise in cable television that the political economy of the entertainment industry began a process of reconstruction and redefinition. At this time, the businesses of film, broadcast, and cable were largely separate and distinct. The studios, television networks, and cable companies were legally, strategically, and structurally disconnected. Regulatory constraints ensured that vertical integration (ownership of all phases of a business from production to distribution and sale, as with the classical Hollywood studio system) and, to a lesser degree, horizontal integration (ownership of multiple companies at the same stage in the supply chain, such as numerous cable networks) were pursued only with extreme caution, and in small measure.

Furthermore, these industries were fierce competitors, still largely operating independently of one another in the broader media landscape. Their rivalry led to many colorful exchanges in the press, in front of Congress, and in regulatory hearings as film, cable, and broadcast battled one another over the issues of media ownership and concentration throughout the 1980s and 1990s. Motion Picture Association of America (MPAA) President Jack Valenti was singularly eloquent in his contempt for the broadcast industry and their appeals for regulatory concessions, likening them in an appearance before Congress to "a scene out of Oliver Twist, the three networks, in baggy clothes, living among the homeless, tin cups in their calloused and scrawny fingers, crying out for 'more gruel, more gruel.' Frankly . . . there is no spectacle so ridiculous as the three networks in one of their periodic fits of desolating poverty."4

As the feuding between media industries intensified, the 1980s ushered in a period of pivotal transformation in the business of entertainment. While technologies such as home video, satellite delivery, and cable television redefined distribution and audience consumption practices, the media industries began a renewed period of global expansion and escalating costs. These changes had executives in all areas of entertainment scrambling to find new efficiencies of scale. At the same time, the interpretation of antitrust policy underwent significant changes and deregulatory policies became widespread; numerous legal and political confrontations ensued with the Department of Justice; and vertical integration made a remarkable comeback in the media industries after almost forty years of government-enforced exile. This time, however, vertical integration was not merely taking place *within* particular industries, such as the ownership of film studios, distributors, and theaters. Consolidation and integration in the new era were now being engineered *across* industries, gradually uniting film, cable, and broadcast properties with a number of distribution pipelines and exhibition outlets across a variety of media. The very concepts of vertical and horizontal integration were being reinterpreted, and conglomerates began to shift from risk management strategies of loose diversification (such as owning film studios and parking lots) to acquiring related businesses in the name of synergy and efficiency.

As the 1980s progressed, previous barriers between media industries began to break down; film studios combined with broadcast networks (Fox), production/distribution entities reunited with exhibition outlets (Universal, Paramount, Warner Bros.), and film companies merged with cable properties (Warner Bros., MCA/Universal, Columbia), thereby creating innovative alliances across formerly distinct industrial boundaries. It was a time of intense merger activity in film and television, and all of it took place with the blessing of the Department of Justice. By 1996, most of the major film studios and broadcast networks had become part of global conglomerates that encompassed some of the largest players in media and entertainment; the result was a handful of empires that controlled the most powerful and strategic interests in film, broadcast, publishing, cable, home video, music, merchandising, and theme parks.

One of the more profound implications of deregulation from 1980 to 1996 was the convergence of media industries. When explaining the complicated and layered processes of convergence, Henry Jenkins has used the term "economic convergence" to describe "the horizontal integration of the entertainment industry," which has resulted in corporate synergies driving cultural production.[5] I would propose the term "structural convergence" to describe the mergers taking place in the media industries from the mid-1980s onward—a mixture of vertical and horizontal integration *and* conglomeration. This label more accurately describes the shifts in political economy and regulatory policy that would make the subsequent mergers of Viacom/CBS (1999), AOL/Time Warner (2000), NBC/Universal (2004), and Comcast/NBC (2011) possible.

A new faith in the concept of synergy brought on most of the shifts that shook the media's industrial foundations during this time. The desire for synergy gripped the collective psyche of the entertainment business and took on enormous importance throughout the 1980s. The concept has been variably defined as "the commercial possibilities of mutually locking commercial ventures,"[6] "tight diversification,"[7] or "a belief that one plus one could equal three."[8] Former FCC Commissioner Nicholas Johnson has described it in far less flattering terms, calling it "the annihilation of competition."[9] In practice, synergy was the principle upon which media conglomerates were built during the 1980s and 1990s in order to exploit the rapidly imploding boundaries between film, television, and cable, and between various production, distribution, and exhibition outlets.[10] Subsequently, the media industries began instituting vertical and horizontal integration throughout the entire spectrum of visual entertainment, forcing a reevaluation of the concepts and uniting heretofore separate industries. Once these changes began taking place, a single company could control production through point of sale not just within, but also across media. The unchecked corporate power that spread across industrial lines created a media environment that was beneficial to private, not public interests. Whatever advantages these strategic alliances might have offered the consumer/audience were far outweighed by the diminished vitality, competition, and the anti-democratic nature endemic to such a concentrated marketplace. After all, the process of empire building in any context—ancient or modern, political or cultural—is about amassing power and centralizing control. Media executives and conglomerate architects were quite successful at both, usually by employing the discourse of synergy and convergence as rationales for building empires while obscuring the vast machinations of power behind their construction.

There was another type of synergy taking place during this era as well: between the entertainment business and the American political climate. Shifts in the interpretation and implementation of antitrust policy and media regulation, along with the many interconnected political and economic imperatives of the Reagan, Bush, and Clinton administrations, were intricately linked with the media industries' ability to merge and reorganize. Indeed, there were several developments that rendered Hollywood and Washington particularly responsive to and supportive of one another. Most significant was the fact that from 1981 to 1988, a former film actor and television star was residing in the White House, and he counted one of the most powerful men in Hollywood (Lew Wasserman, then-chairman of MCA and Reagan's longtime agent) as a close personal friend. President Reagan's connection to the film industry began when he was an actor under contract for Warner Bros. in the late 1930s. He was also a member of the Board of Directors and then president of the Screen Actors Guild in the 1940s and 1950s, and subsequent television star and host, most notably for *GE Theater* from 1954 to 1962.[11] His attachment to entertainment would ultimately serve the industry quite well. During a crucial moment for media deregulation in his first term, President Reagan intervened on behalf of the Hollywood studios—reneging on his commitment to keep the government's hands out of marketplace affairs in order to help his former colleagues. "Film is forever," he said at the fifty-third annual Academy Awards in 1981.[12] During his presidency, he certainly attempted to ensure that the film studios would remain healthy and endure, just like the pictures themselves—if not "forever," then at least for as long as he was in office.

During Reagan's presidency, there was also the increasing power of political action committees (PACs) in Washington, as well as a particularly active MPAA. The MPAA was the industry's primary trade organization and lobbyist, led by Jack Valenti, who had visions of global trade that were perfectly aligned with those emanating from the Oval Office. The Federal Communications Commission (FCC), Federal Trade Commission (FTC), Justice Department (DOJ), and, at times, even the Office of the President supported the deregulation and consolidation of the media industries between 1980 and 1996. This synergy between media and politics in turn helped to fuel a period of dramatic change and to create a history that has yet to be integrated and documented in chronological detail. *Empires of Entertainment* retrieves the many distinct elements of this history and delineates the key moments, players, and dynamics that enacted a monumental shift in the political economy of visual entertainment. This shift was as significant, if not more so, than the end of the studio era. Or, as Stephen Prince has characterized this moment for the media industries, it was "a point of transition that redefines all that follows and separates it from what has come before."[13]

Of course there is an array of colorful personalities, power brokers, and moguls animating this complex story, including Turner himself, Jack Valenti, News Corp. Chairman/CEO Rupert Murdoch, former Disney CEO Michael Eisner, former ABC, Paramount, and QVC executive Barry Diller, FCC Chairman Mark Fowler, TCI Chairman John Malone, Viacom Chairman Sumner Redstone, Time Warner creator Steve Ross, and President Ronald Reagan chief among them. Their impact on the trajectory of this history is undeniable, and the role of individual agency in its construction is certain. Yet the creation of empires involved a variety of stakeholders, interests, and agendas often in tension with one another. Therefore, while this book does recognize the role of various individuals, it is not meant to focus on the primacy of their agency or their "greatness." Rather, my intention is to highlight these individuals' significance as part of a complex dialogue and negotiation of forces that all combined for striking consequences in a relatively short time frame.

To chronicle the rise of entertainment empires at the end of the twentieth century requires that we look at significant moments and events through various perspectives—legal and regulatory as well as industrial, technological, personal, economic, and political. This book examines these often-disparate histories chronologically and conceptually, placing the dynamic birth of the global entertainment conglomerate in the context of a larger transformation in regulatory philosophy and industrial politics. Shifts in this philosophy and in the practice of antitrust and regulatory policy over the past four decades have had tremendous structural and industrial ramifications, essentially creating a political economy of media where empires of entertainment dominate the global landscape. In essence, this was a time that resembled a new "Gilded Age" for the entertainment industry—one that witnessed unprecedented growth, new developments, and economic expansion while spawning its own breed of "robber barons" in the form of media moguls. The media industries also benefited from the same laissez-faire government policies that companies and markets enjoyed in the late 1800s.

A regulatory climate favorable to industry consolidation was crucial to the formation of these empires, as was the politically dependent (re)interpretation of antitrust policy that occurred during the Reagan era and continued through the passage of the Telecommunications Act of 1996. Still, the dance of consolidation, concentration, and regulatory intervention was not an entirely smooth ride for those creating media conglomerates that would endure into the new millennium. In fact, the process was marked by inconsistency and even irregularity across industries, often prompting the questions: What constitutes enough concentration or too much market control? How are markets defined and regulated when their boundaries, products, dimensions, and delivery systems are always evolving? Is Turner's characterization of "victory" the only one, or are there other measures of success for conglomerates and regulators? To that end, at what point should media consolidation and the concentration of ownership be controlled by the government as opposed to market forces or corporate strategy? These questions have been the subject of much debate and negotiation, and scholars including Herbert Schiller, Ben Bagdikian, Eli Noam, Robert Horwitz, and Robert McChesney have brought these issues to the fore of scholarly and public discourse.[14] Nevertheless, as many of them discuss, the language of policy resists any clear or consistent answers. More to the point, the answers have been in constant flux, shifting alongside political winds and adjusting to the prevailing interpretations of industrial concentration and market competition.

This nexus of regulatory practice, politics, and media ownership is the core of this book, and is the foundation for the media industries' decades-long winning streak. These victories are tethered to politicized determinants of policy, and this focused study of the legal and regulatory histories of media conglomerates is an attempt to bring law and policy issues into the fold of humanities scholarship more directly. Law and policy have only been tangentially embraced by film and media studies, but they provide a rich and important foundation for the textually oriented concerns usually occupying the humanities. There is already a vital strand of media scholarship that has embraced legal research and policy analysis. Thomas Streeter, Lawrence Lessig, Mara Einstein, and Robert Horowitz, among others, have illuminated the ways in which law and regulatory policy immediately and directly inform production, distribution, consumption, and textual practice.[15] This book is part of that larger effort to envision a multi-dimensional and interdisciplinary history that opens up new areas of inquiry and evidence for the study of media industries, particularly in relation to conglomeration and deregulation in an era of convergence.

Empires of Entertainment is also part of the effort by media studies scholars to integrate the histories of media industries. Scholars such as Michele Hilmes,

William Kunz, Frederick Wasser, and Douglas Gomery have been among the contingent of media historians who have considered the film, broadcast, cable, and video industries in relation to one another.[16] Indeed, Michele Hilmes has written extensive arguments for trans-media histories, and also notes that "Convergence is not a new phenomenon; it is the very hallmark of modern media."[17] Examining these histories vis-à-vis one another *and* in relation to law and policy also creates a foundation for more explicitly politicized avenues of research—namely those taking place under the umbrellas of media advocacy/reform, media activism, and cultural policy.[18] With exceptions noted above, most media histories tend to consider these industries as separate subjects, thereby distorting regulatory, legal, and political economic histories that became increasingly interrelated. *Empires of Entertainment* argues that any industrial analysis, particularly those focused on more contemporary periods, must view film, cable, *and* broadcast history as integral pieces of the same puzzle, and parts of the same whole. Consequently, the questions animating this study and propelling this specific narrative are similarly integrated: How did Rupert Murdoch and Ted Turner exploit film properties to benefit the broadcast and cable industries? How did broadcast regulation impact the film industry? Why didn't the wages of synergy exact the same price—or create the same dividends—for Disney-ABC as they did for Time Warner? What was the effect of the Telecommunications Act on the film industry? The answers themselves are arguments for re-envisioning contemporary film, broadcast, and cable histories as no longer distinct but rather as fundamentally connected and contingent upon one another.

Antitrust Policy and Deregulation

The policy blueprints for these transformations in media industries are necessarily informed and enabled by larger shifts in antitrust law and regulatory philosophy. Antitrust laws in general are designed to promote fair competition and prevent monopolies; however, it has been widely noted by scholars and those in the legal profession that they are "among the least precise statutes enacted by Congress" and have consequently developed and changed along with current definitions of what constitutes competition, markets, and monopoly.[19] Indeed, antitrust is one of the most politicized forms of legislation, and has even been theorized as a "subcategory of ideology . . . a microcosm in which larger movements of our society are reflected and perhaps, in some small but significant way, reinforced or generated."[20] Further, as antitrust scholar Herbert Hovenkamp has explained, "Almost every political generation has abandoned the policy of its predecessors in favor of something new."[21] Thus, as the delicate task of defining "anticompetitive behavior" in business has cycled in tandem with the prevailing economic and political ideology, the entertainment industry has found itself on both the winning and losing ends of these various interpretations.

Antitrust regulation formally began in the nineteenth century. The Sherman Act, sometimes referred to as "the Magna Carta of the antitrust movement," established federal antitrust policy in 1890.[22] The legislation was a product of the Industrial Revolution and the public outcry over the burgeoning "trusts" dominating industry at the time. It was designed to combat the chokehold on business resulting from monopolistic practices like those employed by Rockefeller's Standard Oil Company. The main provision of the Sherman Act declared that "Every contract, combination in the form of trust or otherwise, or conspiracy, in restraint of trade or commerce among the several States, or with foreign nations, is hereby declared to be illegal."[23] Violations would generally be determined by the courts and sanctions enforced by the Department of Justice and/or the FTC.

The entertainment industry's rich and complex history with antitrust issues dates back to the earliest days of the silent film era, when the courts dismantled Edison's Motion Picture Patents Company (MPPC), also known as "The Trust." The MPPC was a casualty of President Woodrow Wilson's administration, with momentum from the trust-busting populism and progressivism embraced by Presidents Theodore Roosevelt and William Howard Taft. Wilson was committed to a strategy of fighting monopolies through legislation as opposed to using the courts to prosecute individual, high-profile violators of the Sherman Act. His administration oversaw passage of the Clayton Act, a 1914 amendment to the Sherman Act designed to enhance the law's protectionist powers.[24] This was the film industry's first encounter with the Clayton Act and it was not a happy outcome for Edison, and the Trust members, as this legislation was ultimately responsible for defeating the MPPC in the government's case.

Regulators during this era viewed vertical integration as harmful to the competitive health of an industry, and it remained under suspicion through the New Deal era for "increasing entry barriers and thus facilitating monopoly pricing."[25] It was this perspective that ultimately put an end to the Hollywood studio system, when the Supreme Court forced the five vertically integrated major film companies to divest their theater chains with the 1948 *Paramount* consent decrees (so named for the first defendant in the case of *U.S. v. Paramount Pictures Inc., et al*). *Paramount* was emblematic of an aggressive regulatory approach and remains the entertainment industry's most notorious antitrust case. The government's hostility toward large-scale industrial mergers continued for decades, and FTC Chair Robert Pitofsky has characterized the United States during the 1960s as having "the most vigorous antitrust enforcement in the world." That came to an end during the 1970s, when a much more relaxed approach to antitrust enforcement was ushered in alongside economic decline.[26] With President Richard Nixon and then President Jimmy Carter, a trend toward deregulation began, as did a new era of limited antitrust enforcement that would allow for levels of industrial concentration not seen since the early twentieth century. The media industries would be one of the many beneficiaries of this shift, as would telecommunications.

During the 1980s, President Reagan was especially intent on eliminating the use of antitrust enforcement as a means of regulating business, thereby helping the film, broadcast, and cable industries to begin their path toward structural convergence. His conservative, supply-side economic policies involved lowering taxes for investors, resorting to deficit spending, and instituting massive industrial deregulation. A pillar of his economic policy, this "regulatory reform" not only embraced the changes that had begun under Presidents Nixon, Ford, and Carter but significantly extended and expanded their scope. President Reagan translated the popular anti-government sentiment that had been rising throughout the 1970s into his own political mandate, famously joking that "the 10 most dangerous words in the English language are, 'Hi, I'm from the government, and I'm here to help.'"[27] This cloak of populism served as public relations for an aggressive deregulatory agenda, leading many to label deregulation as the "eleventh commandment" of his administration.

The principles guiding antitrust enforcement during his presidency were derived from the "Chicago School" approach. Named for the University of Chicago, where it was largely formulated, the Chicago School applies a single set of operational principles to a wide variety of industrial markets and contexts instead of considering markets on a case-by-case basis.[28] Chicago School theorists assert that markets operate the most efficiently (and most competitively) without regulatory interference, and their philosophy advocates minimal antitrust enforcement and is extremely tolerant of mergers and industry consolidation. The main argument of the Chicago School is that efficiency should be the only goal of the Sherman Act, and that such efficiency will only develop in business when the market is left alone. In other words, antitrust interventions merely hamper the process.[29] Though "free market" ideology was touted during the Reagan era as the only way to preserve true competition, it actually worked to stifle competition by allowing for higher degrees of market concentration and control. This inherent contradiction was at the heart of Chicago School philosophy and would play out in the drama of media industry consolidation throughout the 1980s and 1990s.

The Chicago School's theories were heavily informed by neo-classical economics and became increasingly influential on policy and regulation in the 1970s. They would continue to hold sway throughout the 1980s. It was a turn away from the "Harvard School," which dominated the courts in the 1950s and 1960s—an approach to antitrust that was relatively aggressive toward industry concentration, and focused on detailed case studies and industry-specific analysis. Unlike the Chicago School, which treated most industries exactly the same way, the Harvard School was idiosyncratic, and extremely particularized. It was emblematic of what occurred during the New Deal, when an enormous and varied antitrust apparatus was created. During the 1930s and 1940s, for example, government enforcement agencies such as the Department of Justice and the Federal Trade Commission did studies to determine particular antitrust policies and guidelines unique to each industry. Market-specific agencies were created (such as the FCC) and staffed by experts in the field in order to regulate each different business sector separately, according to their own needs. The underlying notion was that industries are fundamentally different from one another and they needed special rules exclusively applicable to their specific circumstances. The *Paramount* consent decrees were also fashioned in this manner, directed at what the government saw as excessive limits on competition specific to the motion picture business. This view of monopolies was left behind during the Reagan era, as were the consent decrees themselves (as detailed in chapter 4).

Concurrent with a shift in regulatory and judicial approaches to antitrust, there was a movement toward neoliberalism in prevailing political and economic orthodoxy. Neoliberalism advocated for deregulation and linked the principles of individual freedom to the practicalities of market freedom.[30] It placed great faith in market solutions to economic and social problems, and by the end of the 1980s, neoliberalism was the predominant philosophy guiding American political and economic policy. President Reagan himself was the chief proponent of "free market" capitalism, advocating for fewer trade and investment barriers abroad and ensuring the requisite lack of regulatory constraints at home necessary for his domestic policies to flourish. President Reagan's administration fully embraced this doctrine that minimized government's role in economic affairs and promoted a top-down imposition of increased transnational trade. Neoliberal policy, in addition to the worldwide expansion of communications and satellite technologies and the spread of capitalism at the end of the Cold War, all contributed to a great acceleration of global commerce—much of it emanating from the United States and increasingly deregulated. In fact, through a remarkable confluence of economic, technological, and political developments, there came to be three transformative, interconnected forces dominating industrial economics and, in turn, dictating the formation and construction of media empires by the end of the 1980s: globalization, deregulation, and market concentration.

President Reagan's agenda wholly embraced neoliberal ideals, leading antitrust analysts to describe the 1980s as being driven by "free market law and economics scholars" who provided "the theoretical underpinning for the policy of an administration that promised business to get government 'off its back.'"[31] This was enshrined into his administration's dogma in his first inaugural address, when Reagan declared "Government is not the solution to our problem; government is the problem." As former FTC chairman Robert Pitofsky has written, it is unlikely Reagan had antitrust in mind when offering this view, but the net result was that antitrust enforcement "virtually disappeared," effectively staging "a return to the period of neglect of the 1920s."[32]

Accordingly, President Reagan's economic policy was extremely lenient toward mergers, acquisitions, consolidation, and conglomerate growth. The view of his antitrust enforcers was that vertical integration was benign; it was a strategy promoting economic efficiency as opposed to encouraging anti-competitive behavior or restraint of trade, as charged by opponents of this philosophy. It has even been said that William Baxter, President Reagan's first assistant attorney general in charge of antitrust, changed both "the vocabulary and the central paradigm of antitrust," a change that was driven by the deregu-latory and free-market philosophies of the Chicago School.[33] As the scope of acceptable business practices expanded and the parameters of antitrust laws enforced by Baxter narrowed, the media industries were increasingly integrated and consolidated while most regulatory constraints on growth and competition were left by the wayside.[34]

Robert McChesney has explained that "[t]he centerpiece of neoliberal policies is invariably a call for commercial media and communication markets to be deregulated."[35] Therefore, it is important to understand deregulation in the Reagan era not as the mere absence of regulation but instead as the pres-ence of a politicized and carefully crafted government stance of support for the "free market" (which is itself a misnomer, as markets in the United States are subject to government intervention and/or control, i.e., no market is ever truly "free" in a developed economy). The administration's embrace of neoliberalism ultimately produced tremendous social inequities and concentrated wealth and power with a very small class of individuals and monopolistic corporations. And yet, it was precisely this shift in political and economic philosophy that enabled the media industries to merge and converge on such an unprecedented scale.

To be sure, film and broadcast have had a long history of mutual and strategic business interests, dating all the way back to the radio era. Chief among them was RCA, which owned the NBC network and also established the RKO film studio in 1929. Adolph Zukor was also buying up interest in the CBS network, even while his own studio (Paramount) and Warner Bros. were in merger talks. Paramount also had an unsuccessful fling with its own television network in 1949, building stations in Los Angeles and Chicago while investing in the DuMont network, and ABC had merged with Paramount's divested theater chain back in 1953, to offer just a few examples from previous years.[36] However, there had never been the *degree* of consolidation and integration across media industries—or the legal opportunity for such concentration—until the era of neoliberal ideology and deregulation that flowered in the 1980s.

The deregulatory trend during the Reagan era affected nearly all sectors of the economy; between 1981 and 1985, the Department of Justice challenged only twenty-eight mergers (out of thousands that took place every year) and throughout President Reagan's two terms in office, the federal agencies did not initiate a single case that challenged conglomerate or vertical transactions.[37] As business historian William Geisst noted, "Ignoring antitrust actions became a cornerstone of the Reagan administration."[38] Still, while a discernible trend certainly took hold during this time, there was not always a straightforward path to unbridled consolidation in the media industries. Indeed, the manner in which antitrust policy was applied and interpreted was somewhat contradictory and variable. This was especially true at the beginning of the Reagan administration when, for example, the Justice Department broke up (i.e., aggressively regulated) the telecommunications monopoly held by AT&T after seventy years, and also intervened repeatedly in the affairs of the film industry as the studios attempted to encroach on the growing business of cable television.

Despite this uneven progression, deregulation maintained its overall momentum and would ultimately define the relationship between the public and private sectors during this period. Thomas Streeter has argued that this trend was intrinsically linked to the privileging of economic principles (as opposed to more culturally based values, for example) in the policy arena—something also associated with the Chicago School. Streeter explains how "economic arguments about the inefficiency of regulation figured prominently in the deregulation of cable television, but once that deregulation was accomplished, economic arguments about cable's monopoly profits under deregulation were used to support the current regulation of cable."[39] The case of cable in the early 1980s (which will be discussed at length in chapters 1 and 2) is a prime example of the ways in which economic discourse in policy arenas was exploited for political and industrial agendas. Not only does this example point to the importance of economic language in policy decisions, but it is also a perfect illustration of the ironies and contradictions that often characterized de/regulation decisions during the 1980s.

Robert Britt Horwitz explains in *The Irony of Regulatory Reform* (1989) that deregulation incorporated a "surprisingly heterogeneous" political coalition that was aligned *against* continued government regulation. Both liberal and conservative groups attacked the regulatory status quo from their own ideological position. Left-leaning and public interest groups, according to Horwitz, "seeing in traditional regulatory agencies evidence of 'capture' by the very firms under regulation, came to advocate deregulation as a solution to entrenched corporate power."[40] Conservatives and free-market economists attacked regulatory agencies like the FCC for their vast bureaucracies "whose arbitrariness engendered economic inefficiency and artificial protectionism."[41]

Opposite sides of the political fence were strenuously arguing for the same end result, at least in theory. In practice, however, they would remain embattled throughout the 1980s.

After President Reagan, antitrust policy did grow more stringent—continuing the somewhat inconsistent ebb and flow of policy implementation. The antitrust division at the Department of Justice increased its investigations under Republican President George H. W. Bush. Throughout the Clinton administration, the pendulum continued to swing toward more government regulation, away from the traditionally conservative "hands off" approach to land somewhere near the center. The Clinton administration grew more activist in its prosecution of antitrust violations, especially during Clinton's second term—a position most evident in the DOJ's pursuit of the Microsoft case. Even though the court's order to break up Microsoft was eventually overturned and a settlement was reached in 2002, the antitrust enforcement under President Clinton certainly employed a more aggressive approach by the DOJ and the FTC than the previous administration. The Clinton administration also increased regulatory budgets and had more participation from state agencies in the pursuit of antitrust violations.[42]

Still, achieving complete coherence in antitrust enforcement has always been challenging. In addition to the vagaries of policy interpretation, the missions and administrative domains of the numerous government agencies and branches charged with regulating the media industries remain vast and disconnected. The Department of Justice (along with the FTC) has focused on issues of concentration, restraint of trade, and monopoly concerns. These bodies have conducted investigations, reviews, and oversight in the motion picture, music, radio, and broadcast television industries. The FCC oversees broadcast, cable, and telecommunications and regulates (among other things) licensing and ownership, technical standards, conduct, and content to varying degrees, while also protecting the "public interest" by maintaining appropriate levels of competition, diversity, and local character in broadcasting. Even Congress and the Supreme Court are involved with legislation and legal cases that have had significant regulatory impact on these industries. Currently, both the FCC and the Department of Justice review all telecommunications mergers. The Federal Trade Commission also has authority to review such mergers but rarely does, deferring instead to the Justice Department. Nevertheless, although these bodies are not coordinated, they have maintained a somewhat uniform, politicized approach to (de)regulating media industries, especially since the mid-1980s.

While each administration brings its own appointees to enforcement agencies, partisan politics are not always a reliable predictor of procedure in the regulatory arena. After all, it was the Department of Justice under Republican President Nixon that mandated the split of CBS and Viacom in 1970, while

Democratic President Clinton's more activist Department of Justice approved their reunion merger in 1999. However, since the days of the Reagan administration, the Department of Justice has often regarded consolidation in the media as benign—even beneficial to surviving in a competitive global marketplace. Even the FCC has capriciously bent its own rules in order to accommodate the changing parameters of the conglomerate structure. Moreover, some of the foundational principles of media regulation (such as localism, the public interest, diversity, competition) have become disconnected to marketplace realities. The public interest standard, for example, is based on the notion of the broadcast spectrum's scarcity, but new technologies and delivery systems have rendered this model inadequate. Further, the government has yet to successfully force broadcasters to value the public's interest above their own, rendering the vaunted phrase largely an empty rhetorical prop.

Just as there was some residual pro-regulatory initiative in the early years of the Reagan administration, there were lingering deregulatory impulses in the Clinton era—manifesting most notably the Telecommunications Act of 1996, which implemented massive deregulation of the telecommunications and cable industries. President Clinton signed this legislation into law on February 8, 1996, and it was the first major reform of the 1934 Communications Act. As Patricia Aufderheide has asserted, the Telecomm Act "rewrote the basic law that governs communications policy from top to bottom."[43] It also served to "wave the green flag at the convergence race" as one analyst explained, eliminating many ownership limits, cross-ownership barriers, and allowing the telecommunications and entertainment industries to begin cannibalizing each other.[44] This ironic twist in the politics of policy—a massive act of deregulation under a Democratic president—laid the foundation for the global media conglomerates of the new millennium.

The Business of Entertainment, 1980–1996

While antitrust and regulatory policies were being refashioned during the sixteen years between Reagan's election and Clinton's signing of the Telecomm Act, the media industries were concurrently undergoing tremendous change. The 1980s were a decade that saw corporate mergers and consolidation unfold on a staggering scale across the economic spectrum. After weathering a recession in the early 1980s, American business juggled corporate raiders, the stock market crash in 1987, and the hangover caused by a massive budget deficit. The media industries experienced concentration of ownership, fragmentation of markets, and the expansion of production, industrial economy, and global scope. The march toward conglomeration across media began in earnest. The business of entertainment was in various stages of upswing (cable), downslide (broadcast), and acceleration (film), but these industries would soon come together as integral components of media empires, ending their longstanding separation.

Throughout the 1970s, some of the country's highest profile corporations had invested in cable, including Time, Inc. (American Television and Communications Corp.), American Express (Warner Cable), and Getty Oil (ESPN). Often these same companies had ownership stakes in and across multiple sectors of the industry. For example, many programming services (channels) launched in the 1980s belonged to cable system operators (distributors). Time, Inc., for one, owned both ATC, the largest cable system operator in the country, and HBO, the dominant pay cable channel in the industry. Cable operators also funded channels such as The Discovery Channel, Bravo, Nick at Nite, and QVC.[45]

During the 1980s, the cable industry began a new phase of expansion. Regulatory policies started to catch up with marketplace realities, and the FCC finally allowed for the proliferation of cable technology into urban areas. Consequently, every aspect of the business expanded exponentially: operating systems, channel capacity, infrastructure, funding sources, programming, and subscribers. The financing for this expansion was largely through "high yield lending" or junk bonds, much of it engineered by Michael Milken and his firm Drexel, Burnham, Lambert, which was funding cable franchises at that time. According to an interview with longtime industry veteran and media analyst Paul Kagan, "there's no question that the construction of the new [cable] franchises in the 1980's that were given out in '79, '80, '81, would never have happened if Milken and Drexel hadn't have been there. The equity markets weren't ready for it, the bank markets weren't ready for it and there needed to be funding. The cable industry has long said that money will find the right place to be invested. We were it and that's what happened."[46]

The money had indeed found them and concentration became the order of the day quite rapidly. After struggling to get off the ground in the early part of the decade, by 1986–87 the cable industry was showing promise and profits. Multiple system operators (MSOs) began to consolidate, too, and that trend continued well into the 1990s. This was an era of immediate vertical and horizontal integration, as well as unprecedented growth for the cable industry.

Not so for broadcast television, which was experiencing a steep decline. Between 1981 and 1991, the three major networks saw their numbers slide from an average rating of 50 down to 33.9. Cable would continue to wreak havoc on the broadcast industry throughout the 1990s as well: by 1996 the networks only earned a combined average rating of 26.9.[47] Broadcast networks that tried to bolster their competitive positions and enter cable early on met with very little success, and initial attempts at synergy and structural convergence between broadcast and cable failed. CBS Cable, a cultural channel, was launched with much fanfare in 1981, only to lose $30 million and shut down in less than one year.[48] ABC had similar disappointments, especially with its Satellite News Channel designed to compete with CNN.[49]

The film industry, meanwhile, was experiencing ups and downs of its own, but the 1980s would ultimately be an incredibly lucrative time for American cinema. At the dawn of the decade, the "New Hollywood" was in full swing. Commonly used in reference to the post-1975 (*Jaws*) period, this term is usually invoked to describe the U.S. film industry when a specific "economic and institutional structure, mode of production and . . . system of narrative conventions" solidified around one product: the calculated blockbuster.[50] The industry's devotion to the blockbuster initially made the business rather unstable. The well-documented *Heaven's Gate* fiasco that nearly sank United Artists in 1981 was an ominous example of the enormous risks associated with big-budget filmmaking and the increased volatility of Hollywood's business model—especially in the early part of the decade. After all, the film cost over $50 million and took in just over $12,000 in its initial theatrical run.[51] Even though *Heaven's Gate* was not conceived of as a big-budget blockbuster from the start (it was originally budgeted at just over $7 million), it stood as a cautionary tale for decades, and demonstrated that one big-budget film gone wrong could actually bring down an entire studio. Kirk Kerkorian's MGM bought UA shortly thereafter.

Thus, the early 1980s were a bit of a struggle for the major studios, largely due to their inability to control escalating costs and their failure to realize any significant new growth or revenue streams during this time. The film industry gradually began an accelerated production pace that took hold in the latter part of the decade. Soon, ancillary revenues took off and by 1985, they had risen to over 50 percent of the industry's income, and domestic theatrical revenue had dropped to 36 percent.[52] By 1986, home video had become the film industry's chief revenue source, providing distributors with about $2 billion annually and outstripping theatrical revenues ($1.6 billion) for the first time.[53] Television grew much more important to the film business and contrary to the dire predictions circulating in the press, cable and home video were not the end of cinema. Rather in many ways, they were its salvation. As Tino Balio has described, new technologies and ancillary markets actually "stimulated demand for more motion pictures, spread the risk of production financing, and enhanced the value of film libraries," all of which led to a resurgence in the economic health of the film industry.[54]

The performance of the independent sector of production and distribution helped keep numbers up. The major studios were only making roughly one-third of the total films each year, with independents accounting for the rest. Thanks largely to the expansion in independent production and investment from Wall Street, the number of releases had skyrocketed by 1989—there were 501 films released, the most since 1942. Throughout the 1990s this figure would rise and fall, but by 1996, the number of total releases was up to 471 films.[55] This was definitely a boom era for film production, with budgets, releases, admissions, ancillary revenues, and profits all on an overall upward trend.

Disney, Paramount, and Warner Bros. had the biggest success stories of this era. After Michael Eisner and Jeffrey Katzenberg left Paramount to lead Disney in 1984 with Frank Wells, Disney experienced a renaissance and a winning streak no other company could touch. The only one that came close was Warner Bros., and these two studios dominated the box office and market share every single year from 1991 to 1996. The rest of the field was mixed: Twentieth Century–Fox staged a comeback under Australian mogul Rupert Murdoch that took hold at the end of the 1980s, while MGM/UA was eventually reduced to a mere skeleton of its former self. MGM lost executives along with its market share and almost the entire studio, thanks to the *Heaven's Gate* disaster and the breakup of assets during numerous ownership changes. Columbia also fell prey to management problems, going through three chairmen in four years between 1984 and 1988, including David Puttnam, who brought the company many headaches from his well-publicized battles with the studio's parent company Coca-Cola and numerous other Hollywood power brokers.

While the media industries have always looked abroad for a portion of their income, the focus on the international market was amplified during the 1980s and 1990s, as were global revenues. Thanks to worldwide economic expansion, technological advances (especially in relation to distribution), the proliferation of multiplexes, newly opened markets, and the unyielding efforts of the studios to capitalize on these conditions, U.S. film grew even more dominant in the global landscape of entertainment during this period. As communism fell across Europe and American entertainment continued to spread, journalist Carl Bernstein summed the situation up in *Time* magazine: "The Evil Empire has fallen. The Leisure Empire strikes back."[56] In this new media geopolitics, Hollywood was the undisputed superpower.

By the 1990s, there was also a decidedly international character to the ownership of American media, particularly film studios. Rupert Murdoch's News Corporation bought Twentieth Century–Fox in 1985, Sony purchased Columbia and Tri-Star in 1989, MGM was taken over by Pathé in 1990 (and later, Credit Lyonnais), and Matsushita bought MCA Universal the same year. This meant that *half* of the major American film studios were in foreign hands. Paramount and Disney were the only film studios not to change ownership during this decade, while large multinational media corporations bought all the rest. At the same time that foreign companies were taking over the major studios, the international markets for their products were exploding, making domestic film and studio libraries more valuable than ever.

Merger mania had in fact arrived for all of the media industries half-way through the 1980s, with the first big wave appearing in 1985. Thanks to liberalized ownership restrictions in broadcast, there was a rash of buyouts, mergers, and station takeovers. Station groups were bought, sold, and consolidated at unprecedented rates and all three networks changed ownership by 1986. Cable companies continued vertically and horizontally integrating, and film studios went on a buying binge and accumulated the same percentage of first-run theaters that they had owned in the pre-*Paramount* Decree days. The trend was so striking that it seemed, as one analyst put it, like the biggest media companies all "went to dinner in 1985 and ate each other."[57]

A second wave of mergers took place between 1989 and 1990. As Thomas Schatz has described, 1989 (the year President Reagan left office) was a watershed year for media-related takeovers; there were 414 deals struck, totaling over $42 billion, the most notable of which were the Time-Warner merger ($14 billion) and Sony's acquisition of Columbia and CBS Records ($5.4 billion).[58] The sale of MCA to Matsushita a year later added to the tally and the end of the decade turned out to be another landmark in media consolidation. A third wave took place in 1994–1995, as the last remaining regulations separating film studios and broadcast networks fell away, cross-ownership rules were dismantled, and the door was open for the deregulated telecommunications industry to join the global media conglomerates. By the time the Telecommunications Act was signed in 1996, all six major film studios, almost all of the broadcast networks, and most of the highest-rated cable channels were part of media empires that did not exist just sixteen years earlier.[59]

From Premiere to Comcast-NBC

This book offers a chronological, transindustrial narrative that addresses the ways in which philosophical and ideological shifts in policy impacted the media industries individually and in relation to one another. The boundaries of the study are the two ends of the regulatory spectrum during this period: the 1980 battle between the film industry and the Department of Justice over HBO that enforced a separation between the film and cable industries for the last time; and the passage of the Telecommunications Act in 1996, which allowed for the merging of film, cable, telecommunications, and broadcast interests under one conglomerate roof. While this structure may appear to present a linear trajectory, the individual chapters reveal a much more nuanced and chaotic journey toward deregulation and structural convergence, as there were many contradictory forces and stakeholders contributing to this complex history.

For example, early confrontations between cable services and major film studios over expansion and merging across industrial boundaries definitely echoed a more rigidly regulated era. As described in chapter 1, "Film versus Cable," the decade's initial showdown began when the Hollywood film studios appealed to the Department of Justice to investigate HBO's business practices, which the majors claimed were monopolistic. Not only did the Justice Department refuse to halt the development of HBO, it chose to file a lawsuit against four studios instead (Paramount, Universal, Twentieth Century–Fox, and Columbia) in order to block their attempt to create Premiere, a major cable distributor. Furthermore, the Justice Department also prevented Paramount and Universal from buying Showtime and merging it with The Movie Channel, claiming that it would create vertical integration in the rapidly transforming media marketplace. This conflict over the major studios' attempts to create or control a competitive cable distribution service illustrates the pervasive resistance and suspicion that the government still had at this time regarding media consolidation emanating from the film industry. This resistance to transindustrial mergers and consolidation would soon be a distant memory, however, as regulatory philosophy began to shift and new attempts at structural convergence resumed in earnest.

The focus in chapter 2, "Broadcast and the Blueprints of Empire," is the establishment of Tri-Star in 1983, the attendant pronounced change in the federal government's position on vertical integration and monopolistic practices, and the renewed life given to the Financial Interest and Syndication Rules (fin-syn) in broadcast. At issue is the evolving relationship between film, cable, and broadcast in the early 1980s, which was prominently on display as Tri-Star was born. The new studio was a partnership of HBO, Columbia, and CBS. It was a vertically integrated, instant major given the go-ahead by the Department of Justice. This chapter focuses on the creation of a new film company, but given the principal players, the aftermarket dreams, and the significance of television to the success of the studio, the implications transcend traditional media boundaries. That same year, President Reagan intervened with the FCC's plans to eliminate fin-syn, and the rules remained in place. This meant that, much to the delight of the film industry, the broadcast networks would not be able to own their prime-time programming. The major film studios would therefore continue to supply the bulk of television programming without having to face competition from the networks. Through close examination of these two major developments, this chapter illuminates the highly politicized, fundamental contradictions in the deregulatory process and the ways in which the interplay of different media industries affected the implementation of policy (and vice versa).

Looking at Rupert Murdoch and Ted Turner's strategic combinations, chapter 3 discusses how the lack of uniform regulation across media allowed new visions of industry partnerships and consolidation to flourish. By 1984, the Hollywood studios had begun inching toward a new conglomerate era by capitalizing on the DOJ's growing tolerance of mergers and enacting new strategic alliances with the cable industry. As the major studios amassed ownership stakes in the growing medium, Fox and MGM/UA remained notable exceptions, albeit with distinctly different corporate models. However, their outsider status would soon change and these two companies would play a pivotal role in redesigning the political economy of entertainment. As part of their opening act in Hollywood, Turner and Murdoch would use the film assets of the two companies to reinvent what "television holdings" could mean for film studios; in the process, they consolidated and integrated media industries while modernizing the relationship between film, broadcast, and cable—all while evading regulatory constraints that pinned the rest of the major players to blueprints of corporate design conceived in and for a previous era.

At the same time that Turner and Murdoch were uniting media industries, the major film studios were revisiting their golden years and once again purchasing prime theaters across the country. Chapter 4's focus on the "Golden Era Redux" looks primarily at the vertical re-integration of the film industry. The chapter details how the *Paramount* Decrees were quietly transformed from an iron fist wielded by the federal government into a façade of non-enforcement embraced by the studios. Most important was the manner in which that façade solidified the studios' power while keeping potential government intervention at bay. In turn, Hollywood's vertically integrated corporate structure, once the subject of intense government scrutiny and antitrust litigation, was reestablished for the first time after almost four decades, not only with the endorsement but also with the assistance of the federal courts and ultimately President Reagan's Department of Justice. Consequently, 1986 was a watershed year in the march toward a new conglomerate era. The film industry went on a theater-buying binge led by Universal, Columbia Pictures, Tri-Star, Paramount, and Warner Bros. Chapter 4 looks at this underexplored and often misunderstood development by examining the political dynamics, legal cases, corporate restructuring, and shifting industrial economy that returned the Hollywood studios to a state of vertical integration from 1986 to 1988. This includes the informal abrogation of the *Paramount* Consent Decrees, the purchase of theaters by five major studio parent companies, as well as the purchase of production and distribution entities by exhibitor Cineplex Odeon.

Chapter 5, "Big Media without Frontiers," concentrates on 1989 through 1992 and the further integration of the cable and film industries, beginning with the merger of Time, Inc. and Warner Bros. This combination kicked off an unprecedented year for media consolidation and the second big merger wave of the 1980s, while also creating the world's largest entertainment empire. With Time Warner's more focused combination of assets and expansive potential for their cross-promotion, a new model for global media conglomerates was established. By the end of the 1980s, it was clear that the decade-long tide of deregulation had swept in an entirely new relationship between the entertainment industry and government regulators and, along with it, a new paradigm in political economy. This chapter details a particularly intense four-year period, beginning with the birth of the world's largest entertainment conglomerate and ending with the re-regulation of cable in 1992. The creation of Time Warner, combined with the impact of the 1992 Cable Act, the progressive deregulation in broadcast, and the incorporation of global ownership and expanded markets into the film industry's paradigm rendered 1989–1992 one of the most dramatic periods in this brief history of deregulation.

Yet the mergers and conglomeration that followed the Time Warner deal made the 1980s look quiet and uneventful by comparison. After a period of stunning expansion in the global arena, the media industries started making more news on the domestic front when the repeal of fin-syn was enacted in 1995. Once film and broadcast were allowed to join forces and unite under common ownership, the final and most intense phase of empire building began. Chapter 6, "The Last Mile," covers these developments alongside the push from telecommunications companies to grab a stake of the media business by way of the cable industry. Although there were still conflicts over allowing the "telcos" in to the entertainment markets, new combinations of major film studios, cable properties, and broadcast networks demonstrated that the deregulation of media industries had moved far beyond its 1980s parameters.

Still, the politics of convergence kept everyone crying out for "more gruel, more gruel," as new inter-conglomerate turf wars erupted. Cable grew significantly more important to the profiles of media conglomerates, broadcast weathered decades of struggle in the face of more cable competition, and the film industry lost control of their business model, as production and marketing costs spiraled upward with no end in sight. At the same time, telephone companies slowly began the long-awaited process of entering the video delivery business, even as activists and media reformers staged numerous protests against the seemingly endless pace of media consolidation. As former FCC Chairman Reed Hundt once remarked, "Détente is not what the Telecommunications Act of 1996 was supposed to be about."[60] Indeed, the Telecomm Act unleashed another era of structural convergence that created brand new power struggles in the media industries. The book concludes with a look at these current struggles, the uncertain future of these industries, and the policy challenges facing a culture dominated by empires of entertainment.

1

1980–1983

Film versus Cable

The path to fully integrated empires of entertainment first wound through the cable industry, via the film studios. At the outset of the Reagan era, distinct and well-regulated borders kept media industries mostly separate from one another. Because of the Financial Interest and Syndication Rules (fin-syn) and cross-ownership regulations dating back to 1970, broadcast networks and film studios were not allowed to own one another, and broadcast networks were also prohibited from owning cable systems. Therefore, a blueprint for structural convergence would begin with deals between film and cable. This was not a simple or straightforward process; both film and broadcast were very wary of and hostile toward the potentially threatening cable industry during this period. Three decades later, cable properties would become the entertainment empire's royal family, the main profit centers and arguably the salvation of media conglomerates. In the late 1970s, however, cable was still a fledgling interloper that the film and broadcast industries were determined to wrestle to the ground and either take over or litigate into submission.

Deregulating Early Cable

Despite the fact that cable technology had already been in use for decades, Congress and regulatory agencies had only started fostering development and expansion in the cable industry during the 1970s. A variety of government and private foundation studies, including the Sloan Commission Report (1971), were commissioned in the late 1960s and the 1970s to determine how to best regulate cable and adapt this new communications technology and civic resource.[1] The Sloan commission primarily advocated for a more deregulatory approach toward the new medium, often in the name of "the public interest." While the Sloan Commission recognized that cable was beginning to be perceived of as "a threat" to "conventional television," the report promised that cable was actually a "television of abundance" that was "no threat to the power of the total television system."[2] The report did have mixed recommendations and saw the need to regulate the size of distributors, but overall, the Sloan Commission was in favor of allowing cable technology, infrastructure, and programming to expand and grow. It was a prominent early signal of shifting regulatory perspectives and new possibilities for the cable industry.

In light of this and other recommendations, as well as a slow turning in attitudes at the FCC, cable finally got a reprieve in the mid-1970s from policies that had grown increasingly restrictive over the previous decade. The respite from heavy regulation was uneven, localized, and quite slow to develop, but overall, the industry began transitioning into a deregulatory period. Under Presidents Nixon, Ford, and, to a greater extent, Carter, many of the binding restraints on the cable and communications industries were slowly lifted. Over the next few years, political roadblocks related to satellite competition would also be removed, changing cable's outlook and options dramatically. Everything from restricting the programs that pay-television networks were allowed to carry, to preventing the use of satellites and limiting licenses was reexamined with the goal to increase competition in the industry. This made cable more attractive *and* more threatening to film and broadcast.

An early report by Clay Whitehead, the first head of the White House Office of Telecommunications Policy under President Nixon, signaled the government's desire to encourage growth and market-based competition in the cable industry. In 1974, Whitehead submitted a series of recommendations to the president for regulating cable television. They were deregulatory in most respects, and advised, among other things, that no restrictions be placed on cross-media ownership (such as broadcast networks owning cable systems) or multiple ownership of cable systems, and that programming content and pricing be totally exempt from government regulation. The idea was to change the regulatory paradigm from one emulating over-the-air broadcasting and governed by the 1934 Communications Act to one based on print, entitled to First Amendment protections enjoyed by newspapers, magazines, and books. Whitehead's report argued that "cable may never become what it can become if it continues to be constrained by the policy of the Communications Act."[3] The committee wanted cable to be treated as a brand new medium, "not merely an extension or improvement of broadcast television," and as such, brand new policy was required to liberate cable's potential.[4] The committee concluded "that programming, advertising and other information and services on cable channels can be allowed to develop on a free and competitive basis, with no more regulatory power exercised over the content of this communications medium than is exercised over the print or film media."[5]

At the same time that it was advocating for a hands-off approach, the report also recommended that the government get involved and disallow the common ownership of cable systems and programming, or, in other words, separate cable's content from its distribution. "At the heart of the Committee's recommendations," the report highlighted, "is a proposed policy that would separate control of the cable medium from control of the messages on it. The goal of this policy is to assure the development of cable as a communications medium open to all, free of both excessive concentrations of private power and undue government control."[6] This early but very significant report set the tone for what would follow in cable policy: an approach that was predominantly deregulatory, hands-off, and extremely tolerant of consolidation but at the same time, slow to shift paradigms and often inconsistent. Further, the goal to keep cable free of "excessive concentrations of private power" was either abandoned, or simply a failure, almost from the start. Still, the recommendations were similar to those controlling film and broadcast in that these media industries were forced to keep the ownership of content production and distribution separate at this point in time.[7] While Congress did not adopt the recommendations in this report per se (many cable systems acquired ownership interests in programming almost immediately), the government did advance a supportive agenda for cable's growth in this early period and the industry took full advantage while they could.

The separation of content and distribution would have been extremely disruptive for two major players in cable at the time: Time, Inc. and Warner Communications, Inc. (parent company of Warner Bros. studio). These companies had been busy integrating both cable programming and distribution assets into their portfolios for decades. Time owned cable systems since the 1960s and programming services since the 1970s, with a stake in the first underground urban cable system in America (Sterling Manhattan Cable in lower Manhattan) and the first major satellite movie channel, Home Box Office. Warners was also heavily invested in cable systems and channels (in addition to filmed entertainment), and CEO Steve Ross increasingly turned his focus, interest, and finances toward cable during the 1970s. Warner Communications was soon one of the largest cable system owners in the United States. After American Express purchased half of the WCI cable holdings in 1979 to form Warner-Amex Cable, the company developed many innovative cable properties, including QUBE (an interactive cable service that was many years ahead of its time), Nickelodeon, and MTV in addition to The Movie Channel. WCI was the only conglomerate to have such significant interests in film *and* cable, placing Ross and the company well in front of the pack and definitely among the most forward-thinking in the business when it came to expanding the Warners empire across media platforms.

Ross even went to see Whitehead about the issues raised in the 1974 report, as the only studio executive who was actively against the kind of regulation separating content from cable systems promoted by the committee's recommendations. The other studios would have been happy to see cable at a disadvantage of any kind, particularly when it came to distributors owning content. Although the meeting did not amount to much, Whitehead characterized Ross as ahead of the rest, remarking that he was "trying to figure out where the industry was going—in a much more farsighted, strategic way than anyone else."[8] Indeed, Ross's vision would ultimately be the one guiding the trajectory of media industry consolidation through the next two decades, but there were significant hurdles to overcome first—regulatory and otherwise.

The first of these hurdles was a series of crucial confrontations between the film studios, HBO, and the Department of Justice (DOJ) over the concepts of antitrust and vertical integration as they related to the cable industry. The transindustrial battle over pay-cable, as it was known at the time (referring to premium services or "movie channels"), ushered in a decade of power struggles, further consolidation, and dramatic mergers in and across media industries. The initial antagonism between the film studios and premium cable channels also drew the battle lines for the ensuing conflicts that pit the two industries against one another as the construction of entertainment empires got under way.

The studios fired the first shot when they appealed to the Department of Justice in 1979 for an investigation of HBO's business practices. The film companies claimed that HBO was behaving monopolistically, and they sought to have federal regulators scrutinize the channel for antitrust violations. Much to their surprise, the Justice Department not only refused to stem the development of HBO, but they turned around and sued the *studios* instead, for attempting to create their own cable distributor. The Justice Department intervened in the film industry's plans once again in 1983 when the studios attempted to enter the pay-cable business through another series of mergers and acquisitions. From the government's perspective, what was at stake here was more than merely industrial growth or market expansion; it was the very definition of various entertainment "markets" being formulated at this time. As Jill Hills has argued in her study of telecommunications and empire, it was during this time that "regulatory definitions of markets became political constructs created to benefit new stakeholders seizing the opportunity of new technologies."[9] These definitions and politicized decisions would shape the immediate future of regulation for home video and pay-cable, and because the markets were initially interpreted narrowly, the convergence of media industries was controlled and somewhat restrained for the first few years. By aggressively and actively policing studio involvement in the cable marketplace, the DOJ also forestalled the consolidation of the major film, television, and cable companies for the time being.

This chapter examines two early instances of film's incursion into the cable industry with the cases of Premiere and Showtime. Principally, these first conflicts over the major studios' attempts to create or control a competitive cable distribution service illustrate the government's tremendous suspicion of the film industry when it came to matters of competition and vertical integration. After all, the DOJ pursued antitrust action against the film studios twice in three years for their attempts to establish pay-TV channels/services that would compete with the dominance of HBO. There was a definitive separation between the two markets of pay-television and theatrical film, and HBO benefited from this distinction and their perceived "outsider" status in relation to the major studios at this point in time. It is also clear from these early incidents that a stricter, less tolerant interpretation of antitrust policy still maintained a prominent grip on the courts at the start of the 1980s. The striking difference between the enforcement agencies and their approach to antitrust under President Carter as opposed to under President Reagan is abundantly clear from looking at these two cases. This inherent, fundamental shift in regulatory philosophy would become the single most important factor in determining the industrial blueprint of media industries as the decade unfolded.

The Rise of HBO

The relaxation of regulatory constraints in tandem with the launch of the new RCA communications satellite SATCOM I spurred tremendous growth in cable television beginning in 1975. In September of that year, HBO was the television industry's first client for SATCOM I and this new method of distribution put HBO on the map as the dominant force in pay-cable service; within two years, the channel was available on 262 cable systems across the country.[10] Additionally, in March 1977, HBO won a lawsuit against the FCC when the US Court of Appeals struck down FCC rules that essentially protected commercial television broadcasters while restraining cable companies.[11] This decision gave cable television greater First Amendment protection and served to strengthen numerous other cases for the cable industry as the business attempted to expand and leave behind the excessive government restrictions that limited its growth. By 1979, the amount of programming and networks being distributed by SATCOM I had increased significantly; among the numerous services on the satellite were Ted Turner's superstation WTBS, Showtime, Pat Robertson's Christian Broadcasting Network, C-SPAN, ESPN, and Nickelodeon.

The release of two FCC studies in 1979—the Syndicated Exclusivity Report and the Economic Inquiry Report—was another boon to the cable industry. Initiated by Chairman Charles Ferris, who was in fact pursuing a deregulatory agenda even before his successor Mark Fowler, these studies concluded that cable television did not seriously threaten local broadcasting or the public interest. Essentially, the findings eliminated the basis for most of the restrictions and regulations that had developed over the previous two decades and led to the repeal of many remaining federal limitations on the industry. Ferris had also announced his renewed commitment to regulation by market forces—as opposed to FCC mandates—when he proclaimed that on his watch, the FCC would be "allowing new technologies and new entrepreneurs to achieve the potential that burdensome regulation denied them in a previous era."[12] The result was serious growth in programming and a charge by cable operators into new urban markets.

Consequently, by 1980 cable was beginning its ascent, and although less than 10 percent of television homes were pay-television subscribers, basic cable households would more than double from 17.5 million in 1980 to 35.4 million in 1985.[13] Channels ranging from Turner's Superstation TBS (1976); ESPN, C-SPAN, and Nickelodeon (1979); CNN, BET, USA, and Bravo (1980); MTV (1981) and The Weather Channel (1982) had begun to broaden the menu for subscribers, while HBO was the undisputed pioneer and leader in premium channels. After creating a unique, satellite-fed nationwide network in 1975, HBO's sales grew exponentially every year. In August 1980, there were approximately 7.7 million subscribers to pay-TV in the country, being served by 4,200 cable systems. HBO had over half of those and was spreading rapidly; by the end of 1980, HBO had about 6 million subscribers, accounting for 69 percent of the pay-cable market at the time. In the summer of 1980, HBO's programming got a higher share rating than CBS, NBC, or ABC for the first time in its short history.[14]

Meanwhile, two other satellite networks had arrived to challenge HBO's dominance: Showtime and The Movie Channel. Showtime had 1.4 million subscribers, 16 percent of all pay-cable subscribers, by the end of 1980. Teleprompter (a major multiple systems operator, or MSO) and Viacom co-owned Showtime from 1979 to 1982, at which time Viacom took complete ownership. Viacom was a major program syndicator and supplier as well as a growing MSO/cable provider. At the time, Viacom also owned television stations, radio stations, and cable franchises in the United States and was a global syndicator of American television shows. Furthermore, Viacom's cable system was the tenth largest in the United States by 1982 with 600,000 subscribers.[15] The Movie Channel was co-owned by Warner Communications, Inc., and American Express. It was the brainchild of Warner Bros. CEO Steve Ross and was initially introduced as the Star Channel.[16] It had a much slower start than HBO, primarily because it was not on a satellite until 1979, four years after HBO uplinked.[17] It only represented about 5–6 percent of the pay-cable pie with 460,000 subscribers.

These competing services were both part of vertically integrated entertainment companies. Warner Communications and Viacom produced, distributed, and exhibited programming—often for cable systems that they owned themselves. While the film industry was troubled by this growth, it was HBO and its complete market dominance that most upset the studios. Industry executives were incensed by what they perceived to be the service's monopoly and monopsony power in the network program service market. (Monopsony power relates to the power of one buyer over many sellers; it is the power created when a buyer of a product purchases such a large percentage of a producer's output that the buyer can effectively control the price paid.) HBO had so much power over the studios from its unique position in the pay-TV market that it was able to negotiate extremely favorable contracts for Hollywood product and command "artificially low prices," as the studios saw it.[18] According to industry analyst Harold Vogel, by 1981, HBO had surpassed the large theater chains and had become the studios' largest customer, licensing over $130 million of studio product that year alone.[19] As the president of HBO noted, they bought "virtually every movie made in Hollywood."[20]

Furthermore, the cable channel was becoming an increasingly large part of the financing puzzle for new and largely independent film production as well. By the early 1980s, HBO was spending $250 million to finance Hollywood films.[21] In fact, HBO was also leveraging this production financing for more control over the films, which angered the studios even further. Their multiple roles in the industry at this time led HBO Chairman Gerald Levin to profess in 1983, "HBO is now the largest purchaser of motion picture rights in the world. But it is not simply a pay TV network anymore. It's kind of a new style merchant bank."[22] Levin was referring to the practice of pre-selling rights upfront—basically promising exclusive rights to air the film for a specified period in exchange for money that increasingly went to fund the production itself. Pre-selling television rights (cable and broadcast) as an alternative means of financing filmmaking grew very popular in the early 1980s. While HBO was an excellent source of such funding, their dominance in this market worked to steadily shut the major studios out of the fastest growing source of revenue in the film industry. This is because the upfront payments from pre-sales—while limiting risk at the beginning—diminished the long-term payments when they were negotiated in advance of theatrical release, particularly for a big hit.[23] As journalist Thomas Whiteside has written, this practice "tended to undermine the control that big studios had traditionally exercised over the whole chain of film distribution."[24] Michele Hilmes has similarly argued in her study of pay-cable history that "HBO's increasing involvement in film financing affected the studios' hegemony in the field."[25] In general, pre-sales were a boost for independent producers, although they also grew more dependent on HBO. It was a practice that ultimately upset the balance of power between the major film studios and the burgeoning pay-cable industry.

MPAA President Jack Valenti began leveling charges of monopoly at HBO back in 1977, and further complaints finally led to a Justice Department investigation in 1979.[26] The studios' tremendous dissatisfaction with the growing power of HBO, their own inability to break into cable distribution, and the shrinking returns for their films sold to HBO is what ultimately led them to appeal to the DOJ for an investigation. "They have declared war on the studios," claimed then-chief of Paramount Barry Diller.[27] Diller's hyperbolic reaction was typical of the anxiety unleashed by HBO in Hollywood. "If we don't stop them, they will control all aspects of moviemaking," he continued. "There would be no reason for studios to exist."[28] Internal memoranda from the files of Paramount (used as evidence in the government's case) revealed that there was a persistent and pervasive unhappiness and hostility throughout the film industry over the "disproportionate amount of money being retained by the cable operators and programming companies," particularly HBO.[29] As opposed to the forty-five cents on each box-office dollar retained by the studios for every film they distributed in the theaters, the studios only got twenty cents on the dollar paid by each HBO subscriber (with HBO keeping 25 percent of the subscription fee and local cable operators getting the balance).[30]

It was clear that the studios wanted to knock HBO out of the driver's seat and have more power over the pricing and distribution of their product in cable television. HBO was now the middleman, negotiating the relationship between the studios' product and the audience for their product on cable. The rivalry between the studios and the cable service was escalating, and film executives detailed their disgust with HBO's arrogance to anyone with a press credential. HBO executive vice president Michael Fuchs told reporters that he considered that a compliment, given the way the studios had conducted business over the years.[31] When the appeal to the Justice Department did not amount to anything, the studios decided to adopt a new strategy, since their other attempts to conquer this new industry had thus far failed.

Premiere

Inevitably, the Hollywood studios started actively attempting to take some ownership in the pay-cable business since it was now a buyers' market, and the buyer-seller relationship was growing increasingly hostile. Cable regulations were beginning to loosen and HBO was making healthy profits; naturally, the studios wanted to form their own pay-cable service and capture a piece of that market. Of course, they also wanted to slow down HBO. As one analyst noted, "[I]f your biggest customer is becoming bigger than you, you have to go into his business."[32]

Paramount, MCA/Universal, Twentieth Century–Fox, and Columbia thus began developing plans for a new pay television channel in late 1979. The result was the establishment of "Premiere," which would allow the studios to distribute their own films exclusively to their own pay cable outlet. Warner Bros. already had its own deal in the early stages of development (see "Showtime/The Movie Channel" section) and United Artists was concerned about antitrust problems and decided not to participate.[33] With the goals of increasing revenues and gaining tighter control over the pricing and distribution of feature films in pay television, the remaining four major producers created a joint venture in April 1980.

In partnership with the Getty Oil Corporation, the studios planned to launch the satellite-fed program service on January 1, 1981. Getty Oil already owned cable programming after backing the launch of ESPN in 1979. While the studios were each bringing films and $2.5 million in cash to the table, Getty was the principal financier in the company, committing to $30 million.[34] Additionally, and perhaps equally as important, Getty Oil provided access to satellite space. The dearth of obtainable transponder space on existing satellites was a big problem at this stage in cable's development; RCA's SATCOM I, the satellite primarily used for transmission of programming to cable systems, was in tremendous demand and several different programmers had to share space on the twenty-one transponders available. Thanks to its involvement with ESPN, Getty had open space to lease.[35]

The studios' plan was to pool their resources and launch a pay-cable movie network that primarily showcased their own films in the channel's evening-only programming. They also devised a nine-month "window" during which the films contributed by the partners would be available to Premiere *only*, and all other networks (such as HBO) would have to wait for that window to expire in order to license any Universal, Paramount, Columbia, or Fox films. In the meantime, the Premiere partners agreed not to do any business with HBO or Showtime—holding back their films with the idea to release them first on Premiere.[36] This nine-month window was a critical element of Premiere's strategy and was their means of differentiating the service as well as a component that the participants considered absolutely essential to their taking part in the deal.[37]

On the surface, Premiere seemed like a viable, exciting prospect. Armed with a savvy business plan, secured funding, and satellite space, and a marketplace ripe for their services, the studios were ready to begin amassing their share of the pay-cable business. Unfortunately for the studios (and much to the delight of HBO), Premiere's timing would prove to be the crucial misstep. With the Carter administration's antitrust division still at work, attitudes toward the film industry and prevailing interpretations of antitrust statutes were not yet driven by the neoliberal economic philosophy that would guide regulatory practice once President Reagan was in office.

Consequently, the government was not yet inclined to look favorably upon their expansion into another media industry.

Additionally, HBO and Showtime were rallying regulators to their side; they asserted that Premiere was in violation of antitrust law and began concertedly appealing to the DOJ to take action.[38] It worked, and in August 1980, Premiere was dealt a crushing blow when the Justice Department filed a civil suit to prevent the channel from going on the air. The government was trying to shut the service down just three months after the studios announced its formation, claiming that the Premiere agreement was anticompetitive and in violation of antitrust statutes. The original complaint filed on August 4, 1980, alleged that the agreement establishing Premiere constituted price-fixing and a group boycott, both in violation of Section 1 of the Sherman Act. The government argued that Premiere would basically be operating as a cartel, and moved for a preliminary injunction on August 15, 1980, to halt the network's development.

The court's concern over the film industry's foray into this new and rapidly expanding market was evident throughout the case rhetoric and decision. Pay-TV was growing fast and the judge noted the importance of this moment and this case in his opinion, stating that it would determine who could partake of the enormous revenues associated with the pay-cable enterprise.[39] The thrust of the government's case was that the four studio defendants (Columbia, Fox, MCA, and Paramount) were entering into an anticompetitive agreement, based primarily on the nine-month distribution window. The argument focused at first on the size and strength of the studios involved, as their combined market power was formidable. The partners were responsible for distributing some of the biggest box office hits of the previous two years, including *Close Encounters of the Third Kind*, *The China Syndrome*, and *Kramer vs. Kramer* (Columbia); *All That Jazz*, *Alien*, and *Norma Rae* (Fox); *Heaven Can Wait*, *Star Trek*, and *Grease* (Paramount); and MCA/Universal's *Animal House*, *The Jerk*, and *Jaws 2*.

Furthermore, HBO looked to the Premiere partner studios for 33 percent of its product and Showtime licensed 44 percent of its programming from the same studios.[40] Yet, the court noted that although the pay television network services obtained only one-third of their movies from the defendants, they spent a disproportionate amount—over one-half of their budget—for film rentals on these pictures.[41] This was an apparent indication that high prices were a measure of the power and popularity enjoyed by these producer/distributors and their films. After all, in 1980 alone, nine of the year's top-ten grossing films were produced/distributed by Premiere's partners.[42] However, this reliance on their own products began to look dangerously like anticompetitive behavior.

According to legal analysts, the service was also quite vulnerable to charges that it constituted a group boycott because of Premiere's promise to its subscribers that they could get films produced by Fox, Paramount, Universal, and Columbia nine months prior to their exhibition on HBO or Showtime.[43] The original complaint notes that Premiere's rival network program services, such as HBO, Showtime, and The Movie Channel, would be unable to exhibit such films as *Kramer vs. Kramer*, *Coal Miner's Daughter*, *Friday the 13th*, *Star Trek*, or any other recent success produced by the defendants until at least nine months after they were made available to Premiere.[44] Attorneys for the DOJ called the deal an unlawful contract that had the defendants engaging in conspiracy and restraint of trade, activity that could potentially fix prices, restrain competition, and establish a boycott of network services other than Premiere.[45]

Between November 20 and December 8, 1980, the court conducted an evidentiary hearing with testimony from representatives on all sides of the issue, including Premiere's principal partners, other cable program services, producers and distributors, industry witnesses, and economic experts. The defendants contended that there was substantial vertical integration in the market already and that the largest MSOs had already integrated backward from distribution/exhibition into ownership of cable program services (as opposed to going from producers to distributors and/or exhibitors).[46]

This argument involves the very fluid and contested terrain of defining "the market" in question, the main issue upon which most battles in this area hinged and the one that would have enormous impact on future media mergers and activities. According to court documents, the government economists viewed the relevant market as a single chain of distribution:

film producers → film distributors → cable networks → cable operators → consumer

Economists for the studios, on the other hand, viewed this chain as two separate markets:

1) film producers → distributors → cable networks
   and
2) cable networks→ cable operators → consumer

Vertical integration would be much harder to prove or establish using the government's definition, as it was a much longer and expansive chain of buyers and sellers in the "market." Markets are frequently revised and/or redefined based on the demands and goals of a particular argument, and in this case, the government was trying to prove that the pay cable market was currently operating *without* the barriers to entry characteristic of vertical integration, and that Premiere would be ushering those restraints into this market for the first time.

On December 31, 1980—less than four months after the deal was announced and just three days before Premiere was scheduled to begin service—a preliminary injunction was issued that restrained the channel from going on the air, and the launch was abandoned. The court sided with the government and concluded that the exclusive nine-month window was more than an incentive for new subscribers, but was also a "drastic restraint" that created unfair competitive advantage in the marketplace. This window would effectively, according to the court, "withdraw from the network program services other than Premiere about one-half of the most desirable first-run films."[47]

It was also determined that Premiere's pricing mechanism was anticompetitive and potentially subject to manipulation by the participating studios. This "boycott" of other services for the nine-month period would likely drive up prices in the industry, the court reasoned, and these increases would eventually be passed on to the consumer. Additionally, the judge reasoned that if Premiere were allowed to continue, the effects could be damaging to HBO and devastating to Showtime and The Movie Channel, perhaps even putting them out of business. The judge delivered a ruling that privileged or protected the largest and most established players in the pay-cable business, referring to "the harm Premiere would probably cause the existing pay television industry" and the "disastrous" effects that the service could have on the cable market.[48] Consequently, the preliminary injunction was ordered to prevent such harm and "irreparable alteration of the marketplace."

In so doing, the judge attributed more gravity and importance to the potential for monopolistic conduct than to the potential for competition introduced by Premiere. He agreed with the prosecution and asserted that there was "virtually no complete vertical integration" in the market under consideration.[49] However, Warner Bros. was indeed already vertically integrated in cable—a fact that the opinion even mentioned, despite the contradiction. Warner Communications, Inc. owned Warner Bros., The Movie Channel—a joint venture with American Express—and they were also partners with American Express in Warner Amex Cable, the nations' fifth largest MSO at the time.[50] Additionally, the opinion noted further vertical integration in that Time, Inc.—which owned HBO—also owned American Television and Communications Corporation (ATC), the nation's second largest MSO, and Manhattan Cable Television.[51]

Furthermore, at the time Showtime was co-owned by Teleprompter and Viacom, the nation's largest and seventh largest MSOs, respectively. Together, they had ownership interests in 149 cable systems with 1.7 million basic subscribers and over 600,000 pay-cable subscribers. Showtime had 1.4 million subscribers at the end of 1980, one-third of which were Viacom or Teleprompter customers.[52] Thus, all of these companies (Time, Inc., Warners, Teleprompter, and Viacom) were functioning as producer/distributors and exhibitors, as they were creating programming for the marketplace with a guaranteed safety net in the form of their cable systems that were hungry for new product.

The judge also conceded that HBO had obtained affiliations with large cable systems by using volume discounts and that certain business practices (such as exclusive licensing and selective purchasing tactics) "do suggest the exercise of monopoly or monopsony power."[53] This did not seem to trouble the court, however, as the judge reasoned that "it is to be expected that the first entrant in the industry would have a substantial head start and that new entrants would have some catching up to do."[54] The court concluded that there seemed to be no shortage of those willing to take that risk.

Ironically, all of these examples point to the fact that the market was indeed well on its way to being a vertically integrated oligopoly (many—especially the major film studios—argued that it was already there), but this time the players were not just the usual Hollywood suspects. Now, the MSO's and large corporations such as Time, Inc. were involved and even benefiting from the studios' history and reputation for corruption. It was Time, Inc. that owned the largest pay-TV channel (HBO) and the largest cable system operator in the country (ATC). According to cable historian Megan Mullen, "[b]y 1980, Time already was more vertically integrated than any of the Hollywood studios had been since the 1948 consent decree."[55] Yet, the studios could not escape the stigma of their previous track record; Judge Gerald L. Goettel himself compared the nine-month window to the illegal practice of "clearances"[56] banned by the court in the *Paramount* case, noting that historical "joint attempts to control the initial issue of motion pictures have already been condemned . . . [in cases] ironically, involving some of the same defendants as in the [present case]."[57] Apparently the film industry would be forced to continue paying for their sins of the studio era with the sacrifice of Premiere.

The Justice Department's actions are also indicative of how crucial HBO was to the cable economy at the time as the cornerstone of the entire pay-TV market and a tremendously important source of revenue to cable operators. As Michele Hilmes has noted, Premiere threatened HBO's power and strength, which in turn threatened the health of the entire cable industry. "If HBO were to be weakened seriously by Premiere's corner on product," Hilmes explained, "cable operators unable to receive Premiere—for reasons of channel space or lack of appropriate satellite hardware—would lose subscribers."[58] The government was not willing to jeopardize such a burgeoning commercial force.

Still, the Premiere partners filed a reply with the U.S. Court of Appeals in February 1981, but the court upheld the earlier order; thus, on January 28, 1982, Judge Goettel officially dissolved the joint venture. As it was conceived and delivered into the world on the wrong side of the law and on the losing end of the antitrust battle, the studios chose to just drop the deal. The five companies involved lost over $20 million as a result of the lawsuit,[59] while pay cable subscriptions increased over 100 percent in the two years that the drama played out in court—from 8.9 million in 1980 to 20.6 million in 1982.[60] Adding insult to injury, the following year HBO named its new original programming division "HBO Premiere Films."

The court's ruling preserved HBO as the single most powerful player in pay-cable and kept the studios from getting their foot in the door of that market, at least until the formation of Tri-Star in 1983. This decision also maintained a vision of the marketplace that relied upon increasingly anachronistic definitions of the film and video industries. Although these lines blurred considerably by the end of the decade as markets bled into and fed off of one another for survival, federal regulators staunchly preserved the age-old demarcations and boundaries at this point. Attempting to maintain or respect the same market definitions, regulatory approaches, and industrial hierarchies that had been in place for the previous twenty years would prove to be impossible for the government in light of the shifts in technology, converging entertainment forms, and media usage. The new regulatory paradigms based on Chicago School economic philosophies embraced by the Reagan administration also presented the Justice Department with a new mandate before long. Nevertheless, the studios were still determined to break into the cable business while the government remained steadfastly opposed to them doing so. Another confrontation was brewing over these two industries merging and it would play out once again in the arena of pay-cable, but this time it was focused on HBO's other competition.

Showtime/The Movie Channel

In 1983, the Justice Department was investigating the Hollywood studios once again on potential violations of antitrust statutes related to their activity in the cable industry. This time, it was because of the studios' involvement in the impending merger of HBO's two primary competitors in pay-TV: Showtime and The Movie Channel. Although the film industry was left out in the cold by the failure of Premiere, the major studios remained determined to break into the pay-cable business. They just needed to find—or create—the open door they needed. Not surprisingly, they quickly began knocking out new walls to create their entryway into the market.

It was at this time that Columbia, Fox, and ABC had negotiated to buy a majority interest in Showtime in an attempt to break into cable distribution and loosen HBO's iron grip. But, at the last minute in late November 1982, Columbia decided to back out. It soon became clear that something big was going to materialize from their outside negotiations with HBO. And indeed, after Thanksgiving meetings between Columbia's chairman Faye Vincent Jr., Time's chairman J. Richard Munro, and CBS chairman Thomas Wyman, Columbia decided to work out an entirely separate deal. They renegotiated a long-term renewal of their pre-sale contract and, more significantly, entered into an alliance with HBO and CBS to form a new studio, Tri-Star (detailed in chapter 2). The Columbia executives had been presented with an offer they apparently couldn't refuse, igniting the fury of their jilted Showtime partners as well as the disdain of the Hollywood community for joining forces with HBO while the company was such a thorn in the side of the film industry.

The next proposal that entailed significant structural convergence was for a five-way merger that would link three major film studios and four cable giants to form one powerhouse pay-TV service, launching an all-out assault on HBO's unrivaled position in the field. Announced in January 1983, the plan entailed the participation of MCA, Inc. (parent company of Universal Studios), Warner Bros., and Paramount Pictures buying into a partnership deal with Viacom that essentially had Showtime purchasing The Movie Channel and merging into a new combined channel. Paramount, MCA, Warners, and Viacom (parent company of Showtime) would each own 22.58 percent of the new service and American Express would own 9.68 percent.[61] Initially, Showtime had been courted to join the attempt to form Premiere back in 1979. However, no agreement was reached because, according to court documents, Showtime's owners were concerned about the antitrust implications of an agreement with numerous film studios.[62]

Once this Showtime deal was made public, the DOJ and Anti-Trust Division chief William Baxter began a four-month investigation, extending their traditional first look at mergers by ninety days. HBO was up to 12 million subscribers by this point and extremely lucrative—its revenues for 1982 were roughly $500 million and it was Time, Inc.'s fastest growing division.[63] The service also accounted for 24 percent of Time's overall profits.[64] Profits were something neither Showtime (with 4 million subscribers and just breaking even on $192 million in estimated revenues) nor The Movie Channel (2.3 million subscribers and still in the red) could boast yet.[65]

The deal would have created a combined subscriber base of about 6.3 million, just about half of HBO's subscribers. The participants in the Showtime/Movie Channel deal argued that the merger would actually help competition because it would strengthen the second- and third-place services against the supremacy of HBO. Their position was that they could mount a stronger challenge to the quasi-monopoly of HBO as one channel as opposed to two individual companies. Attempting to avoid the pitfalls of the Premiere case, the business plan put tremendous emphasis on the fact that the service would take films on a non-exclusive basis and there would not be any special exhibition window in place for films produced by the participating studios. Nevertheless, the players in this deal still presented a major problem from an antitrust standpoint and government was unhappy with the terms. It was rumored early on that the merger would have problems getting the DOJ's blessing.

Representatives from Showtime met with the Justice Department to try and find a way to save the deal, arguing that the merger would help *strengthen* competition in the pay-TV industry, but the DOJ refused—ultimately, they found the proposed combination too big and too potentially powerful.[66] And, despite an eleventh hour presentation to Chief of Anti-Trust Baxter by the participants in the plan, on June 10, 1983, the Justice Department announced that they would indeed file a civil antitrust suit to block the proposed merger. The deal was sounding alarms because of the numerous dimensions and directions of consolidation that it involved: a horizontal merger between pay-TV services, a horizontal merger between film studios, and vertical merger between film studios and pay-TV services.

Just six months earlier, the Justice Department's antitrust division released updated government standards for judging the legality of mergers and industry concentration.[67] As defined by the 1982 Merger Guidelines, horizontal mergers in general were more problematic and more likely to create "competitive problems" than vertical ones.[68] The guidelines stressed, as Lawrence White has noted, that "a vertical merger should have antitrust significance only if it has *horizontal* consequences in one or more markets."[69] The DOJ thus focused on such consequences in their case, reasoning that a horizontal merger between pay-TV services (Showtime and The Movie Channel) could threaten the nature of competition when selling these channels to cable systems and to subscribers. They also asserted that the merging of two of the country's three largest pay-TV services could inhibit competition in the sale of their programs to cable systems.

A horizontal merger between major film studios was also a serious sticking point. The DOJ was concerned that the three studios could use their collective power to control the pricing structure of fees charged to cable services for licensing films and in turn, also create a barrier to entry for new companies. In their argument, the Justice Department primarily reasoned that the joint ownership by MCA, Paramount, and Warners could greatly reduce the competition between and among those studios and studios in general, especially in relation to licensing films for exhibition on cable.

However, with the involvement of MCA, Paramount, and Warner Bros., the merger took on a horizontal character and kept growing, expanding even beyond this dimension. Because of the studio participation, there were also elements of vertical integration, since their production capacities in film would be linked with the distribution/exhibition elements of the pay-TV services. The Justice Department noted this problem and reasoned that a vertical merger between studios and pay-TV services could have threatened competition in terms of supply and demand; buying programming for the joint Showtime/Movie Channel and/or selling MCA, Paramount, or Warners product to other pay-TV services would have been in danger of becoming compromised or anti-competitive at a critical state in the industry's development. Accordingly, most of their objections were focused on the horizontal implications of this arrangement, as dictated by the 1982 Guidelines.

It is important to remember that both Viacom (Showtime's parent company) and Warner Bros. already operated local cable systems at the time. Warner Amex alone owned approximately 120 cable systems with 665,000 subscribers.[70] This added another element of vertical integration—involving the merger of studios and pay channels with MSOs. As a result, this element of vertical integration had more severe, transindustrial consequences than merely those involving cable channels, which were the most troubling element to the Justice Department. Strangely, even with all of these concerns on the table, the government still did not acknowledge the fact that competition in the pay-cable industry was *already* inhibited. HBO had 53 percent of the market at the time, and Time, Inc.'s other pay cable channel, Cinemax, had about 9 percent of the market. With a combined share of almost two thirds of all pay-TV viewing in the country, they dwarfed Showtime—the nearest competitor with 18 percent of the market—and the Movie Channel, which only had 13 percent.[71] Moreover, in addition to HBO's interest in Tri-Star pictures and Silver Screen Partners, the company had acquired "exclusive pay-TV rights to an estimated 1/3 of all theatrical films in production" in 1983.[72] HBO's parent company, Time, Inc., also owned the country's second-largest cable system provider, American Television and Communications, not to mention many influential news and entertainment magazines that could directly (or indirectly) promote HBO and its programming or investments.

Again, the definition of the "market" was the key component to both sides' arguments. The 1982 Merger Guidelines (which did not speak of "industry" concentration at all, but instead of "market" concentration, a concept that was easier to redefine in order to suit the purpose/argument at hand) said that the appropriate market includes "those products that the merging firm's customers view as good substitutes at prevailing prices."[73] However, this characterization is purposefully vague and demands the crucial step of explicitly defining the parameters of any industry or market before determining the degree of concentration.

The studios thus maintained, "the marketplace was broadly defined as the home entertainment market, including broadcast television, pay television and video cassettes."[74] This looser, more expansive view of the market would certainly allow the studios greater leeway in combining their resources, conducting collaborative activities, and entering into mergers/acquisitions before arriving at any type of structural concentration or collusive behavior that could be considered anticompetitive; the bigger and broader the market, the less concentrated it is, even when consolidation takes place. Additionally, the attorneys for the Showtime–Movie Channel partners were arguing that the "market" for *entertainment product* was much broader than the government had characterized it to be. They contended that the attraction of the services was more than merely theatrical films, but it extended to any type of "first-run, network-quality programming," thus widening the product market and lessening the importance of the film studios in this context.

Unfortunately for these partners, the Justice Department's conceptualization of the market in question was much more narrow—limited only to the pay-television industry. This was directly opposed to the manner in which the "market" was defined by the government in their suit against Premiere two years earlier; in that case, the studios, cable networks, *and* cable distributors were all lumped into a single market in order to demonstrate the threat that Premiere's consolidation would pose to such "wide-open" competition. Nevertheless, the DOJ now found that the Showtime–Movie Channel deal had too many horizontal consequences in relation to the specific pay-TV market alone to be approved. Ironically, the fact that there were significant vertical arrangements that would have impacted the market just as much—if not more so—was not a chief concern.

Still, there was an increasing urgency and awareness among studios about the necessity for integrating first run motion picture exhibition with the various other markets for entertainment, regardless of their legal definitions. This synthesis was especially applicable to cable television. Domestic theatrical was still the most important venue, as it would determine the value of the film in all other markets—home video, foreign exhibition, syndication, and cable. As one studio executive noted, "not to have a piece of the action in those other markets you've helped create just doesn't make a whole lot of sense."[75] Consequently, Warners, Paramount, and MCA came up with a new proposal for the DOJ to consider that, they believed, would eliminate the government's antitrust concerns with the merger. The proposal provided numerous assurances about their business conduct, namely that the studios would not license their own films on an exclusive basis to the new channel, that they would license their films to other pay-cable services at the same rates that they charged Showtime/The Movie Channel, and that they would exhibit films from studios not involved in the merger. Legal counsel for the studios met with William Baxter in Washington, D.C., to present this new proposal and, they hoped, to prevent the impending lawsuit.

Nevertheless, again on July 28, 1983, the DOJ issued a statement declaring that regardless of these promises, the department would move forward with its civil antitrust suit to block the proposed joint venture. The concern over price-fixing and barriers to entry presented by the participation of three of the biggest film studios in the industry was its primary motivation. The department was also worried that "such a combination would increase the incentives and abilities of motion picture distributors (possibly including distributors not associated with the service) to increase the price at which they license their motion pictures to pay television."[76]

Still, while Baxter's Antitrust Division refused to allow the merger, they did leave the door open for potential approval in case the deal was restructured. Although the new Merger Guidelines were much more focused on the potential problems arising from horizontal mergers as opposed to vertical ones, the Justice Department was still committed to challenging any mergers that threatened a competitive marketplace. In its estimation, this merger of major studios and pay-TV companies would do just that by virtue of the collusive arrangements that might arise between production and distribution/exhibition. This regulatory approach would change, and rather quickly, but at this point in the decade there was still significant government intervention in the mergers and acquisitions of media industries.

Even after the DOJ had rejected the proposed merger *twice*, Showtime and The Movie Channel remained determined to join forces against their nemesis, HBO. Shortly thereafter, the two cable companies revised their plan and proposed to unite under their present ownership alone and leave their partners from the film industry out of it. With that, the Justice Department finally relented and announced on August 12, 1983—after MCA and Paramount withdrew as partners—that the government would not challenge this restructured company. Warner Bros. remained as the sole film studio involved in the deal because of its partnership with American Express in Warner-Amex. As it was reconceived, the plan would be a radically different one from its original incarnation. Warner Amex and Viacom would be the main partners, each owning 50 percent of the combined Showtime and Movie Channel services. In early September, the transaction was completed and the government closed its investigation on November 10, 1983.[77]

The two studios that withdrew from this partnership, MCA and Paramount, had also been defendants in the Premiere case. Interestingly, they had found their way into cable ownership shortly after that debacle in 1981 when MCA, Paramount, and Time, Inc. became co-owners of the USA Cable Network. USA was a basic cable network seen in 10 million homes, shown on 1,600 cable systems by satellite feed. It is one of the many inconsistencies in the history of media regulation that the studios were not able to partner with Showtime or other studios to challenge HBO, yet they were allowed to combine with HBO's parent company to create a new basic cable network.[78]

One of the most significant aspects of these cases taken collectively is the manner in which they force a reevaluation of the deregulatory characterization often blanketing "the 1980s" both in and outside the media industries. Neoliberal philosophy would soon hold sway over policy decisions, but this transformation was neither instant nor unilateral. In fact, it was at this very moment that the government broke up the monopoly enjoyed by AT&T for seventy years. In 1982, the antitrust lawsuit that the Justice Department began eight years earlier finally resulted in the dismantling of the world's largest and most successful telecommunications network. AT&T and its twenty-two local subsidiaries were restructured into one long-distance company (AT&T) and seven regional local carriers (what became known as the "Baby Bells") effective January 1, 1984. This Justice Department victory would be regulation's last hurrah for some time, as the Reagan administration would bring a new approach to antitrust rooted in the market-based solutions embraced by the Chicago School and its adherents. There was immense pressure on the DOJ to drop the AT&T suit, but the case had too much momentum at this point, not to mention the time and resources invested, to simply be dropped. On the same day that the Reagan administration finished with AT&T, they also settled a longstanding antitrust suit against IBM. Essentially, William Baxter dropped the IBM case after thirteen years because it no longer had merit, according to the new administration. That was a decision that spoke more to the future of regulatory practice during the Reagan Era than either the Premiere or Showtime rulings (or, for that matter, the AT&T settlement).

Cable and Early Empires

Although it was the feature film and its audience that helped to fuel the initial explosion of "pay-cable," the major film producers—notoriously savvy about controlling distribution—were originally shut out of this all-important profit center. This was quite unfortunate for the studios, as they were facing some difficult times. The cost of producing a feature length film had soared from $9.3 million in 1980 to $11.8 million by 1982 (an increase of 25 percent in just two years), and marketing added another $4 million to the price as the box office was going through a wave of instability.[79] The studios needed to establish a foothold in this new distribution market, but the government was not yet ready to cooperate.

In 1983, however, Paramount entered into a five-year distribution agreement with Showtime/TMC that was hailed by Viacom as "the most important product acquisition agreement in pay-TV history."[80] Viacom touted the deal to its shareholders, explaining that the company would have exclusive national pay TV service rights to Paramount's theatrical releases over the next five years, as well as to recent blockbuster titles such as *Flashdance* (1983), *Terms of Endearment* (1983), *Trading Places* (1983), and *Staying Alive* (1983). Interestingly, the $500 million agreement was the realization of exclusive licensing practices—the very same kind that broke the deal for Premiere. Such exclusive deals would soon become commonplace in the industry; by the end of the 1980s, Fox, Warner Bros., Columbia, Orion, and Tri-Star all contracted with HBO for the sole distribution rights to various films, sometimes in exchange for initial production funding.[81] Columbia was the first major studio to make a major pre-sale agreement with HBO; in 1981, the two negotiated an arrangement by which HBO essentially guaranteed at least 25 percent of Columbia's production costs through 1984 in exchange for longer-term cable rights to its films (five-year deals instead of the typical one-year agreement), including several "exclusive" rights.[82] This would become a more typical mode of film financing by the end of the decade.

HBO actually had deals with all Hollywood majors by the end of 1984—except, of course, Paramount and Universal. The two studios refused to admit that this had anything to do with HBO's hard-nosed negotiations, but it was quite a shock when Paramount announced the agreement with Showtime/TMC in the winter of 1983. Effectively, the studio was denying cable's biggest giant any of its pictures and heating up the war between Showtime/TMC and HBO just in time for the new year—all while continuing on its odyssey for a bigger stake in pay-cable even after the government shut Paramount's dreams down twice in 1983 alone. Still, Michele Hilmes noted that while Paramount's arrangement with Showtime/TMC did help the second-place service to gain subscribers during the five-year period from 1983 to 1988, the studio did an about-face when the deal was up and switched to a non-exclusive arrangement with HBO for another five years.[83]

There were other significant corporate shifts taking place in the film industry: MGM announced in May 1981 that it would acquire the United Artists Corporation from its parent company, Transamerica, and in January 1982 Coca-Cola announced it would purchase Columbia Pictures for approximately $820 million.[84] Fox was also rumored to be on the block; and all of this takeover activity was due to the revaluation of these companies because of their film libraries. Wall Street was suddenly very interested in what previously had seemed like a minor asset that could only be exploited on broadcast television in chopped up, censored form. Paramount and Warners had both made the enormous mistake of selling the negatives of many of their early films in the late 1950s—Paramount sold 750 features to MCA in 1958 for $50 million and United Artists bought a package of 700 Warner Bros. features and several hundred other shorts and cartoons in 1957 for just $30 million.[85] With the advent of cable, particularly the premium channels, these dormant properties were reinvented, reborn, and revalued as a major profit center.

And thus began the shift to a more tolerant attitude toward matters of concentration, vertical/horizontal integration, and antitrust in media industries. From the Premiere and Showtime cases, it becomes evident that there was an implicit understanding or unspoken acceptance regarding the issue of vertical integration in cable, as long as the film industry remained at arm's length. This tacit agreement preserved the market as one defined by the powerful interests of HBO for the time being while the film studios clamored to stake their own claim in this rapidly exploding ancillary arena.

In 1983, *Variety* estimated that the six major studios (Universal, Paramount, Fox, MGM/UA, Warner Bros., and Columbia) controlled 89 percent of the domestic exhibition market.[86] A film's main profits still were overwhelmingly derived from its domestic theatrical release; in 1984, the revenues from pay-TV typically accounted for only 15 percent of a film's earnings.[87] The general feeling about cable at the time of the Premiere deal was echoed by one executive who explained that in terms of revenue and corporate policy, "[T]hese new markets are still small potatoes."[88] That would soon change, however, as cable quickly became the main staging ground for redefining the film industry's perspective on all matters from political economy and business strategies to expanding the previously articulated boundaries of antitrust policy and industrial structure.

2

1983–1985

Broadcast and the Blueprints of Empires

In the Premiere and Showtime cases, the Antitrust Division at the Department of Justice had established an antagonistic position toward the film and cable industries' joining forces. With Premiere shut down and the major studios all but eliminated from the Showtime/Movie Channel merger, it was clear that the Justice Department frowned upon horizontal integration within or between these particular markets at the dawn of the decade. This was largely due to the antitrust interpretation and regulatory philosophy that still lingered from the Carter administration. However, the remaining traces of this resistance to transindustrial consolidation would abruptly disappear in 1983, when a new phase of empire building began with the formation of Tri-Star.

Tri-Star was a joint venture of three separate media industries: pay cable (HBO), broadcast (CBS), and film (Columbia Pictures). This partnership would receive the blessing of the Justice Department and create an instant major—a vertically integrated studio and brand-new Hollywood player with $400 million in start-up funds. Unlike the other mergers involving film studios that were previously evaluated by the Department of Justice in 1983, this one was finally given the green light; the formation of Tri-Star thus began a fundamental shift from an antitrust policy rooted in hostility to concentration and horizontal integration, to one based on the looser and less restrictive Chicago School approach. This would be the key to the expansion and merging of the film and cable companies throughout the rest of the 1980s and into the 1990s.

The same year Tri-Star was born, President Reagan delivered a tremendous boon to the major Hollywood studios by intervening in the regulatory arena to maintain the fin-syn rules and thus preserve the competitive position of the film studios in the television production market. This was a noteworthy departure from Reagan's traditional philosophy regarding government intervention in marketplace economics. This move was curious, but more understandable when taking into account his history and affinity for the Hollywood studio system, and his longstanding relationship with Universal mogul Lew Wasserman, whose MCA empire (and personal fortunes) stood to benefit tremendously from these directives.

Although he may have helped the film studios in the short term, the president's machinations actually stymied their future expansion by securing the regulatory foundation that anchored film and broadcast as *separate* industries. Consequently, the studios were not able to take full advantage of the potential synergies available to integrated media industries until the mid-1990s (with Fox as the notable exception, due to its early status as a "part-time" network). This government-enforced boundary between the ownership of film and television was one result of the film industry's hard-won political victory that, ironically, the studios would benefit from most once it was dismantled.

Tri-Star

In December 1982, HBO, CBS, and Columbia Pictures announced their plan to create the "eighth major studio" in Hollywood.[1] The new venture, initially code named Nova, eventually became Tri-Star Pictures and was slated to produce twelve to fifteen films in 1983, including *The Natural*, *The Muppets Take Manhattan*, and *Places in the Heart*.[2] It was the first major film studio produced in over fifty years, since the formation of RKO in 1927. Tri-Star was set up to essentially release and distribute their films through Columbia, show the films on HBO when they moved to pay-cable, and air them again on CBS when they finally made it through the pipeline to broadcast television. Victor Kaufman, former Columbia executive, was set to run the studio and assume the position of chairman. (Columbia had been bought by Coca-Cola earlier that year, making the studio among the first to be bought by outside corporations in the 1980s.) Tri-Star's combination of co-owners was a design of fully exploitable vertical integration through multiple markets and industries—feature film, home video, pay-cable, and broadcast television—that was unlike any other media corporation in 1982.

Interestingly, the deal was formulated to capitalize on the same benefits of exclusivity that the Department of Justice had determined to be "anticompetitive" in the Premiere venture just two years earlier. The Justice Department had shut down the Premiere deal because of the perceived dangers involved with the nine-month window, during which the service would enjoy sole access to Universal, Paramount, Columbia, and Fox films. While HBO, CBS, and Columbia were not proposing to restrict access for a specific amount of time (although HBO actually did have exclusive pay TV rights for a period), they would enjoy first pick of the rights for many of the films moving through their pipeline on home video, cable, and broadcast television.[3] HBO also had an existing deal

with Columbia, exchanging financing for cable rights, which gave this association its initial foundation.

Even in light of these considerations, the accusations of price-fixing and
group boycott that stopped the Premiere partners were not leveled at Tri-Star.
This is because Tri-Star's timing was impeccable. Their desire to develop the
obvious synergies across media industries would be sanctioned by the Justice
Department quite swiftly, thanks primarily to the palpable shift in regulatory
philosophy that began taking hold at this time. Ironically, their arrangement
was actually a greater potential threat to competition in the media industries at
large. Tri-Star was comprised of powerful film, television, and cable companies,
all three of which could affect competition in their respective businesses (as
opposed to Premiere, where the leverage—and perceived threat—was primarily
limited to the film industry).

At this point, the political economy of entertainment began a transformation as companies began to respond to the deregulatory swing that started in
the 1970s and found its full expression during the Reagan administration. In the
film industry, the formation of Tri-Star was a pivotal moment that truly signaled
the arrival of Reagan-era deregulation in the media industries. As Stephen
Prince has noted, the birth of the studio heralded "the inexorable movement
throughout the decade toward greater concentrations of media ownership and
control of interlocking markets."[4] Tri-Star also indicated a paradigm shift in
the philosophy of the Justice Department in relation to antitrust enforcement
in entertainment: from this point forward, the Antitrust Division would no
longer aggressively challenge mergers, acquisitions, and/or consolidation in
the media industries.

There was even a noticeable change in the film industry's public commen-
tary on the subject, as Tri-Star's owners used rhetoric in newspapers and trade
magazines that demonstrated they were largely unconcerned with the issue of
antitrust. This shift from traditional deference and caution when discussing
potential government intervention or regulation was quite striking and indicative of a definite change in the attitudes and confidence of studio executives.
They no longer anticipated any problem from the Department of Justice,
despite the recent beating that Hollywood took from the Premiere episode.
The fear of government regulation that had lingered for thirty-five years since
the Supreme Court handed down the *Paramount* decision was fading fast, and
in its place was a new, emboldened, and aggressive approach to mergers and
acquisitions.

Inspired by both the relaxed regulatory climate and the laws of basic supply
and demand, Tri-Star was thus quickly and efficiently created. The plan was to
establish financing packages that reduced the studio's risk to practically zero;
half the cost would be from outside financing, while pre-sales would cover the
rest of production plus half of distribution costs.[5] The studio was left with just

about $3 million per film to cover, which was easily possible for this operation. Because of its guaranteed distribution pipelines and deep pockets, every Tri-Star film was essentially paid for in advance, thanks largely to the promises of cable. Such carefully designed security had not been an organic part of a studio's structure since the industry's golden era.

In addition to the rights fees from HBO and CBS, Tri-Star also secured funding from advance sales to other ancillary markets such as home video (which was fast becoming a very fashionable financing method in the early 1980s). The studio pre-sold $500 million worth of properties even before the company was formally operating! With another $200 million from the three partners, $200 million from a bank line of credit, $150 million from HBO and partnerships with individual investors, Tri-Star would begin its corporate life with a capitalization of nearly $1 billion.[6] HBO was by far the most heavily invested player in the deal, pledging nearly twice the funds of any other individual company.[7]

Tri-Star took on numerous functions as the new hybrid studio in Hollywood, one of which was helping to fill the significant programming void in pay-TV. In 1982, HBO was striving to find more first-run films, as well as vertically integrate for efficiency and profitability. As the world's largest pay-cable service, HBO was significantly outstripping all of its competitors at the time, but the channel was still hungry for new exclusive product. The largest six studios were only putting out approximately sixty films per year at the time, along with distributing another sixty or so made by independent producers. Tri-Star's new capacity to produce and distribute first-run product offered HBO more supply while significantly enhancing the synergy of HBO's investments at the same time.

The rest of the film industry immediately began crying foul over the eventual unfair advantage that such a studio would enjoy, given its pedigree, its inherited distribution networks, and of course, its association with HBO. Potentially, the studios argued, Tri-Star would be able to use Columbia's distribution power to gain prime exhibition access in theaters, funnel films directly to HBO, and reach the highest number of pay-TV subscribers available, and still have the guaranteed broadcast outlet on the CBS network.

Furthermore, the studio chiefs complained that this alliance would bolster HBO even further, and the service was already much too powerful and dangerous in their view. "If HBO and Time go unchecked," complained Barry Diller, then-president of Paramount, "the motion pictures industry, without exception, will be under the total control of one company in less than five years."[8] The studios had already pressed the Justice Department to investigate the service for monopolistic practices and their complaints were growing louder. President of MCA Sid Sheinberg was quoted as saying that "HBO had become so powerful that it determines whether or not a film will be made."[9]

Now the association between HBO and Tri-Star made the situation even more threatening, as this new alliance would be making films *and* exhibiting them on their own cable service. Whether in response to governmental concerns about market competition or those raised by the studios, the Department of Justice began an antitrust investigation of the new studio and its three partners at this time, albeit without any fanfare or major announcements.[10]

However, on September 14, 1983—nine months after the company's initial formation—the Justice Department informed the three partners that the government would terminate their antitrust investigation of Tri-Star. The Antitrust Division had concluded that "the joint venture and licensing agreements were not likely to lead to a significant lessening of competition in the distribution of pay television programming services to cable operators or in the licensing of motion pictures to pay television programming services."[11] Thus, with the formation of Tri-Star in 1983, the studios had finally made some headway into the terrain of cable ownership and, more importantly, apparently succeeded in redefining markets in a manner more palatable for regulators than the arguments put forth a year earlier.

The Department of Justice also announced at the same time that they were dropping their investigation of HBO and its series of exclusive agreements for the same reason. One such arrangement was between HBO and Columbia, allowing HBO to retain exclusive rights to 50 percent of Columbia's films in production prior to June 30, 1986, and additional films on an exclusive basis in exchange for HBO's participation in financing those films. Another deal involved HBO and Orion Pictures—the second "instant major" studio HBO would become involved with after Tri-Star in order to increase their profit participation in the films they licensed. Their deal with Orion allowed HBO exclusive rights to thirty Orion films over several years in exchange for financing and an additional $10 million in various securities.[12] Additional agreements related to independent producers and to HBO's Silver Screen Limited Partnership (an entity established for financing film production) were also investigated and dropped.

Antitrust chief William Baxter went even further to say that instead of inhibiting competition, Tri-Star's presence might actually *increase* competition among film producers and distributors by creating a new competitor in the industry. Referring to the rejected proposal for the Showtime/Movie Channel merger that involved the participation of Universal, Paramount, and Warner Bros., Baxter also noted in his press release that the Tri-Star deal did not involve the collusion at the level of production or distribution in the motion picture industry that led the department to disallow the Showtime merger.[13]

Again, the concept of market definition was the critical factor in determining the venture's legality and potential for anticompetitive behavior. Baxter's characterization of the "motion picture industry" in this case was one that considered aftermarkets and ancillary industries as separate and discrete entities—exactly the opposite of the way it was defined by the government in the Premiere case. Such a narrow market definition as that applied to Tri-Star—much the same as it was applied to pay-TV in the Showtime/Movie Channel deal—was beneficial to the companies desiring this merger. HBO's partners, CBS and Columbia Pictures, were not in the pay-TV business and thus the potential for reduced competition was not perceived to be as great. Had the market definition been expanded to cover home entertainment and include broadcast television or home video, the partners in the Tri-Star deal would have encountered more problems with regulators.

In fact, if it were not for the Department of Justice's limited and narrowed vision of the entertainment product and market, Tri-Star would probably never have been born. The Chicago School approach was based on an increasingly outdated understanding of the entertainment industry and its markets, and this was the key to the studio's success with the Justice Department. In Baxter's view, it was more acceptable to have the single largest pay television player, one major film distributor, and the number one broadcast network combine forces than to see three film studios participate in the same pay cable venture. The focus was on preventing concentration *within* markets as opposed to *across* them, which proved to be rather myopic and provided a startling example of how media industries were evolving much faster than those in charge of regulating them.

The other studios were quite upset about Tri-Star's foothold in pay-TV—with good cause—as Tri-Star's association with cable would prove to be one of their most important strategic assets. The company's formation was taking place as the cable industry was experiencing its initial explosion; from 1980 to 1983, there was an increase of more than 1,000 percent in consumer spending for cable television and those numbers were continuing to grow.[14] Cable's subscriber base had averaged an astonishing 75 percent growth rate every year from 1975 to 1983.[15] It was also becoming increasingly important to the studios: rental fees returned more than $500 million to the film studios in 1983, and income from licensing those films to pay-TV was growing at a rate more than twenty times faster than box office returns.[16] These numbers were not lost on an industry desperately trying to stabilize its earnings in uncertain times.

This explosion in cable revenues was also beginning to diminish a different source of income for the studios. The once insatiable market for feature films on network television was quickly drying up as viewers began turning on their cable boxes for uncut, commercial-free movies. So, while pay-TV profits were on the rise, broadcast licensing fees were declining steeply; CBS, for example, cut their order for feature films by 41 percent in mid-1984 in an attempt to scale back. This placed even greater emphasis and importance on cable as a key element in the film industry's business strategy beginning in the early to mid-1980s. There was also evidence that the primetime marketplace in broadcasting was in turmoil, as the expenses for news, sports, and other programming were seeing dramatic spikes, hiring freezes were starting, and large layoffs were looming. Advertising sales were flat in the broadcast industry, and CBS even began slashing its prices for advertising time, admitting that its "overall pricing strategy was a failure and its promise of making 1983 a 'turnaround year' would not be met."[17]

At the same time, Tri-Star was exceedingly well poised to take advantage of theatrical exhibition, which had also grown by $800 million during the same period. The partnership with Columbia guaranteed Tri-Star films distribution and marketing muscle that would be virtually impossible for a newcomer to attain. The deep pockets of Columbia's parent company (Coca-Cola) provided the venture with yet another measure of security and strength in this arena. As Stephen Prince has noted, Coke's assets were also quite helpful to Columbia in marketing and promoting films, especially because of Coca-Cola's power to buy advertising time at a tremendous volume discount.[18] These advantages would naturally benefit Tri-Star as well.

Many elements of Tri-Star's business plan served as a model for a new generation of media industries and moguls. The partnership itself was a monument to the necessity of exploiting new and varied forms of distribution, and also a demonstration of how significant cable holdings would be to entertainment companies of the future. Furthermore, Tri-Star was an early portent of how important it would become to exploit both film and television holdings when formulating future blueprints for media conglomerates; taking advantage of transmedia distribution pipelines and cross-promoting assets would be the guiding principle for mergers and acquisitions like Rupert Murdoch's purchase of Fox in 1985 to some degree and most definitely for the Time Warner merger in 1989. This model would continue to proliferate throughout the 1990s.

Additionally, Tri-Star ushered in a new type of studio mogul: executives with Ivy League credentials and former careers in management, advertising, or law. This was a dramatic difference from the previous generation of studio chiefs, who largely eschewed formal education and began as East Coast exhibitors, working their way through all facets of the business. Jeff Sagansky, Tri-Star's production president, went to Harvard Business School before working as a programming executive for NBC. He would eventually go on to become president of CBS. In fact, many of the New Hollywood moguls would come from the ranks of ex-agents and attorneys, including Kaufman himself, Arthur Krim (United Artists, Orion), Tom Pollock (MCA/Universal), and Frank Wells (Disney), among others.

The spiraling costs of making films during the 1980s was one possible reason for this shift in executive pedigrees; with the average cost of a film's production closing in on $15 million, business savvy was a vital quality to have in a studio's leadership to ensure its survival. "In 1986 America, you cannot run a major studio without a financial/legal/investment type high up in the hierarchy," noted Frank Rothman, former chairman and CEO of MGM/UA.[19] With films so expensive to produce, studios had to rely on their chiefs for their contacts and investment knowledge more than anything else; borrowing the cost of a film from the bank was no longer an option with the stakes so high. The complicated financing arrangements evolving in the 1980s that shared risks by pre-selling video and cable rights in exchange for production financing required a new type of skill set to make a deal.

Almost immediately, Tri-Star's leaders announced an ambitious production schedule. They were hoping to produce and distribute twelve to fifteen films per year with an average budget of $12 million—a bit less than industry standard at the time but extremely competitive for a brand new company.[20] *The Natural*, starring Robert Redford, was Tri-Star's first production and a fitting one at that. It seemed that the new studio, much like Redford's character Roy Hobbs, was facing formidable odds. Still, it was determined to either hit a home run or go down swinging. It was Redford's first film since *Brubaker* in 1980 and was booked into 1,000 theaters, a rather wide release at the time.[21] With luck on their side, the first Tri-Star film was indeed a (qualified) success. The $5 million they paid Redford for his role in *The Natural* was top dollar at the time, but it seemed worth it when the film grossed over $50 million.[22]

The Natural provides an excellent example of the Tri-Star business strategies that quickly began to aggravate the rest of the film community. The studio's attempts to buy their way into the market had them overbidding for screenplays, talent, and finished product to distribute ("negative pick-ups"), driving up costs for everyone else. The paycheck for Redford on *The Natural* was a good example. The bidding war Tri-Star initiated for *Rambo: First Blood Part II* is another, and one that also paid off handsomely: an estimated one-third of the film's $150 million box office was returned to the studio for its role as the film's distributor.[23]

The studio first showed a profit in 1985, but that same year CBS sold its share to Columbia when Tri-Star began trading publicly. Cable and the VCR were steadily eroding the promise of a distribution windfall for the broadcast network, and they opted out of the partnership rather quickly. However, CBS was still legally bound to pay for licensing fees to air Tri-Star's films through 1989, so their exit did not cause much damage to the company at all. Furthermore, once CBS sold its share, Tri-Star began producing television shows—something the studio was barred from doing before because of its association with the CBS broadcast network, and which proved to be extremely profitable.

Tri-Star had some reasonable early successes, including *Rambo* (1985), *About Last Night* (1986), and *Peggy Sue Got Married* (1986) but overall its initial performance was disappointing for investors. By the end of 1984, the studio had released only twelve films, with just three box-office hits (*The Natural*,

The Muppets Take Manhattan, and *Places in the Heart*) and Tri-Star only gained a 5 percent share of the domestic theatrical market during its first year.[24] However, by 1986 insiders were finally considering Tri-Star a "major," once it produced five movies that grossed more than $25 million each and captured a "7–8 percent market share without having a bona-fide 'blockbuster'"—which was then defined as a film that earned more than $50 million in rentals.[25] Tri-Star also set up a home video company, like most of the other majors were doing, and also regained control of its own movie sales to TV from Columbia in 1987.

The ownership stake continued to shift until 1986 when the company was equally owned by Coca-Cola (owner of Columbia) and the public (each 43 percent) and to a lesser extent by HBO, which had reduced its stake by half to 14 percent after Time, Inc. sold shares to Columbia in 1986.[26] By 1987, Columbia's stake was at 30 percent and HBO held 10 percent of the company, with the rest owned publicly.[27] Coca-Cola was actively involved in entertainment acquisitions in the mid-1980s, as owner of Columbia Pictures from 1982 to 1989, also becoming the industry's largest television program supplier through a series of acquisitions, including pieces of the Weintraub Entertainment Group.[28]

Tri-Star's blockbuster-sized bomb *Ishtar* (1987) is known as one of the biggest flops in movie history and was also the impetus for Coke to spin off Columbia and Tri-Star, which were set to merge by the end of that year. The studio lost more than $35 million on the film and soon thereafter Coca-Cola sold off its $1.4 billion entertainment unit. Columbia had been having a very difficult year; in 1986, only four of the thirteen films released by the studio made a profit. By June 1987 the studio had released only three films for the year.[29] The company was also experiencing a dramatic exodus of senior management, with the biggest loss coming from the top: Fay Vincent, Coke's entertainment division head, was moved to the bottling unit at the company.[30] British producer David Puttnam (*The Killing Fields*, *Chariots of Fire*) was brought on to run the studio in the spring of 1986 only to be ousted after less than a year, having alienated many key players with his disdain for the "blockbuster," his attempts to cut costs and elevate the artistic merit of Columbia's films, and his maneuvers to leverage more control over the production process.[31] At this point, Tri-Star was worth over $250 million.[32]

Thus, in December 1987, Columbia merged with Tri-Star and the two became known as the $2 billion Columbia Pictures Entertainment, Inc., run by Tri-Star chief Victor Kaufman. Coca-Cola cut its ownership to 49 percent.[33] Eventually, the soft-drink giant would sell the entire studio to Sony for $3.4 billion in 1989,[34] neither one of the companies having profited in any lasting way from their seven years together.

The greatest legacy of Tri-Star is the ushering in of a new era for anti-trust enforcement in the media industries. The days of aggressive regulation and policing "non-competitive arrangements" were over. After Tri-Star was established, the Justice Department did not challenge any vertical, horizontal, or collaborative industrial structures in film or television for the rest of the decade. Instead, consolidation and synergy would quickly become an accepted reality of doing business, and the government assumed their new position as "casual observer" of the marketplace.

Tri-Star would also play a primary role in the rebirth of vertical integration as it related to film studios. As will be explained in chapter 4, Tri-Star and Columbia were among the first to purchase exhibition outlets in the post-*Paramount* era, and Tri-Star was actually the first company to successfully repeal their consent decree, which prevented them from owning movie theaters. The studio also reinvigorated vertical integration as a viable strategy by helping to transport the rest of the industry—along with the attitude of the Justice Department—back to the pre-*Paramount* mindset where all facets of the business could coexist peacefully under one roof. Now that roof just had to be enlarged to accommodate the conglomerate-sized house of assets.

The Vagaries of Broadcast Regulation

The television networks had already faced some serious antitrust issues of their own. Accused of monopolizing the airwaves, they had been under the scrutiny of both the FCC and the Justice Department for over a decade. In 1970, the FCC enacted the Financial Interest and Syndication Rules (commonly referred to as "fin-syn"), a key piece of television regulation that essentially functioned as the *Paramount* Decrees for the broadcast industry. Fin-syn mandated that the broadcast networks were not allowed to produce or have an ownership stake in their own prime-time entertainment programming, nor were they allowed to participate in syndication revenues from programming that they aired. Further, the networks' activity in foreign distribution was limited to those programs of which they were the sole producers.

The rules forced the networks out of the syndication market and also separated production from distribution and exhibition in a sense. A lawsuit brought forth by the Justice Department for similar reasons was settled in a series of consent decrees in 1978 (for NBC) and 1980 (for ABC and CBS) and limited the amount of programming that the networks could own and produce. The FCC's rules and the Department of Justice consent decrees shared many of the same restrictions, but fin-syn was the public face of that regulation and most often the focus of discussions about the networks' restrictions on program production.

These rules also present an interesting paradox in 1980s regulatory philosophy, as fin-syn's enforcement by the Reagan administration was a complete aberration in the faithful adherence to the principles of the Chicago School. Fin-syn was the linchpin ensuring that film and television remained as separate industries, unable to merge until the repeal of the rules in the 1990s. Yet, the Reagan administration's refusal to eradicate fin-syn stands as a most unusual break in its remarkably cohesive approach to antitrust enforcement, especially after Tri-Star was born. Instead of minimizing government regulations, as was the case in most industries (including media), President Reagan chose to enhance regulatory restrictions in this particular case and preserve fin-syn until after he left office. As will be explained later in this chapter, the result was a complicated battlefield over the right to produce and own programming that pitted the Hollywood studios against the broadcast networks, the broadcast networks against the FCC, the FCC against Congress, Congress against the president, and even President Reagan against his own handpicked FCC chairman.

Fowler and the FCC

The foundation of regulatory policy in the American broadcast industry is based on "the public interest, convenience or necessity," as defined by the 1927 Radio Act, which considered the airwaves a public trust.[35] There is a marked ambiguity to this phrase that has been attributed to everything from a deliberate design in the legislation to accommodate changing economic conditions and technologies (allowing the FCC to adapt policy as needed), to less benevolent intentions such as undercutting regulators and making them more susceptible to congressional influence or attack.[36] Patricia Aufderheide characterizes the "public interest" as both "the favorite invocation of every stakeholder in the regulatory process" and "the notorious fudge factor in the FCC's rule making."[37] Other scholars have also noted that over time, a well-documented and controversial shift in this foundation has taken place: the public interest has become equated with corporate interests and maximum profitability. Essentially, this view holds, the FCC has lost sight of their "public." The agency has increasingly become the steward/patron of major corporations and big broadcasters, or, in the words of media critic Ben Bagdikian, they have "gone from their original purpose of protecting consumers against unfair or dangerous industry behavior to an opposite role of protecting industries from their consumers."[38] When discussing the deregulation of telecommunications, Robert Horwitz has similarly described this transformation in the concept of the public interest during the Reagan era as "a shift away from concern with stability and a kind of social equity to a concern with market controls and economic efficiency."[39] The indeterminacy of the construct has certainly allowed regulators a great deal of latitude over the years, but the loose interpretation of the notion of "public interest" was particularly beneficial to private interests during the 1980s.

With President Reagan's appointment of Mark Fowler as chairman of the FCC on May 18, 1981, that deregulatory swing which began during the late 1970s under such chairmen as Charles Ferris was institutionalized. Suddenly "there was a sense that you could do whatever the hell you wanted" in the broadcast industry, according to then CBS News president William Leonard.[40] It was during this period that the FCC began to be described as the industry lap dog instead of the watchdog it was intended to be, and Fowler became known as the steward of the broadcast industry. This intensified as Fowler aggressively pursued a pro-network agenda throughout his term of office and maintained a deep commitment to marketplace economics as a means of regulating television. This would serve the networks at first, but eventually it would undermine the stability of the industry and deregulation would issue an open invitation for corporate raiders.

Fowler was wholly determined to stimulate competition by eliminating FCC regulations. The FCC signed on to President Reagan's deregulatory agenda with little conflict, as Reagan and Fowler shared the common vision of an unfettered marketplace. Fowler, a communications lawyer who had worked on Reagan's presidential campaign, was indisputably one of the most significant (and controversial) proponents of deregulation during this era. He said openly of Reagan: "His philosophy is my philosophy. And our task has been nothing less than to make America once again a free enterprise zone."[41] Immediately upon taking office, he promised to perform "radical surgery" on the commission, proposing to do away with all unnecessary rules and policies and immediately begin instituting his policy of "unregulation."[42] He even kept a Mao cap in his office to use as a dunce hat for the FCC staffer who offered "the most regulatory idea of the week."[43]

Fowler's seminal 1982 article in the *Texas Law Review* outlined his vision for what broadcast policy should be. It involved disavowing the "public trustee" model on which regulation in the United States had been predicated, and embracing a marketplace model, which replaced government regulation with basic economic principles of supply and demand. Fowler argued "the perception of broadcasters as community trustees should be replaced by a view of broadcasters as marketplace participants. Communications policy should be directed toward maximizing the services the public desires. Instead of defining public demand and specifying categories of programming to serve this demand, the Commission should rely on the broadcasters' ability to determine the wants of their audiences through the normal mechanisms of the marketplace. The public's interest, then, defines the public interest."[44] This articulation of his philosophy also foreshadowed what was to come during his tenure at the commission.

Once Fowler was appointed, the move toward a "free market" (as defined by a lack of regulatory constraints) was under way and with it, a FCC emphasis on competition and profit as opposed to scheduling mandates or programming requirements. The eradication of structural and content regulations proceeded rapidly under his leadership. He claimed that he wanted his agency to step aside and allow what he called the "marketplace magic" to take over. However, Fowler remained extremely active despite his expressed desire to minimize the role of the FCC. By the end of his first four years as chairman, Fowler's FCC had reviewed, changed, or deleted 89 percent of the agency's approximately 900 mass media rules and, in his own words, simply "scrapped a lot of the rules that didn't make any sense."[45] Fifty years worth of regulation wound up on the chopping block when he arrived in office.

Fowler was the antithesis of Newton Minnow, President John F. Kennedy's FCC chairman. Minnow crusaded against the "vast wasteland" of violence and commercialism that he saw taking hold of the spectrum in the early 1960s. Minnow actively fought for public television, educational television, and tighter restrictions on network-affiliate programming practices and threatened to take away broadcasting licenses if the industry did not become more responsible to the audience. Fowler, on the other hand, famously equated television to any other household appliance, calling it a "toaster with pictures" and reasoning that if viewers didn't like what they saw, they could simply pull the plug. When considering the implications of deregulating the medium on a grand scale, he insisted, "If I had to choose, I'd rather have free than fair."[46] Consequently, the agency was relegated to playing the role of a passive, glorified traffic cop instead of actively patrolling the airwaves for violations of the public interest.

Fowler was also a strong advocate of what he called "the print model," endowing broadcasters with the same First Amendment freedoms as newspapers or any other print medium. In his fervent condemnation of the government regulating television content, he often took his views to the extreme. Basically characterizing his own job as reckless and illegal, he told reporters, "I don't think that anyone who reads the First Amendment—and reads the language that 'Congress shall make no law abridging freedom of speech and press'—and then looks at the whole gamut of content regulation that we have on the books right now can avoid the conclusion that what we do is unconstitutional and, I think, dangerous."[47] Most notable about Fowler's tenure was this way that he challenged the basic and foundational assumptions of the regulatory agency that he chaired; he actually questioned whether or not the FCC should continue on its path of policing the airwaves and industry conduct in the name of the "public interest." FCC Commissioner Dennis Patrick summed it up best when he said that the FCC's threshold question had become whether it should regulate at all, not what sort of regulation might be appropriate.[48] With this, Fowler basically equated the public interest with the profit interest, changed the terms of the entire regulatory debate, and to some extent, even redefined the mandate of the FCC. Deregulation was officially sanctioned and, as a result, the concept of the broadcaster as public trustee swiftly deteriorated.

However, the process of deregulation was not always a simple or monolithic one for the Commission. The complications of developing technologies, new competition, rapidly evolving corporate holdings, and the industry's renewed global emphasis made maintaining a free, unregulated, *and* profitable market very tricky. The varied investments and interests of the networks, producers, and cable companies naturally clashed with one another and with government regulators, and hostilities increased as the playing field grew. There were even conflicts between and within the different branches of government involved, due to competing politics and varying responsibilities to outside pressures. Thus, the FCC was often engaged in intense political struggles, lobbying Congress with varying degrees of success as the agency pursued Fowler's agenda.

One of the FCC's most contentious campaigns was waged to raise the ownership limits for a single company from seven broadcast stations to twelve. The current limit of seven stations per owner was unacceptable to Fowler—so much so that, according to his press spokesman, he began to discuss repealing the rule with his policy advisors even before he had been confirmed as the FCC chairman.[49] Overturning this was one of Fowler's main goals, and thus the "rule of sevens" (also known as the 7–7–7 rule because it applied to the number of television, AM, and FM radio stations one company could own) was consequently changed to the "rule of twelves" in 1985. This was allowed with the provision that the twelve stations together reached no more than 25 percent of the nation's homes. Although it was a victory for Fowler, it was nevertheless a compromise with Congress—he originally wanted all ownership restrictions lifted after five years to pave the way for new network formation.[50] Fowler encountered major resistance from Congress on this issue and the Senate even threatened to cut off funds to the FCC if Fowler carried out his original plan. The chairman was forced into major negotiations with congressional committees, particularly those in the House of Representatives that were still controlled by Democrats, such as Commerce and its Subcommittee on Telecommunications. These conflicts with lawmakers ultimately highlighted how strained Fowler's relationship with them had become and how much resentment there was toward the FCC in Congress, particularly in the House.

As Alex Ben Block noted in his chronicle of the Fox network, *Outfoxed*, the change in ownership limits opened the door for larger station groups with more economic clout to add to their positions in the industry, "resulting in an increase in programming made by station groups themselves."[51] With a larger base over which to amortize production costs, these "mini-networks" were able to lower their expenses involved in creating first-run syndication shows and, in turn, lower their expenses as distributors. Furthermore, renewing licenses became practically automatic on Fowler's watch and more pro forma than ever before with the institution of postcard renewals. All it required was a twenty-cent stamp; there was no longer even the pretense of broadcasters having to prove that they were operating in the public's best interest in order to continue accessing the airwaves. License tenure was also increased from three to five years for television and from three to seven years for radio.

The repeal of the "anti-trafficking" provision was another move by the FCC that made potential buyers sit up and take notice. Owners had been required to retain stations for three years before selling them, but the reversal of this law in 1982 eliminated that requirement altogether. This ruling subsequently encouraged the practice of "flipping" stations for a profit and further inflated station values. After the FCC also decreased the processing time for broadcast licenses and increased ownership limits, the industry was primed for corporate raiders. Station prices kept creeping higher, even as the broadcast playing field widened. The Tribune Co., for example, bought Los Angeles TV station KTLA for $510 million in 1985—roughly double what the station went for three years earlier.[52] These relaxed rules presented a tempting opportunity for well-bankrolled speculators and outside investors to buy up station properties to fortify their own empires, similar in nature to the corporate takeovers in the film industry during the late 1960s.

Changes in ownership were just the beginning; the real transformation would come when the FCC attended to the critical piece of regulation that lingered: the Financial Interest and Syndication Rules. This was the key—the fin-syn rules could open the gates to entirely new dimensions of industrial structure, efficiency, and synergy in broadcasting. Fin-syn's requirements prevented vertical integration and kept the Hollywood studios out of the network ownership game for as long as the rules remained effective. Fowler's determination to eliminate these rules caused numerous clashes on Capitol Hill and fin-syn would prove to be an albatross for the chairman and his commission throughout the 1980s.

Fin-Syn and PTAR

In 1970, the three broadcast networks had a financial interest or syndication rights to 98 percent of their programming and independent producers were practically shut out of the market.[53] The networks maintained complete control over the industry, and this control was a goldmine; in 1983 alone, the syndication business was valued at an estimated $800 million.[54] Program suppliers, mainly consisting of the major Hollywood studios, were furious over the terms extracted by the networks for airing their products—often a stake in the profits or distribution rights for reruns in other markets. It was a true oligopoly, much in the same sense as the vertically integrated Hollywood studios had once been. The FCC performed an exhaustive inquiry of the networks' monopolistic behavior in the late 1960s and, in response to the abuses of power that they perceived, the FCC established both the Financial Interest and Syndication Rules and the Prime Time Access Rule (PTAR).

Enacted in April 1970, PTAR basically prohibited network-affiliated television stations in the top fifty television markets from broadcasting more than three hours of network or "off-network" (rerun) programs during the four prime-time viewing hours of each night (at this point, prime time was a four-hour block of programming). According to the FCC:

> PTAR was promulgated in 1970 in response to the concern that the three major television networks—ABC, CBS, and NBC—dominated the program production market, controlled much of the video fare presented to the public, and inhibited the development of competing program sources. The Commission believed that PTAR would increase the level of competition in the independent production of programs, reduce the networks' control over their affiliates' programming decisions, and increase the diversity of programs available to the public.[55]

By limiting the hours of network programming on affiliate stations, PTAR established a protected, one-hour block during prime time in which it was assumed that individual stations would have more freedom to schedule locally produced, community interest, or independent shows. This was also expected to expand the market and opportunities for independent producers. According to J. Fred MacDonald, this group had seen their share of network programming slip from 33 percent in 1958 to just 5 percent ten years later, thanks to the network oligopoly.[56]

PTAR also came to be viewed as a means of promoting the growth of independent stations in that they would not have to compete with "top fifty" market affiliates in acquiring off-network programs to air during the one-hour access period. Further, PTAR was expected to increase the advertising revenues of independents and bolster their position in the market. The rule was to be implemented in the fall 1971 season.

The Financial Interest and Syndication Rules were enacted at the same time with similar goals: to loosen the grip of network power over the industry and expand the market for independent producers. They were formulated largely in part as a response to insistent lobbying from the film studios, who were having severe troubles of their own in the late 1960s and were increasingly dependent on their revenues from television production. Fin-syn dictated that the networks could not own the programming that they aired or syndicated, forcing them to look to the Hollywood studios for product.

Due to network appeals to the courts and various legal entanglements, the FCC delayed implementing the rules. Consequently, the Justice Department filed suit against all three networks in 1972, charging them with antitrust violations and monopolistic conduct. Because of this legal maneuvering and the concurrent Department of Justice lawsuit, fin-syn was not fully enforced until the mid-1970s. The consent decrees between the Justice Department and the three networks signed between 1976 and 1980 enforced and further solidified fin-syn and also severely limited the hours of "in-house" prime-time programming the networks could produce. The impact of the lawsuits (and eventual consent decrees) against the networks and fin-syn were virtually indistinguishable, as the issues, resolutions, and time periods were almost identical. The one significant difference was that the consent decrees had an expiration date of 1990.

Nevertheless, all of these regulations prohibited the broadcast networks from vertically integrating the production, sale, and distribution of syndicated programming—preventing them from creating a schedule that privileged their own products. It was further argued that separating the networks from syndication would strengthen independent stations, removing the networks' ability to stock-pile popular rerun material (second-run, off-network series) or funnel hits directly to their owned and operated affiliate stations.

In reality, however, the rules did not significantly tip the scales in favor of the independent sector, although there were some major exceptions, as the fortunes of independents such as Tandem (*All in the Family, Sanford and Son*), MTM (*Hill St. Blues, St. Elsewhere*), Carsey-Werner (*Roseanne, The Cosby Show*), and Lorimar (*Dallas, Knots Landing*) can attest. Producers of first-run syndication shows, such as *Wheel of Fortune* and *Entertainment Tonight*, also flourished as syndication revenue swelled from about $520 million in 1980 to over $2 billion in 1994.[57] While fin-syn did help keep the independent producers in the game and at times phenomenally successful, fin-syn mostly strengthened the position of the major studios; according to Mara Einstein and her in-depth study of the rules, the major film studios were responsible for approximately 70 percent of prime-time programming in the early 1980s.[58] The fin-syn rules essentially solidified a balance between two powerful economic forces: the film studios and the broadcast networks. The net result for the film industry was a secure position as the largest supplier of television shows as well as what looked to be permanent, guaranteed access to this all-important market.

As for the networks, fin-syn seriously damaged their collective and competitive position and rendered them dependent on the film studios for programming. After all, there were few pockets outside the studio system deep enough to accommodate the system of deficit financing (whereby the producer receives a license fee from the network that is far below the cost of the program's production, and gambles on the unlikely prospect of syndication for future revenues to earn back the difference). With the advent of cable, the fin-syn rules were becoming even more profound in terms of their restrictions because cable introduced an expanding pool of riches that the networks were barred from earning as the market exploded. The channels that would require product—syndicated product—continued to grow and the networks were forced to watch the spoils go to the film studios. Consequently, producers and distributors became instantly deadlocked, waging a lobbying war over fin-syn's existence and legitimacy in what one FCC commissioner referred to as "a battle between the very rich and the very wealthy."[59]

Policies such as these would logically be prime candidates for elimination by Reagan's deregulatory agenda. From his former career in the entertainment industry, and especially his term as president of the Screen Actors Guild (SAG) for seven years (1947–1952, 1959–1960), the president was quite well versed in the issues at hand. Consequently, the Hollywood film community made strenuous appeals directly to the White House while the broadcast lobby converged on Washington, hoping that the FCC would eliminate fin-syn and cut them in on a piece of the billion-dollar syndication pie. At this point, the FTC, the FCC, the Commerce Department, the Office of Management and Budget (OMB), and the Justice Department all concurred that the rules were no longer necessary, and the OMB even wrote a memo of support to Mark Fowler, endorsing his position. New technologies and delivery systems were beginning to erode the networks' share of the audience, and the rules were now becoming anachronistic in a rapidly changing industrial landscape. The networks were facing limited revenue growth, soaring costs, and shrinking audiences by 1983 and it appeared to be the beginning of the end for fin-syn.

However, the film studios had other plans. Jack Valenti, MPAA president and chief lobbyist for the film industry, began a vigorous, rather ironic verbal mudslinging against any modification of fin-syn in order to stem what he characterized as the networks'"anti-consumer grab for monopoly power."[60] He quickly shifted the narrative on Capitol Hill from this battle being between two giants (the television networks and the Hollywood studios) to one focusing on the evils of the networks against the helpless independent producers. If the networks retained their syndication rights, Valenti argued that they could—and would—warehouse their programs, act anticompetitively, and destroy the independents. Valenti wrote letters to Mark Fowler, as well as Presidential Counsel Edwin Meese, Chief of Staff James Baker, and Deputy Chief Michael Deaver (also known as "The Troika")[61] pleading the case of the Hollywood studios and beseeching them to forestall the repeal of the rules. Valenti depicted an industrial climate in which the networks were on the verge of "absolute and total dominion over programming," all competition for programming and audience members for independent TV stations were endangered, and "every independent producer in the field is on the verge of hysteria."[62] He argued to Fowler that network prime-time television was a "marketplace NOT in equilibrium." In a letter to the chairman bemoaning the state of competition in the market, he wrote "There is no chance for new entries. The three networks sit astride the program funnel and no one else can intrude."[63]

The studios had more on their side than Valenti's powers of persuasion. There was also a strong anti-network bias coming to a boil on Capitol Hill. It was always popular in Congress to attack the television industry; that platform has been used as a way to advance careers since the days of Joseph McCarthy and then-congressman Richard Nixon. An anti-broadcast bias had resurfaced once again and observers noted that "some members of the Senate and House would vote for any legislation viewed as anti-network."[64] Another asset to the pro fin-syn forces was, ironically, Chairman Fowler himself. Fowler had extremely rough relations with Congress, and was constantly criticized for failing to carry out their will. Fellow Republicans were no exception, participating in the chorus of discontent and even initially refusing to support Fowler's nominees. In this case, Fowler was said to have "precipitated a direct confrontation with the Hill by not consulting with its members."[65] He neglected to show Congress the deference that would have fostered better relations, and his uncompromising spirit engendered a strained relationship at best. Fowler often acted on his own accord, vigorously pursuing policy that was most favorable to the networks and failed to take into consideration the alienating effects and political ramifications of his actions. As he forged ahead with his plans to eliminate fin-syn, Fowler's work was actually angering Capitol Hill and fortifying the position of the studios and other opponents of the repeal.

Variety reported that the "furor over the repeal of fin-syn is about to reach circus proportions" as Congress prepared to get involved in March 1983. The debate over this piece of regulation that was critical to the future of entertainment empires went into high gear at this time. The FCC had issued a "tentative decision" to repeal the rules but would encounter major roadblocks and opposition along the way. The battle went on for most of the year, with celebrities, politicians, and studio executives lobbying anyone in Washington who would listen, with the hopes of maintaining the status quo and keeping the networks in check. Yet many industry observers were predicting some victory for the networks, perhaps in the area of financial interest but not syndication rights.

Those prognosticators apparently had not accounted for President Reagan's personal ties and loyalties to Hollywood. This is the element that ultimately proved to be the most important one for the studios—and the deal-breaker for the networks. Trade magazines had been rife with speculation about Reagan's difficult position, surmising in advance that "the President will heed the expressions of concern he has heard from his friends in the movie industry—even if it would mean turning his back on the deregulatory policy he has vigorously pushed and that the Commerce and Justice Departments, as well as the FCC and FTC, have indicated is correct."[66] Indeed, according to the Office of Policy

Development, the Commerce and Justice Departments, the Office of Management and Budget, and the Council of Economic Advisors (CEA) all studied the arguments and agreed that "the rule should be repealed, on grounds that it restricts competition and diversity in both the financing and distribution of television programming."[67] The Commerce and Justice departments filed comments supporting repeal. Additionally, the cabinet council on commerce and trade unanimously recommended that the administration support the repeal of the rules.

The president himself received a host of letters on the issue, many from California and the Hollywood community. Senator Pete Wilson of California was among those who wrote the president and urged him not to repeal the rules. "Simply releasing the networks, under the guise of deregulation, to further dominate the programming landscape seems counter to your Administration's goal, which I share, to promote genuine competition," Wilson wrote in September 1983.[68] Two weeks earlier, Charlton Heston—one of the most outspoken and active opponents of repealing the rules—had also written personal letters pleading with White House Counsel Edwin Meese and President Reagan to maintain fin-syn. Fearing that unless the White House got involved, "the networks will achieve total victory," Heston implored Reagan in grandiose fashion to intervene through his Cabinet council and the Department of Commerce. If he didn't, Heston wrote, "Unhappily, the public will be the ultimate loser. Unleashed by the FCC, the networks will quickly move to entrench their dominance of the marketplace. The public will suffer, the creative community will suffer, in the end I believe the nation will be less well served by vital resources within your influence."[69] Reagan also met with Heston to discuss the matter in person.[70]

President Reagan also had a rare and unusual meeting with his FCC chairman to discuss fin-syn in the fall of 1983. This was quite controversial, as it is illegal for the president to try to affect an independent agency and its rulings on pending matters. While there is no evidence to prove what President Reagan's intentions were, this meeting of September 28, 1983, was indeed to discuss fin-syn. The *Washington Post* reported that it was called by the president and cited official sources who characterized the meeting as a "briefing" by Fowler and not anything inappropriate.[71] This was Fowler's first meeting with the president since being appointed as chair of the FCC, and there was another meting scheduled three weeks later. After that, Congressman John Dingell, the chair of the Committee on Energy and Commerce, wrote the president expressing concern regarding his meetings with Fowler. Dingell authorized an investigation to see if there was indeed interference by the White House and concluded that the president was "injudicious" in calling Fowler to the Oval Office to discuss a matter pending before the commission, stating that "it was particularly unwise given the President's personal interest and the financial interest of his friends in the rulemaking proceeding." Furthermore, the investigation determined that President Reagan "acted improperly, and undermined the fairness and the integrity" of the proceedings, but no action was taken.[72]

Also at this time, Congress had introduced legislation that would prohibit the FCC from changing or repealing the Financial Interest and Syndication Rules. This would allow Congress to trump the FCC's authority and slow down Fowler's deregulatory steamroller. Their reasoning was that even less competition among networks would not necessarily serve the public interest, and that Fowler was moving too quickly on this front. Congress was basically entering the fray on the side of the Hollywood studios, in large part because of their distaste for Fowler's approach. The House passed their bill, which put a six month moratorium on any changes to fin-syn, and the Senate introduced a similar bill, with hearings to begin in November.

On November 2, 1983, the Antitrust Chief William Baxter, Secretary of Commerce Baldridge, and Assistant Secretary of Commerce David Markey (head of the NTIA) were preparing to testify before the Senate Commerce Committee to oppose this legislation that would have prevented the FCC from repealing the fin-syn rules. Essentially, the administration was going to go on record as backing the FCC in their bid to change the rules. However, Baxter and Markey were summoned to the White House the day before and, while the president was not there, Dingell's investigation revealed that "a clear message was communicated to them that the President wanted a unified Administration position in support of the legislation . . . and that Justice and Commerce should testify accordingly."[73] On an issue that the administration had never taken a position on before, President Reagan (indirectly) directed the Commerce and Justice Departments to immediately switch sides, putting those who had been arguing for the repeal of the rules in an extremely compromised position. The next day, they carried out the instructions of the president, reversed course, and testified in support of the legislation that would *prevent* the FCC from repealing the rules. In other words, the administration was coming out against the FCC and against repealing fin-syn.

That same day, through his counsel Edwin Meese, the president made a remarkable declaration at the hearing. Meese read a letter from Reagan and stated that although President Reagan favored "vigorous competition," he now supported a legislatively mandated two-year moratorium on changes in the rules to permit further study. "In this instance," the statement read, "in light of changing market conditions in the television and program production industries . . . additional review of the consequences of repeal of the rules is necessary."[74] It was quite unusual for the president to get involved at this level, and moreover to be involved and advocating *against* deregulation.

This rather shocking statement can be attributed in some ways to the power of his former agent, personal friend, and MCA/Universal chief Lew Wasserman, who came to lobby on behalf of maintaining the rules the night before the Senate hearings.[75] Reagan had a long history with Wasserman, who had much to lose if the rules were repealed and the networks were able to produce their own programming.[76] It is not a coincidence that one day after his closed-door meeting with Wasserman, Reagan stepped in and came out against Fowler's commission. Yet it was surprising that suddenly the hands-off president was getting involved with re-regulating the broadcast industry and directly contradicting his own FCC. The network reaction was one of astonishment and harsh criticism, while Fowler was left to hang his head and waffle his way through the rest of the proceedings without the support of the president. In the end, Reagan's allegiance to the studios prevailed and the rules were not modified during his administration. There was a reprieve on any modification of the rules, which was supposed to last six months. Both sides were sent to the negotiating table immediately after the hearings and as Mara Einstein has detailed, the networks progressively walked out over the next three months until there was nobody left on the broadcasters' side.[77]

The FCC began to consider modifications at the end of Reagan's tenure, largely due to lobbying pressures by the networks and the undeniable changes in the industry that had taken place since the rules were implemented. By the late 1980s there was a fourth network settling into place and various new forms of competition (cable, home video, satellite services, pay-per-view movies, etc.) were steadily eroding the dominance of the broadcast networks. None of these elements represented any significant threat in 1970 when fin-syn was enacted and the networks' combined share of the television audience was around 90 percent (as opposed to the low of 57 percent that they hit in the early 1990s).

Taken together, the amnesty granted to fin-syn and the birth of Tri-Star represent the often-paradoxical nature of antitrust policy as it relates to the media industries. Fin-syn's reprieve meant *more* regulation for the broadcast industry and *less* tolerance for transmedia mergers. This would prove to be the exception to the rule. The creation of Tri-Star, on the other hand, was a sign of things to come. It was emblematic of a more relaxed and permissive regulatory attitude toward concentration and the same transmedia mergers that were the building blocks for entertainment empires. These two case studies are also testaments to the everlasting importance of distribution. Tri-Star itself was pieced together as a mighty and varied distribution pipeline. The films that the studio produced (or acquired) would be distributed by Columbia, then shown on HBO and CBS. The Financial Interest and Syndication Rules remained a thorn in the side of the networks because they separated production from distribution. However, the rules' larger power was actually in their ability to separate the *markets* and *industrial structures* of broadcast from those of filmed entertainment at the same time that they prevented networks from owning their prime-time programming. Their influence and impact was much greater than previously understood by the networks and studios, and fin-syn prevented the union of the film and broadcast industries for as long as the rules remained in effect.

Two additional significant moments in law and policy for media industries took place in 1984. First, the lawsuit filed by Walt Disney Productions and Universal against Sony in 1976 for designing and selling a device that the studios claimed was infringing on their copyrighted materials was finally settled on January 15, 1984. The Supreme Court ruled that videotape did not constitute copyright violation and the studios (and their future conglomerate parents) were handed the luckiest legal defeat in their history. That same videotape which they were trying to outlaw would soon overtake theatrical revenue and become one of the most critical elements in their balance sheets. The "Betamax case" would also pave the way for ancillary revenues to assume their place of major importance for the corporate strategies of media industries in the immediate future.

Later that year, Congress passed the Cable Communications Policy Act of 1984. This was an amendment to the Communications Act of 1934 and the first national policy regarding the regulation of cable television. This comprehensive act represented the attempt to incorporate federal legislation into the efforts to police cable. It also represented a major shift in regulatory policy toward the cable industry vis-à-vis broadcasters. For twenty years, the FCC had restricted the growth and power of cable, thus preserving the security of the networks from the threat of this new technology and medium.[78] In 1984, however, the preferential treatment for the networks was coming to an end and cable was freed from many restrictions preventing its expansion. Once the administration's deregulatory agenda took hold and the economic implications of cable's continued growth became more apparent, the FCC grew more lenient toward the cable industry in order to promote its development.

This legislation was more a transference of authority from state and local authorities to the federal government than a specific act of deregulation; however, the effect was profound in terms of enhanced stability and freedom for the cable industry. It provided a new framework for regulation and eliminated restrictions and oversight on most aspects of the industry, putting cable under federal jurisdiction for the first time. Moreover, the act also legally prohibited the telephone companies—cable's sworn enemies—from providing cable service in their areas, restating the ban that was enacted by the FCC in 1970. The thrust of the act was toward less regulation and more weight given to the voice of the "market" for important decisions, consistent with the administration's overall tenor. It also ensured that the cable companies could continue to develop without the threat of competition from the "telcos."

The manner in which cable became the driving force for the media industries at this point in the 1980s was transformational. As cable grew, so did the tolerance of the Department of Justice for mergers, acquisitions, and structural convergence in entertainment. Film and broadcast would soon expand beyond their previous lines in the sand and begin to incorporate cable holdings into their portfolios on a larger scale. It would have seemed logical for the networks to be investing heavily in the mushrooming cable medium. After all, each one had at least thirty-five years of experience producing, scheduling, and selling televised entertainment and information. The potential synergies of collaboration were myriad. Nonetheless, the networks remained largely on the outside of this revolution looking in, primarily due to the fact that deregulation was applied in different measures and with different outcomes to film, cable, and broadcast. This variance enacted a transfer of power in the middle of the decade that wound up emboldening cable and preventing the broadcast networks from fully participating in the early cable windfall.

The big three broadcast networks as well as local broadcast stations had been prohibited from operating cable systems since 1970, when the network/cable cross-ownership rules were adopted.[79] They were not, however, prevented from ownership in cable programming services (channels), and they had all purchased interests in programming services between 1981 and 1982. ABC was the most active in this arena. One of the network's early forays into cable ownership was the Satellite News Channel in 1982, a service that was established in partnership with Westinghouse to compete with CNN. ABC soon sold out to Turner, settling on $25 million to abandon the Satellite News Channel and get out of the cable news business to avoid an antitrust suit Turner had initiated.[80] ABC also began the ARTS network (Alpha Repertory Television Service) as a joint venture with the Hearst Corporation in April 1981. The "network" was essentially a three-hour evening programming block that aired on the Nickelodeon channel and specialized in cultural programming related to visual and fine arts.

NBC's parent company RCA started a service similar to ARTS—the Entertainment Network—with the Rockefeller Group in 1982. Both ARTS and the Entertainment Network were devoted to showcasing programming for audiences interested in fine arts, ballet, opera, and other live performances, but the Entertainment Network was sold to subscribers for a separate fee. NBC and Rockefeller also had an exclusive deal with the BBC, which was very important to establishing their primacy in this particular market. ARTS bought the Entertainment Network in 1984 and the merged service became A&E.[81] From that deal, ABC and NBC were co-owners (along with Hearst) in one of the most prominent burgeoning cable networks.[82] ABC and Hearst also partnered to launch the Daytime programming service in 1982, which was a four-hour block of shows that were basically televised versions of Hearst magazines (such as "A View from *Cosmo*" with Helen Gurley Brown, and *Esquire*'s "About Men for Women"). Daytime was reformatted in 1984 to become Lifetime Television. With that, ABC owned 33 percent of Lifetime and 38 percent of A&E (along with NBC) as well as 80 percent of ESPN (a very successful purchase for ABC made in 1984).[83] In the early 1980s, ABC was far ahead of the rest of the broadcast industry when it came to integrating with cable services.

CBS had also started its own basic cable network devoted to arts and culture in October 1981—CBS Cable—programming twelve hours a day[84] of dance, drama, music, and other cultural interests.[85] The network produced 60 percent of its own material and acquired the rest from a combination of domestic and overseas sources. The programming was ambitious and sophisticated; it included everything from a twenty-five-program history of modern jazz and a series set in New York cabarets to the Vienna Philharmonic Orchestra playing all nine Beethoven symphonies. The schedule even showcased some live drama, a genre not seen on television since the 1950s.[86] Largely due to enormous expenses incurred to produce its large lineup of original programming and its inability to find its affluent, culturally minded audience, CBS Cable had failed by the end of 1982, losing $30 million in its first year.[87] Nevertheless, many critics and industry insiders acknowledged that CBS Cable was the superior arts programming service.[88] Each one of these network-founded cable services was basically an attempt to reach a very highbrow and niche audience interested in the arts. Instead of sticking with their time-honored strategy of reaching for the mass audience, these new ventures were all essentially rivals of PBS.

In the meantime, cable and film were beginning to formulate the seeds of empire with some of their own mergers. By the time that the media industries finished 1984, both Fox and MGM/UA were the only film studios left unallied with cable interests. Warner Bros. had a slew of cable systems and networks, Paramount and MCA (parent company of Universal) along with Time, Inc. were the co-owners of the USA Network, Disney had launched their Disney Channel cable network in 1983,[89] and Columbia was involved with HBO on a number of ventures including Tri-Star. However, Fox and MGM/UA would not be on the outside of the cable industry for long. Ted Turner and Rupert Murdoch would soon acquire these studios and with their new purchases, would reinvent what "television holdings" could mean for film. Together, Turner and Murdoch modernized the relationship between film and TV for the future of media conglomerates . . . all while evading the long arm of fin-syn, which kept their competitors shackled to outmoded blueprints of industrial design.

3

1984–1986

Outsiders Moving In–Murdoch and Turner

In 1983, a yacht sponsored by Rupert Murdoch crashed into Ted Turner's vessel during the Sydney to Hobart race, causing Turner and his crew to run aground just six miles from the finish line. After returning to dry land, Turner challenged Murdoch to a live, televised fistfight in Las Vegas.[1] While Murdoch did not take Turner up on his offer, this "exchange" between the two moguls in the early 1980s established the tone for their relationship over the next twenty years and kicked off the definitive rivalry in media industries—one that would even spur the pace of empire construction at times.

Turner and Murdoch became extremely important to the development of media conglomerates just as cable acquisitions started to drive their expansion and growth. Horizontal *and* vertical integration became key strategies for the cable industry during the 1980s. Program distributors were also suppliers, and cable channels were increasingly controlled by MSOs. Unlike in broadcasting, the efficiencies of teaming production and distribution were readily available to this burgeoning industry. Cable companies were aggressively taking advantage of those opportunities, with Murdoch and Turner leading the way. As cable was increasingly deregulated, the broadcast networks were at risk of losing their privileged position in the entertainment landscape along with the government protection they had enjoyed in the marketplace since the days of radio. It was at this moment that Murdoch and Turner found a way to use broadcast to enhance their own cable and film properties, making the struggling industry newly valuable to empires of entertainment.

Broadcast's Downward Slide

Unlike broadcasting, the cable industry was free to grow and/or consolidate in a variety of ways that allowed for production and distribution to combine. Cable's approach often seemed to brazenly defy antitrust policy as it was applied to other media industries, highlighting the discrepancy among regulatory standards. Cable systems could own financial stakes in cable channels, for example, and many of them, including John Malone's TCI (the nation's largest cable provider in 1982 with more than 2 million customers) and ATC were heavily invested in programming.[2] This stake that MSOs had in the content shown on their "networks" was precisely the type of vertical integration that fin-syn was designed to prevent in broadcasting.

As discussed in chapter 2, the broadcast networks were forbidden to produce or have any financial stake in their own programming. They could own cable channels (e.g., ARTS or ESPN), but thanks to the 1970 network/cable cross-ownership rules, they were prohibited from owning the cable delivery *systems* (or provider/distributors, commonly referred to as MSOs, such as TCI), which were the center of power in the industry. As a result, by the mid-1980s the "big three" were left watching helplessly as their cable competitors availed themselves of business strategies that were illegal for the networks to employ. Much the same way that the major studios were excluded from television owner-ship in the 1940s, the broadcast networks were shut out of the distribution game once cable took off.[3]

What's more, at this point the solvency of the broadcast television industry was being assailed on multiple fronts, as competition from new technologies and Chicago School regulatory philosophies threatened the stability of the business. Network profits had been shrinking since 1980 due to increased pro-gramming costs (for both news and entertainment) and declining advertising revenues (thanks to cable, a recession, and rising interest rates). Audiences were also diminishing as cable slowly began draining broadcast viewership and all three networks began instituting massive layoffs amid desperate budget crises. These threats brought corporate raiders circling, and the walls began closing in by 1985. ABC chairman Leonard Goldenson presciently complained in late 1984, "the FCC has so deregulated the industry that broadcasters are no longer insulated from unfriendly takeovers."[4]

The environment of deregulation created by the Reagan administration made the 1980s a time when there were more hostile takeovers, mergers, and buyouts than any other in U.S. history. This new emphasis on the neoliberal principle of "the market regulating itself" drastically reduced the power and budget of numerous government agencies, including the FCC, the Federal Trade Commission, and the Antitrust Division of the Department of Justice. At the same time, cable and home video were proliferating. This combination caused tremendous anxiety in the broadcast networks—while they certainly did not want to be regulated, they did want their growing competition to be closely policed.

With the introduction of cable and the VCR, the market shares of the networks began to quickly erode. Cable siphoned off more of the broadcast audience with each new fall lineup and by 1985, nearly half of all network viewers received their programs through a cable system.[5] Broadcast networks saw their market shares drop to 75 percent, down from 89 percent just ten years earlier.[6] Eventually, the networks saw a third of their audience defect to cable. It would continue to worsen throughout the decade as VCRs found their way into two-thirds of American homes and gave Hollywood a new inroad to encroach on the television audience.[7] These new choices and markets steadily chipped away at the networks and also signaled the end of television's image as a "free" source of entertainment, now that consumers were increasingly willing to pay for basic cable, premium channels, and pay-per-view movies.

Additionally, broadcasters were now being threatened by the regulatory agency that had historically safeguarded their power. The FCC was moving away from the traditionally protectionist role toward broadcasters; this former "guardian angel" of the networks actually opened the door for new owners to take control during President Reagan's second term. By 1985, the networks were facing a financial crisis (largely attributed to spiraling costs, poor management, and growing competition from new technologies), stock prices were depressed, and ratings were sliding.[8] The combination of the agency's relaxed rules and abandoned regulations provided the crowning impetus for what was termed by the industry trades as "merger mania" during the mid-1980s, as the FCC essentially invited and encouraged more exchange and concentration of ownership.

The increase in television ownership limits is most commonly understood as the last shoe to drop before the merger craze in broadcasting that started in 1985. Almost immediately after ownership limits were raised from seven to twelve (allowing the networks to nearly double the number of their "owned and operated" stations, which were traditionally big profit centers and essential to financial health for the networks), the "big three" were targeted for takeover. The result was a brisk increase in station sales and within two years, all three major networks had new owners and a fourth was born to challenge their market share. The new owners that had been watching the industry's declining market values and underperforming assets were able to take advantage of lowered interest rates to finance their acquisitions. This was the first change in ownership ever for CBS and NBC, and the first time for ABC since control of the network went to United Paramount Theaters in 1951.

ABC was the number one network in the 1970s—it had the best ratings and the best "quality demographics"—but it had fallen back to its familiar third-place territory by 1984. Profits were declining, the network's stock price was depressed, and, consequently, it was the first to fall victim to a hostile takeover. The new owner was Capital Cities, a group of ABC affiliates that had invested in magazines and cable. With the help of Warren Buffett, Cap Cities became known as "the little fish that swallowed the big fish" when it bought the vulnerable ABC in March 1985 for a bargain rate of $3.5 billion, a price that analysts say was grossly below its market value. Cap Cities took control of the network in January 1986.[9] Around the same time, General Electric worked out a deal to buy RCA, the parent company of NBC. The deal—the largest non-oil-related merger in U.S. history—was announced in December 1985 and government approval was finalized in June 1986. It was a $6.28 billion merger that GE touted as an excellent strategic combination that would "help America's competitiveness in world markets."[10] This comment is interesting in that, even though broadcast networks are inherently linked to constructs of "the national," GE was connecting the acquisition to international commerce, and also anticipating the growing importance of "the global" to media industries.

Shortly thereafter, in September 1986, real estate magnate and chairman of Loew's Corporation, Laurence Tisch, gained control of CBS from network founder William S. Paley, while preventing a hostile takeover by Ted Turner. CBS was the number-one network for the first half of the 1980s, but its hits were quickly becoming tired, with shows like *Dallas, Murder She Wrote*, and *Falcon Crest* now losing in the ratings to new hits on NBC like *The Cosby Show, Cheers*, and *Hill Street Blues*. By 1985, CBS was in trouble—showing a quarterly loss for the first time in the modern era—and vulnerable to takeover, which happened by the next year when Tisch became the controlling shareholder. He had started buying up the company's stock in 1985 and was made president in September 1986 when Loew's owned 25 percent of CBS.

While the existing broadcast networks were changing hands, Rupert Murdoch was buying up prominent independent stations so he could start a network of his own. One month after Capital Cities bought ABC in 1985, Murdoch purchased Metromedia's stations to launch the Fox Network (as discussed later in this chapter). Without the increase in station ownership limits and relaxed regulations, these properties would have been less attractive, less accessible, and it would have been highly unlikely that they would have all fallen victim to hostile takeovers.

Promoting Efficiencies

The 1984 Merger Guidelines certainly helped to set the stage for what was unfolding behind the screens. These newest articulations of antitrust policy by the DOJ were purposefully ambiguous but more focused on emphasizing economic analysis in the application of antitrust policy.[11] Consequently, the new guidelines allowed for most vertical mergers, as they were generally viewed as "promoting efficiency." As one policy analyst has noted, "Antitrust complaints based on exotic vertical and 'shared monopoly' theories came to a virtual halt—the focus of Reagan policy shifted to more traditional horizontal restraint-of-trade matters," and even those were given a much wider berth with the new rules.[12] After all, a fair share of very large, high-profile horizontal mergers were taking place beyond the cable industry, including several in the oil and auto manufacturing industries. Some of these mergers were among the largest in U.S. history, such as the one valued at $10 billion between Texaco and Getty Oil in 1984.

One other policy of importance to the shifting terrain in television was the Cable Communications Policy Act of 1984. As noted in chapter 2, the Cable Communications Policy Act—the first substantial act of deregulation in the cable industry—was just the spark the growing industry needed, and a wave of consolidation and growth quickly followed. The act also tried to establish a compromise between the cable systems operators and the city governments by giving the municipalities authority over rates and regulation, although that authority was severely limited. Essentially, the MSOs were freed from the majority of the regulatory restraints that had hampered the industry's growth up to that point and the act took most of the power to set rates away from local authorities as of December 29, 1986. Local rate control was largely going to be a thing of the past; municipalities could still set rates for "basic" service, but national cable systems could basically write their own check for rate increases. State and federal regulation of rates would be prohibited and local authority granted only in cases where "effective competition" did not exist. However, according to the FCC's distorted definition, competition existed everywhere so the agency framed the issue "in such a way as to insulate nearly all local systems from local control."[13] At this point, the government turned the reigns over to the MSOs and the "free market," which were primed and ready to unleash the cable industry.

With the notice of this newfound power to increase cable rates at will, the cost of cable systems skyrocketed, along with their anticipated earnings. MSOs used the rate deregulation to borrow more money and expand their operations. "What [deregulation] did was create liquidity, which we used to acquire additional cable operations, rebuild plants and invest in programming," said TCI President John Malone.[14] TCI alone owned nearly 25 percent of the country's cable systems after a binge in which Malone bought 150 cable companies in the three years following the 1984 act.[15] TCI also acquired significant interests in Turner Broadcasting Systems, the Discovery Channel, AMC, and BET. Malone and the rest of the cable industry would ultimately pay for their exuberance with the 1992 Cable Act, but they would have eight years of deregulated growth to enjoy in the meantime.

Thomas Streeter has noted the ironies of the 1984 act—a work of deregulation that intended to create competition in the industry but instead wound up creating local monopolies by allowing cable franchises to be exclusive.[16]

Streeter has argued that the most important (if not the most obvious) irony of the 1984 Cable Act is the fact that "the economic conditions driving cable and generating pressures for passage of the 1984 act are the same ones that have motivated most regulation of the corporate economy in general: economies of scale that generate pressures toward vertical integration, oligopolistic behavior, and the practice of using regulation to generate industry stability and political legitimacy."[17] However, this irony was lost on federal regulators and the industry was thus *deregulated* according to and inspired by principles traditionally spurring *regulation*.

Even after the 1984 act, cable systems still had to live with the "Must Carry" rules. These rules originated in 1972 and mandated that the cable systems carry all local television stations, regardless of whether the station had low ratings or duplicated another network/channel that was already on the system.[18] While cable owners chafed against these rules and—led by Turner himself—later fought them all the way to the Supreme Court, the rules did allow for the proliferation of independent and new UHF stations, which might have otherwise been lost or ignored due to inferior signal strength. Now, the reach and coverage of these UHF stations dramatically increased and they were able to attract significant audiences with distribution over cable. While Turner distributed his channels via satellite, Murdoch's channels used the broadcast spectrum, and, in turn, benefited tremendously from this cable policy. In fact, thanks to both Ted Turner and Rupert Murdoch, the "Must Carry" rules took on even more significance. In essence, Turner and Murdoch were able to use their UHF stations to do exactly what the networks were forbidden to do: have a financial stake in the broadcast programming that they distributed and aired. This lack of uniform regulation across media industries was the linchpin in cable's ability to expand during this time, and also the reason Turner and Murdoch were able to begin building their empires in the mid-1980s. Both relative outsiders before that time, they would bring a new vision to entertainment industry partnerships and consolidation, combining film and television content and distribution into singular companies.

Ted Turner—Cable before Cable Was Cool

NBC chairman Bob Wright has summed up Ted Turner by saying that "he sees the obvious before most people do . . . [a]nd after he sees it, it becomes obvious to everyone."[19] Turner saw television's future before most people did . . . and he saw that it was in cable, not broadcasting. Never one for subtlety, Turner drove this point home in 1982, with a giant billboard image of himself playing guitar, proclaiming, "I was cable before cable was cool."[20] Turner relished in his image as an outsider and pointed to the struggles of the networks—the ultimate insiders—whenever possible. "I consider the networks kind of like the Germans were in late 1942," he said in the mid-1980s. "They held a lot of territory very thinly. Two out of three of them are unprofitable now."[21]

Like the moguls of the studio era, Turner built his company from scratch. He inherited a family billboard business in 1963, moved on to radio five years later, television by 1970, and, ultimately, helped jump start the cable revolution in the mid-1970s when he recognized the potential of satellite technology. He began Turner Broadcasting in 1976 once he decided to send his local programming to the rest of the nation via satellite.

His first television station, WJRJ in Atlanta, was losing money when he acquired it in 1968. WJRJ was an independent UHF station that Turner bought and renamed WTCG (for Turner Communications Group). It would eventually become SuperStation TBS in 1979, and it was the first of its kind on cable—a hybrid broadcast/cable property using satellite distribution. Once Turner persuaded the FCC to give him approval for the venture, he began using RCA's Satcom I satellite to bounce his signals to the rest of the country, following the lead of HBO. By December 1976 it was renamed once again and the new WTBS was the second network on the RCA satellite and the first cable "superstation," billing itself as "The SuperStation that serves the nation."[22] Turner immediately began with a corporate strategy of amassing programming assets that could be exhibited on his station and replayed often, lowering operating costs and creating a vertically integrated model from the start.

The major film studios were vehemently opposed to Turner's venture, as were the broadcast networks and local stations. For once, the film and television industries agreed on something: Ted Turner was a threat to the way they did business. The studios protested the fact that Turner would be paying local rates for their films and then exhibiting them nationally. The networks did not like the idea of his imposing on their territory. The FCC was not too friendly, either; while the agency was established to protect the "public interest," it had largely evolved into a steward of the broadcast networks' interests and Turner did not fall into that category. However, Turner lobbied congressional leaders with the argument that he, a broadcaster, was merely "trying to help the nascent cable industry provide consumers with more [and better] choices."[23] They were convinced, and TBS was the first basic cable service to go on the satellite and one of the foundations of cable programming, along with HBO. As Eric Guthey has noted, however, "the FCC's decision to allow Turner to beam his station's signal nationwide to cable systems via satellite flew in the face of the principle of localism," but Turner exploited that contradiction all the way to the bank, using it "to dismantle the regulatory protection of the network broadcasting system" at the same time.[24]

Turner was also instrumental in getting federal restrictions relaxed for the rest of the cable industry in the late 1970s. He was one of the very few broadcasters who supported cable's growth and expansion, which made his position uniquely compelling. On the whole, broadcasters were united against cable and the threat that it posed to their audience, but Turner could not afford to be so limited in his thinking; as the owner of an independent UHF station, cable viewers represented more than half of Turner's customers.[25] In fact, it was because of the manner in which he combined UHF broadcasting properties and cable (via satellite) that he was able to get his empire off the ground. However, he did identify himself primarily as a cable entrepreneur and fought the "Must-Carry" rules—rules that mandated cable carriage of his own broadcast stations—all the way to the Supreme Court. He also continually fought for the importance of cable as an alternative to the stranglehold that the networks held on the American broadcast industry and, he argued, on American public opinion. He emphasized the need for "family-oriented" programming, diversity in the marketplace, and options in news and entertainment for the viewing public. With this, he won a favorable audience in Congress and great support from the cable industry, forging an alliance that would save him from bankruptcy ten years later.

From the start, Turner thought in terms of owning *content*. Turner even envisioned the Atlanta Braves and Atlanta Hawks as programming inventory for WTBS, while admitting that they were "the world's worst two sports franchises" when he acquired them in 1976–77.[26] He first paid $1.3 million in 1973 for the rights to broadcast three years of their games and then wound up buying the Braves when the owners threatened to sell to Toronto after net losses entered the seven-figure territory.[27] Turner saw hundreds of hours of a relatively inexpensive programming disappearing and quickly bought the team, saving Atlanta's franchise *and* securing his own scheduling niche in sports. Although he went into debt to pay the $10 million asking price (for a team that was losing $1 million a year), Turner was happy to maintain his channel's continuous baseball coverage.[28] He was not the first to combine ownership of a television network and a sports team (CBS owned the New York Yankees from 1964 to 1973), but he was the first network owner to maintain all of the broadcast rights for his own team. This turned out to be quite a sound investment and a primer for how to successfully cultivate corporate synergy as well: after using the team to boost his independent channel, and vice versa, the Braves would be worth $200 million by the mid-1990s.[29]

Turner then bought the Atlanta Hawks and tenaciously held on to the franchise, despite the fact that he was unable to realize a profit on the team. Advisors had finally convinced him to sell in early 1983, but Turner changed his mind after the Hawks beat the Celtics in the hallowed Boston Gardens that year. Even though he lost $3 million in the 1981–82 season and $5 million in the 1982–83 season, he stubbornly continued airing all of their regular season games on his superstation.[30] Still, he could indefinitely broadcast the games on WTBS or sell the rights to other stations. Turner's philosophy was to aggressively extract all possible value out of his assets, exploiting all potential channels of synergy. As he told *Forbes* magazine, "Modern chicken farmers, they grind up the feet to make fertilizer, they grind up the intestines to make dog food. The feathers go into pillows. Even the chicken manure they make into fertilizer. They use every bit of the chicken. Well, that's what we try to do over here with the television products, is use everything to its fullest extent."[31]

With this approach guiding his investments, Turner began amassing more and more "television products." In fact, Turner was looking to own a library of programming, "a fine library, so that we could control enough programming that we could program a really fine entertainment network, not only in the United States but globally, to position ourselves in the global business."[32] He was tired of being at the mercy of the film studios for programming. He wanted to become a modern media giant. Often citing Standard Oil as a model, since Rockefeller owned the oil fields, gas stations, pipelines, trucks, and distribution networks, Turner very clearly saw from the start that "controlling everything" was the path to power. This philosophy eventually became the mandate and mantra for empires of entertainment.

His launch of CNN in 1980 was a big step in gaining more control. However, it required that he secure more space on RCA's satellite to transmit the service across the country (and eventually, the globe). Of course, as owner of NBC, RCA was not keen on assisting one of their competitors. Turner then sued RCA when they refused to give CNN space on the satellite. He also launched a major offensive against Congress and the FCC to convince them of the importance of CNN. He donated a $13,000 satellite dish to the House of Representatives and wired all of the members' offices so they could see for themselves.[33] Turner got his space on the transponder and this would help him turn CNN into the most watched and authoritative news service in the world. Turner also offered to present the White House with an antenna and receiver system to receive satellite transmissions in order to provide CNN to the president and his staff around the clock.[34] That plan did not work out because of severe interference in the area, but Turner's many efforts were enormously important in cable's struggle for acceptance by the White House and Congress.

In the process, he also turned to antitrust law to help the channel get established. Turner sued the White House (President Ronald Reagan, Chief of Staff James Baker, Deputy Press Secretary Larry Speakes, and Secretary of State Alexander Haig) *and* the three networks for excluding the CNN crews from the White House press pool. He charged that the networks were employing monopolistic practices and that the president and his staff were treating CNN unfairly. Turner claimed they were attempting to eliminate competition and monopolize the market, thus violating the Sherman Act. His suit had a mighty list of complaints against the "network defendants," including:

> Excluding CNN from pools, establishing membership terms for partici-
> pation in pools that are so onerous as to effectively preclude participa-
> tion in such pools, preferential treatment to themselves, discriminating
> against CNN, knowingly providing CNN pool material not suitable for its
> needs, forcing CNN and others to subsidize the [networks'] coverage of
> newsworthy events, interfering with development of CNN's relationships
> with foreign and international news and transmission services by doing
> business as "North American pool" and excluding CNN, interfering with
> CNN's arrangements to cover various news events.[35]

Eventually, after about a year of acrimonious litigation, Turner won an out-of-
court settlement in March 1982. The settlement allowed CNN to join the rest
of the journalists in the pool.

Still, Turner continually had to fight for respect in the early days. Even after
the settlement, CNN continued to be slighted by the White House. In one letter
dated January 27, 1983, CNN's senior vice president wrote to White House Communications Director David Gergen:

> The two musketeers? The six dwarfs? The three networks? It was with no
> little dismay we learned that CNN was not invited to the pre–State of
> the Union noon briefing along with the anchors of the older networks.
> Candidly, one wonders what is required to acquire parity. Certainly we
> have the audience. Surely we cover the White House. Without question
> we bring more live coverage of the President to our seven time zones
> than the other networks combined. We are also members of the network
> pool. Nevertheless, CNN shall stay the course.[36]

Turner added a second CNN service (then CNN2, soon to be Headline
News) in early 1982 while taking on two formidable powerhouses of broadcasting: ABC and Westinghouse. The two companies had announced a plan for
a headline news channel called Satellite News Service (SNC) to rival Turner.
Turner decided to create CNN2 in retaliation, and get the channel up and running before SNC launched. ABC and Westinghouse had a combined net worth
of $4 billion and Turner was only valued at $200 million.[37] Turner went after
them anyhow (after all, he had just sued the President of the United States and
won) and charged the two companies with illegally keeping Headline News off
of Westinghouse-owned cable systems.[38] The following year, Turner reached an
out-of-court settlement with ABC and Westinghouse. Essentially, Turner bullied
(and bribed) them into selling out, which they did for a payment of $12.5 mil-
lion each, much to their stockholders' relief. For that, Turner bought out their
service and their 7.5 million viewers. *Time* magazine explained it as "David
conquered Goliath with his checkbook."[39] In his autobiography, *Call Me Ted*,

Turner writes that "Turner Broadcasting defeating ABC and Westinghouse in the early 1980s was like Luxembourg going to war with both the United States and the Soviet Union—and winning."[40] However, this victory, which Turner claimed to be more important than launching his SuperStation or CNN, did not come cheap.

All told, it cost Turner $100 million to go to war with ABC and he could not afford it again. Consequently, when a cadre of leading cable systems operators threatened to work with NBC as the network was attempting to move into cable news programming, Turner laid it on the line for the industry, telling John Malone (head of TCI), "You put NBC in business, I'm gone." He told Malone, "You have to choose, you want them or you want me. Just that simple."[41] They wanted Turner, because without him, they would lose many popular cable channels to sell to potential subscribers. So, with regulators looking the other way, Malone and the cable companies stood with Turner and all refused to buy NBC's cable news, putting the service out of business by February 1986. Thanks to TCI and the other MSOs, Turner wound up spending only $10–12 million to fend off NBC, instead of the $100 million it cost to keep ABC out of the cable news business.

Turner's antagonistic relationship with the networks continued—and telling the press that CBS founder William Paley had "turned the network into a whorehouse" with sleazy programming certainly didn't help.[42] Still, he had longed to own a broadcast network. In March 1985, Capital Cities acquired ABC in a stunning $3.5 billion deal—a relatively friendly merger among longtime business associates (many ABC affiliates were owned by Capital Cities) but a massive one for the media industries, nonetheless. Yet, the Justice Department paid little attention. According to Turner's CFO Bill Bevins, the ABC takeover "crystallized where the various regulatory agencies stood, and that the timing was propitious for media takeovers."[43] Turner saw this as an opportunity to realize his dream. ABC was off the market and NBC, while reportedly ripe for takeover, was too problematic as a subsidiary of RCA, according to Turner.[44] That left CBS, and Turner quickly launched a hostile takeover bid for the network with $5.4 billion in junk bonds.

Turner characterized his raid as a humanitarian mission of sorts, instead of merely a business prospect. He was going to save America from the corporations running the networks, explaining that "the greatest enemies that America has ever had—posing a greater threat to our way of life than Nazi Germany or Tojo's Japan—are the three television networks and the people that run them, who are living amongst us and constantly tearing down everything that has made this country great."[45] It was an ironic, and still characteristic move for Turner, as CBS was the one network he continually singled out as all that was wrong with television. Yet, it was also the one he constantly emulated and it was well known to everyone as the "Tiffany network." Turner also likened himself to the founder of CBS, often reminding people, "Paley was an outsider when he started, too."[46]

Turner naturally wanted to integrate his strengths in program ownership and production with distribution, and was one of the first new-era entertainment moguls to actually have the vision, resources, and capability to do so. Casting himself as the underdog once again, Turner spent time consulting with the FCC and worked with former FCC head Charles Ferris lobbying congressional leaders and trying to open the doors for his takeover. In addition to expanding, he wanted to protect his interests from studios that were aligning themselves with television properties; he saw the potential dangers in Paramount and MCA having interest in the USA Network, which was becoming the main rival of TBS on basic cable. He also saw the writing on the wall once Murdoch purchased Fox and began his own network (as detailed later in this chapter). Turner's supply of programming that came from Viacom was also in jeopardy once that company began to expand into network ownership, and by 1987, Viacom had five cable networks, including MTV, VH1, Showtime, The Movie Channel, and Nickelodeon (after buying Warner-Amex in 1985). Turner needed more content-based assets and a larger distribution pipeline to remain competitive.

However, CBS shareholders, the FCC, and the network were all very hostile toward Turner. Shareholders would not profit from the deal, and the network claimed Turner was ill-equipped and unfit to run a network. CBS appealed to the courts and the FCC while simultaneously engineering a stealthy buyback of their own stock to regain control. The network was also well represented on Capitol Hill and had fiercely lobbied regulators to prevent the takeover. CBS hoped that the FCC would refuse Turner much the same way that they turned Howard Hughes away when he attempted to buy ABC in 1968.

In the end, CBS was able to fight Turner off. A federal judge in Atlanta allowed the company to buy back 21 percent of its shares for about $1 billion; CBS wound up incurring enormous debt but nonetheless, decisions by the courts and the FCC forced Turner to abandon his mission.[47] The "white knight" financing of Laurence Tisch ultimately saved the network, but even with this failed bid, Turner had finally established himself as a force to be reckoned with in the media world. "We've created havoc for the big three networks over the years," Turner crowed. "All three of them had to change hands. How much more havoc can you have than that?"[48] His lost battle might have even been a blessing after all, as Turner was able to focus his energies on the budding cable industry and create his empire outward from there. Critics have also suggested that had he succeeded with the CBS takeover, Turner might have been dismissed by history instead of regarded as a visionary pioneer.

After being foiled by entrenched network forces and FCC regulators, Turner was stinging and more anxious than ever to become a respected major player in the entertainment industry. He had often talked about buying a film studio, and soon began seriously thinking of purchasing MGM/UA from Kirk Kerkorian. At the time, Turner's broadcasting system was strapped for product and he was powerless against the major studios, which were continually increasing the licensing fees for old films. His profits were shrinking and Turner knew that MGM/UA's rich library would be exactly what he needed to guarantee the lifelong supply of product necessary to sustain his distribution networks and ensure his survival. Turner saw it as a lifeline for his core business (WTBS). MGM/UA was also struggling, having posted an $82 million loss (their worst ever) in the second quarter of 1983.[49] So, unlike CBS, they viewed Turner and his money as welcome relief.

On August 6, 1985—one month after his failed bid for CBS—Turner made a deal with Kerkorian to buy MGM/UA for $1.2 billion. Junk bond king Michael Milken and Drexel Burnham Lambert financed the deal, finding a way for Turner to pay the $1.2 billion that he could not really afford. For this, Turner received the studio, lot, and library of 3,500 MGM films (including 750 pre-1948 Warner Bros. titles), over 700 RKO features, and numerous shorts, television series, and specials.[50] By 1986, he owned many of the most treasured titles in American cinema, such as *Gone With the Wind, Casablanca, Citizen Kane,* and *The Wizard of Oz,* to name a few. With that, Turner made the first acquisition of a major motion picture studio since 1969 (when Kirkorian bought MGM/UA for the first time and Kinney bought Warner Bros.) and began feeding into a new wave of conglomeration in the entertainment industry.

However, instead of lauding his business acumen, the industry laughed at Turner, deriding the deal and predicting that the days of "Captain Outrageous" had come to an end. Even *Newsweek* commented that Turner was "unanimously regarded as 'a pigeon' in Hollywood," with analysts noting that "he took a bath . . . he came to town fully clothed and left in a barrel."[51] Insiders said he paid $200–300 million too high. Yet, it was Turner who would have the last laugh. This purchase essentially filled 60 percent of Turner's programming needs. "We've got Spencer Tracy and Jimmy Cagney working for us from the grave," he pronounced with his customary bravado.[52] He proceeded to pump these films directly into his expanding distribution pipelines, beginning with his SuperStation WTBS. He no longer had to deal with rising licensing fees and now he had control over thousands of quality entertainment hours that could be programmed at will. What might have been overpaying for someone else turned out to be an extremely good deal for Turner. By 1988, Turner used the MGM library to form the basis for an entirely new network, Turner Network Television (TNT), which he launched in October 1988 with a showing of his favorite film, *Gone With the Wind.*

Unfortunately, the MGM deal put Turner in a precarious position and, suddenly, he found himself in dire need of capital. He was nearly $2 billion in debt with $1 million in interest compounding *every day.* He began talking with Rupert Murdoch (who would eventually become his arch nemesis) about merging. He tried to convince Steven Spielberg to run MGM. He was wildly scheming to find a way to hang on to his new asset but coming up empty handed. Almost immediately after buying his new studio, a debt-ridden Turner was faced with losing his entire company. He realized quickly that there was no way to bail himself out and insurmountable debt forced him to turn around and sell the entire operation that he had just purchased in the MGM/UA deal right back. He sold the MGM film/TV production and videocassette business and United Artists back to Kerkorian for $300 million (far less than he paid for it) and the MGM facilities and headquarters to Lorimar for $190 million. The film library was the one asset that he retained and he still owed over a billion dollars for that.

Even after the buyback, Turner Broadcasting was still in danger of collapsing under the MGM purchase in 1987. However, after counseling Turner to walk away from that deal which he could ill afford, John Malone (chairman of TCI) led the charge to Turner's rescue, lining up thirty-one cable operators (including his own TCI, ATC, Cox, Continental, United, and Warner) to help bail him out. "I was terribly afraid he would have to liquidate," Malone was quoted as saying, "The cable industry felt he was far too important to let that happen."[53] They did this by purchasing a 37 percent stake in Turner Broadcasting for $562.5 million, leaving Turner with the majority of shares in his company.[54] Turner also had to grant the group seven out of fifteen board seats and veto power over expenditures exceeding $2 million.[55] Malone agreed to this not because they were personal friends, but because of Turner's importance to the cable industry, explaining that "Turner would have been owned by Rupert Murdoch if the cable industry hadn't rallied. . . . [W]e really did not want to see the most valuable programmer converted to some other industry."[56] Turner was already "too big to fail," according to the cable industry.

This was an interesting reconciliation of sorts between cable program-mers and distributors, which had traditionally been enemies—at least those that did not own one another. The cable operators wanted to protect Turner's programming assets, which were extremely valuable to them. They did not want these services to fall into network hands, nor did they want Turner to go out of business . . . that would not have been in their best interest. So, they decided to institute more of a collaborative spirit to their relationship, which also had the effect of stimulating the growing vertical integration in the cable industry. With this bailout, the nation's largest cable system operator (TCI) was now part owner of Turner Broadcast System, as were thirty other major distributors. And it created a tremendous bond (and obligation) between Turner and his bene-factors, as he confessed that while he might have had his sights on broadcast before, "our primary loyalty lies with the cable industry now even more than it did before."[57]

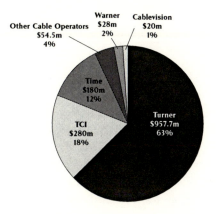

FIGURE 3.1.   Turner Cable Accord, 1987

Sources: Information used to generate this chart comes from Annual Reports and other SEC Filings by Turner (1987–1988); TCI (1988–1996); "Cable Firms Buy 37% Turner Stake, Completing Accord," *Wall Street Journal*, June 4, 1987, 49; and other stories from *The Wall Street Journal*, *New York Times*, *Los Angeles Times*, and *Washington Post*.

With the security of the MSOs behind him, Turner was able to expand and thrive. By 1989, CNN and WTBS would each be earning more than ABC and CBS combined.[58] By the time of the buyout, cable's advertising revenue was exceeding a billion dollars a year, up from just $380 million in 1983. This was a billion dollars that, according to a CBS executive, was "coming out of [the networks'] hides."[59] Turner was enjoying rolling over the networks this way and publicly predicted their demise, largely attributing their state of chaos to his own company and calling broadcasting a "second class medium" in terms of the financial picture. "We're like the Allies after Normandy . . . [w]e have landed. We are there. The beachhead cannot be obliterated."[60] At this point, Turner owned the largest vertically integrated media company in the world. He owned and produced enough programming to run three networks for twenty-four hours a day, something nobody else could claim.

After TNT went on the air in 1991, Turner had truly hit his stride . . . his SuperStation TBS, CNN, and TNT were three of the nation's six highest-rated basic cable stations. When his Headline News channel was added into the mix, these four networks of Turner Broadcasting accounted for 31 percent of all basic-cable viewing.[61] He then bought Hanna-Barbera's library in late 1991 for $320 million, a deal which Disney CEO Michael Eisner reportedly told Turner was the one he most regretted not making. Turner's strategy paid off again, and he described his resolve to purchase The Flintstones, The Jetsons, Yogi Bear, and Scooby Doo as unwavering: "When he said $315 million, I replied, 'Do you take cash?'"[62] Turner immediately began showcasing these animated programs on WTBS, TNT, and eventually on his new Cartoon Network, the first twenty-four-hour all-animation channel, launched in October 1992. Turner Classic Movies was established in April 1994 and created yet another outlet for his massive library.

Turner's approach to building his vertically integrated company was unique because of his primary emphasis on content as opposed to distribution. His vision was pieced together from the bottom up, acquiring programming *first* and then developing the networks, instead of the other way around. Also, the configurations of most of the other major entertainment companies in the 1980s were an amalgamation of distribution networks, creative production arms, and exhibition outlets in various media. Turner's vision was more focused, streamlined, and tightly diversified, sticking to film libraries and cable programming/networks.

Turner and his paradigm of vertical integration eventually became the future of cable and, as he predicted for the networks in the mid-1980s, the future caught up with them. The networks would continue their downward spiral as Turner took cable to new heights while creating the core of an entertainment empire that would endure into the new millennium. He started with a bankrupt UHF station and transformed it into a company that now stands as the heart of the Time Warner global entertainment conglomerate. He did this by unconventional means that combined media in ways that had never been done before, but would become standard industry practice just ten years later. There was only one of his contemporaries who could match his skill and creativity in constructing entertainment synergies while also exploiting loopholes in federal regulations: Rupert Murdoch and News Corporation.

Rupert Murdoch—Vertical, Horizontal, and Global

Back when Turner was going after CBS and buying MGM/UA, Australian mogul Rupert Murdoch also had his eyes on American media properties. Murdoch was busy designing his own aggressive blueprint for a vertically and horizontally integrated entertainment empire *and* he was taking it global. The media referred to him as an "Australian-born Ted Turner" for his role in keeping the majors on their toes and watching their backs. With his aggressive and very strategic acquisitions (plus special treatment by the government), Murdoch was able to skirt decades' worth of antitrust policy and broadcast regulations. Put another way, Douglas Gomery wrote, "The case of Rupert Murdoch illustrates how this version of 'free market' deregulation works for a small group of very wealthy individuals and corporations."[63]

Like Turner, he also started with a small business and took major risks, but while Turner had big, creative ideas, Murdoch was much more disciplined, orderly, and a bit more conservative with his deals. He inherited an Australian newspaper company from his father and the core of his company has been in publishing ever since. He began with newspapers and television stations in Australia during the 1960s and then moved on to British and American media in the 1970s and 1980s. By the end of the 1980s, he had expanded into a global communications empire.

His first American paper was the *San Antonio Express* in 1973 and then he launched the tabloid paper *The Star.* Soon thereafter, his conquests brought him to New York with the purchase of the *New York Post* and *New York Magazine* in 1976 and the *Village Voice* (which he would sell by 1985). News Corporation was formed in 1980 and by 1984, Murdoch and his company were well established in American publishing with papers in San Antonio, New York, Boston (the *Herald Examiner*, purchased in1982), and Chicago (the *Sun-Times*, acquired in 1983) in addition to *The Star.*

Murdoch became more focused on U.S. properties once entertainment and electronic media began to take precedence over news and publishing in the global fortunes of News Corp. He began aggressively building his American assets in the 1980s, even trying (unsuccessfully) to take over Warner Communications in 1984. After that, he went on a buying binge that "stunned media industry executives, some of whom worried that their companies might be next on his shopping list."[64] Murdoch finally made his mark on Hollywood and the American media landscape one year later when his News Corporation bought Twentieth Century–Fox from Marvin Davis in 1985.

Fox was a perfect candidate for takeover in 1981 when billionaire oil baron Marvin Davis bought control of the film studio for $725 million.[65] However, the investment did not work out well for Davis. Even though the studio was the leading supplier of network series and had the biggest home video business in America (in a joint venture with CBS called CBS/Fox), Davis was losing a great deal of money—between 1982 and 1985, the studio was $189 million in the red, largely because of expensive films that bombed in the theaters.[66] Murdoch saw this as an opportunity and made Davis an offer.

After four years of watching the studio consistently underperform, Davis was ready to sell. He was clearly falling behind the curve in terms of growing into other media industries and Davis was unprepared to expand the way he needed to; he had minimal holdings outside the studio and its licensing operation, as his primary dealings were in oil wells. On top of that, Fox posted a net loss of $90 million in 1984.[67] The time was right for Davis to unload, so he took a loss and sold the studio in two stages for total of $575 million. Murdoch acquired half interest in April 1985 for $250 million and bought the rest of the studio in December of that year for $325 million.[68]

Part of the funding Murdoch used to finance this deal was a hefty "buyback" profit he made during his failed takeover bid for Warner Communications, Inc. Murdoch had been acquiring Warner shares since October 1983 and by early 1984 he owned over 5.5 million shares, or 7 percent of Warners stock, and had "publicly stated he wished to take control of the corporation."[69] It was thought that he was going after Warners assets for programming—the film library, television production, and cable interests. However, in late December—in fact, just hours after Murdoch ran Turner aground in the Sydney race, according to Neil Chenoweth—Warner Bros. CEO Steve Ross arranged a stock swap with Chris-Craft Industries to fend off Murdoch's takeover. The swap gave Warner Bros. 42.5 percent ownership of Chris-Craft's broadcast stations, which protected Warners from the Australian-based News Corporation, as Murdoch was prohibited from having more than a 25 percent interest in Warner Bros. once they owned American broadcast stations.[70] Later, in March 1984, Warner Communications bought back Murdoch's stock and solidified an agreement with Murdoch stating that he would "not seek to control or influence Warner for 10 years."[71] Murdoch earned a tidy sum of $41 million in "greenmail"[72] for relinquishing his interest in the studio, and Warner Bros.-News Corporation would join the ranks of the "almost rans" in the media merger annals. Murdoch would have to look elsewhere to add a film studio to his holdings.

Barely six weeks after his Fox purchase was official, Murdoch came out with another deal, this one triple the size: on May 6, 1985, even before the Fox purchase was completed, Murdoch and Davis announced a plan to buy six stations from major group owner John Kluge of Metromedia for $1.85 billion. These were popular, independent, successful properties in Washington, D.C., New York City, Chicago, Los Angeles, Houston, and Dallas and would form the core of the fourth broadcast network. Interestingly, two of the Metromedia stations (New York and Washington, D.C.) were originally spun off by DuMont, the *other* fourth network that failed in 1956. Despite these grand plans, however, Murdoch was still an Australian citizen, and the Communications Act of 1934 prohibited foreign citizens from owning more than 20 percent of a TV license or 25 percent of the licensee's parent company. He had been a "resident alien" in the United States for ten years with a green card but it was still illegal for him to buy Metromedia. And yet, this did not stop Murdoch. In order to make his purchase of the stations, he actually renounced his Australian citizenship and became a naturalized American citizen in September 1985.

Metromedia had also attempted to form a fourth network—and had commitments for stations that would have potentially covered 35 percent of U.S. households—but it never panned out for the company.[73] Other Hollywood studios had been interested in the properties for some time as well, and Murdoch faced competition from Gulf + Western (parent company of Paramount) and Coca-Cola (owner of Columbia Pictures). In the end, Murdoch had the resources and was willing to commit them. Over the summer, Davis backed out of the deal. Nevertheless, Murdoch outbid his competitors by far, bought the stations on his own, and walked away with one of the strongest groups of independent stations in America and all the makings of a brand-new network.

Paying far above market value (fifteen times cash flow as opposed to the customary nine to ten times cash flow that most independent stations were going for at the time), Murdoch created the first new television network in over thirty years.[74] Fox was the only network rival that ABC, CBS, and NBC had seen since the demise of DuMont. More importantly, he managed to structurally integrate the film and broadcast industries for the first time, creating a blueprint for entertainment empires that would endure. Now, Murdoch could funnel his guaranteed supply of entertainment into the lucrative arms of theater exhibition *and* television programming.

Immediately, Murdoch put Barry Diller, former ABC executive and head of Paramount, in charge of his new company. Diller, as CEO of Fox, Inc., would help Murdoch integrate his multifaceted empire into a new model for media industries. Barry Diller had been cultivating the dream of a fourth network since his days at Paramount in the late 1970s. He had pioneered the concept of the modern made-for-TV movie and the "movie of the week" during his days at ABC. He was also chairman of Paramount Pictures for ten years from 1974 to 1984, making him uniquely qualified to run a company with a major motion picture studio and a television network. Leonard Goldberg (Barry Diller's former boss at ABC) was brought in as president and COO.

They began lining up more affiliates for the new network and came away with an assorted team of local UHF and VHF stations that would carry their two nights of prime time programming by 1987. To these independent stations, it was much-needed relief; they were thrilled to have new access to network-quality shows during a time when programming costs were increasing every year, and they got to keep nearly half of the advertising time to sell for themselves. To Murdoch, the stations represented the lynchpin in his vision of vertical integration. Fox already owned, produced, and distributed films and television programs. Now, Fox would have new outlets for these products in the form of a broadcast network, owned and operated stations (O&Os), and affiliates.

The FCC's definition of a "network" was key to Murdoch's successful exploitation of the Twentieth Century–Fox library and the integration of his resources as program supplier and exhibitor. The commission defined a network as "providing 15 or more hours per week to at least 25 affiliates in 10 or more states."[75] This of course had significant implications for Fox and its relationship to fin-syn (and the prime-time access rule). Murdoch started with just eight hours per week, broadcasting during prime time on Saturday and Sunday, then adding an episode of *The Late Show Starring Joan Rivers* on weeknights. With this minimal schedule, he was able to avoid being labeled a network and evade the regulatory policies that restricted the rest of his competition. Fox was able to produce its own programming and was free to syndicate its hits, and begin mounting a growing challenge to the established networks in the face of widespread industry skepticism and doubt.

The Fox network was up and running in 1986 on ninety-nine stations across the country that reached into more than 80 percent of U.S. television homes.[76] Thanks to the combination of cable technology, practically unlimited financing and resources available from his global media ventures, and a government committed to deregulation, Murdoch was primed to explore the new possibilities of horizontal and vertical integration in the media industries. Still, Murdoch was facing an uphill battle with his plans for a fourth network. He had to contend with the entrenched oligopoly of ABC, NBC, and CBS. He also had to face the rather protectionist FCC that policed them. Even the initial manner in which the FCC parceled out the airwaves basically guaranteed that there could only be three networks—in the FCC's 1952 *Sixth Report and Order*, a station allotment plan was articulated that limited the top 100 markets to an average of three commercial VHF stations only. Thus, as historians Laurie Thomas and Barry Litman have noted, "the FCC regulation created a structural barrier to entry which essentially assured the dominance of the network triopoly."[77]

However, there was a significant confluence of factors in the economic and industrial climates working to Murdoch's advantage. First, the explosion in independent (unaffiliated with a network) and UHF stations along with the attendant increase in demand for programming were extremely important developments in Fox's favor. At the onset of the Reagan administration, the Fowler FCC was licensing new broadcast stations in unprecedented numbers and the industry began to change shape. Since most markets already had a full slate of network affiliates, most of these newer stations were independent. As a result, the number of unaffiliated stations more than doubled between 1980 and 1985, from 120 to 283—more than enough to support a fourth network and almost all positioned on the UHF spectrum.[78] This growth inspired tremendous competition for programming amid increasing costs. Independents typically filled their airtime with movies, sports, children's programming, local newscasts, some religious shows, and a host of syndicated reruns. For these new stations, the idea of affiliating with a new network that had a library of 2,500 shows in the vault certainly became more attractive in this competitive environment.

This dramatic increase was also aided by the spread of cable technology, which negated the independent stations' built-in handicap that came with a weaker signal and undesirable position on the channel spectrum. Cable carried UHF stations into homes with an improved signal and moved the channels from their less-than-desirable position somewhere in the "40s or 50s" to a channel assignment approximating a place on the regular VHF dial below 13, in closer proximity to the established networks that the audience was habitually watching. Consequently, Murdoch was able to take advantage of this threat to broadcasters and use it to expand his network's reach into American homes.

The other industry trends that were plaguing the broadcast networks, including a viewership down more than 20 percent, new home video technologies that were eating into profits and stability, and falling advertising revenues also benefited Murdoch. The broadcast business was significantly weakened, creating an opportunity for him to strike. "There may be no better time to come in than when three fat and happy guys find themselves in trouble," said one top TV executive. "[Just] ask the Japanese automakers."[79] Fox Broadcasting president Jamie Kellner echoed this sentiment when explaining how Fox was able to take advantage of the networks' misfortune. "[The networks] got fat when they became successful," he said, which exposed "a weak underbelly to competitors who can operate more efficiently."[80] Also helping Murdoch was the fact that Fox did not have the overhead of the established networks when they went on the air, having a staff of only fifty people, or "the size of the ABC research department," in 1986.[81]

The network had a new attitude toward programming, targeting a younger audience, focusing on cheaply produced "reality" shows and promoting tabloid-esque entertainment (*A Current Affair, Married . . . With Children*, and *America's Most Wanted*). Murdoch was content to program with a specific niche market in mind, aiming for a narrow demographic, as opposed to the masses, as his competitors did. The Fox target audience of young males made things much simpler and more efficient for Murdoch and also spawned a new age of appeal for niche marketing in broadcasting. John Caldwell has discussed how seductive the idea of niche marketing became for the rest of the networks, particularly during the era of cable's ascendance and success with more narrowly defined target audiences. In their attempts to position themselves as reaching out to particular niches, Caldwell points out, "the networks were now desperately invoking the very same buzzwords of diversity that had fueled the competitive emergence of cable." He also labeled these claims as "preposterous—given the generic and historical variety of programming on the majors."[82] Nevertheless, it demonstrates the degree to which the networks were scrambling for strategies in the face of declining revenues. Murdoch, however, was the only one actually putting the concept of niche marketing into practice as a broadcaster.

Of course, the timing of the new Fox network was in perfect synchronicity with the relaxed regulatory climate in Washington. The elimination of the station-trafficking rule and the regional concentration rule, in addition to the FCC's implementation of increased station ownership limits again in 1985, further supported the growth of the Fox network and bolstered Murdoch's ability to compete with the established networks. What's more, Rupert Murdoch and

Mark Fowler shared a mutual admiration and an ideological affinity. While Murdoch praised Fowler as "one of the great pioneers of the communications revolution," Fowler saw Murdoch as representing marketplace competition, new choices for viewers, and a valuable challenge to the big three networks.[83] Fowler therefore went out of his way to assist Murdoch in his bid to establish the Fox network, including granting Murdoch temporary two-year waivers from FCC newspaper/broadcast cross-ownership regulations in 1986. These rules prevented one company from owning a newspaper and television or radio station in the same market,[84] which Murdoch did after purchasing stations in New York (WNYW-TV) and Boston (WFXT-TV) as well as the *New York Post* and the *Boston Herald*. In fact, Fox was given the only waivers for cross-ownership since the rules were adopted in 1975, which led some in the media industries to nickname the FCC "The Fox Communications Commission." President Reagan himself also endorsed the waivers for Murdoch in an address to Congress, in order to preserve "First Amendment freedoms."[85]

In May 1990 the network was granted another waiver by the FCC—this one from fin-syn—allowing Fox to expand its programming schedule to eighteen and a half hours, which posed a greater competitive threat to the "big three." With this waiver, the network would have one more year free from the restrictions of the rules. "Fox has been a bright and innovative force," said one FCC commissioner; "the existence of a fourth network is certainly in the public interest. . . . Fox deserves to be encouraged."[86] Ultimately, Fox never had to abide by the restrictions of fin-syn because they were given another exemption in 1993 when moving to a full prime-time programming schedule, and the rules were fully repealed in 1995. This allowed Murdoch to program twenty-two prime-time hours a week like the other networks and continue his lucrative syndication operation without having to choose between maintaining that income stream and expanding his network programming operation. The networks were, of course, furious that Fox was exempt from the regulations that had been binding them for nearly twenty years by that point.

There would be other studios linked with television properties during the 1980s, but none of these collaborations came close to what Murdoch was creating. In 1986, for example, MCA/Universal bought New Jersey–based independent station WWOR for $387 million.[87] WWOR played primarily to the New York market and was a cable superstation, much like Turner's WTBS. Universal exploited the property largely as a showcase for its own library. Three years later, Paramount—a leading television producer and syndicator with network shows that included *Cheers* and *Family Ties* as well as the syndicated *Star Trek: The Next Generation* and *Entertainment Tonight*—bought a controlling stake in five television stations. These independent stations, broadcasting in Philadelphia, Washington, Houston, Dallas, and Raleigh-Durham, N.C., were part of the struggling TVX broadcast group.[88] That same year, both MCA/Universal and

Paramount would join forces and attempt to form a fifth network, Premier Program Service. This network would have been a rival to Fox, particularly when it came to battling for affiliates. The two studios planned to use WWOR and Paramount's five stations as the core affiliates for the new network. Murdoch, of course, fought them aggressively, but in the end, the studios' plan folded without ever coming to pass. While this did represent some incursion of the film studios into broadcast, on the whole, these ventures were rather isolated and much more limited collaborations than anything approaching the scale of Murdoch's vision or the strategic possibilities of his assets.

It took less than one year from his arrival in Hollywood for Murdoch to become a major player in American film and television, and just two purchases for him to integrate these industries that the government had labored to keep separate for the previous forty years. He also worked in tandem with the threats posed by cable and federal regulators to chip away at the monopolistic power that the networks had enjoyed since their inception. Once Murdoch began his fourth network, strengthening the independent stations and eroding the grip of ABC, CBS, and NBC, the "big three" had to make major adjustments in light of their new competition and the changes now visiting the broadcast industry.

Ultimately, Murdoch's impact in the Reagan era was to change the rules of business in television. He revalued syndicated programming, expanded the broadcast industry, instituted new competitive measures in the relationship between cable and the networks, and redefined the medium for advertisers, audiences, industry players and former competitors in the media industries. Interestingly, he also bought a studio and amassed a mini–television network of independent broadcast stations in much the same spirit (and at the same time) as Turner did, yet Turner was far more maligned by the industry and the press at the time.

Fox's tremendous success would be the first of such strategic alliances between film and broadcast; the rest would have to hold out until the mid-1990s to find government approval (see chapter 6).[89] But thanks to his vast fortune, impeccable timing, stomach for risk, and remarkable ability to avoid federal regulations, Murdoch did not have to wait to make such deals. He did not have to choose between content or distribution, film or television, programming or ownership—he owned it all. Former Fox chief Peter Chernin explained his boss's approach by looking at his roots in publishing. "The real model of vertical integration is the newspaper business. That's a business that creates, organizes, markets, and distributes its own content. It's no accident that Rupert was the guy who bought a studio and built a network out of it."[90]

Further, as Albert Moran has noted, Murdoch's purchase of Fox in 1985 was more than just acquiring product for his media outlets in the United States, Europe, and Asia; instead, it was also a move toward solidifying the global character of the new generation of media corporations. Moran suggested that

in buying Fox, Murdoch "caused an abandonment of the strategy of disaggrega-
tion in favour of a new round of integration along vertical as well as horizontal
lines."[91] These lines were also stretched across the globe by the end of the
decade, with his properties in Australia, Europe, and North America. Today,
Murdoch has holdings everywhere except Antarctica. He has an interest in over
100 newspapers, some of the most profitable magazines in the world, book publishing, sports teams, broadcasting, cable networks, film, internet providers,
and satellite distribution systems that reach all over the planet.[92]

Overall, empire building in the modern era has worked best when companies combine assets to originate new revenue streams, creating instant
economies of scale. The values of the MGM library and a cable channel cater-
ing to cinephiles instantly skyrocketed once Turner brought them together
in Turner Classic Movies, for example. Rupert Murdoch's arranged marriage
of Metromedia's underperforming UHF television stations with the ailing Fox
studio jump-started the creation of the new Fox television network. In this vein,
Turner and Murdoch used film to breathe new life into television, increasing
the value of both in the process and redefining the potential for synergy in the
media industries. Their prescience and trailblazing predated the birth of two
more studio-owned broadcast networks—Paramount's UPN and Time-Warner's
WB Network—by almost a decade. These networks were forced to wait until
the final repeal of fin-syn before they could be on the air. The fact that fin-syn
remained in place ensured that while the industrial economy was shifting in
the late 1980s, the real seismic activity was yet to come. Once the Financial
Interest and Syndication Rules were repealed, the earthquake would soon follow: another wave of mergers, takeovers, and strategic media combinations
propelled by the seemingly unlimited opportunities of structural convergence.

4

1986–1988

Golden Era Redux

Alarming headlines in the trade papers ("Distribs Buy Cash Cow Chains," "Majors Chase Fat Cat Circuits," "New Economy of Scale in Hollywood") trumpeted the mergers and acquisitions—specifically the widespread purchase of theaters and exhibition chains by the major film studios—that shook up the film industry in 1986. This wave of takeovers was a new, and rather surprising, phase in the construction of entertainment empires. Suddenly, the government was allowing the film industry to return to a state of vertical integration, after preventing the studios from doing so for nearly forty years. This was due to the Reagan administration's newly established position for the handling of the *Paramount* consent decrees. The political tenor had moved the Department of Justice and the courts away from the vigorous enforcement that they had maintained over the last four decades and toward a much more tolerant view of vertical mergers that would allow for the studios to reinvest in theater holdings after all of these years. Ultimately, the Department of Justice determined that the marketplace had changed enough to make unnecessary the continued enforcement of the decrees. Choosing not to expend the resources to formally dismantle *Paramount*, the former watchdogs at the DOJ instead relinquished their post as ruthless guardians of the court's decision and adopted the laissez-faire spirit of the day. Almost immediately, the studios began purchasing theaters and the industry was given a laissez-passer to return to a state of vertical integration, thus rendering the *Paramount* decrees on the books powerless and hollow by default.

This particular case of deregulation in the film industry is a shining example of how far the parameters of antitrust policies shifted during the 1980s and the extent to which their reinterpretation was the result of political ideology as opposed to any specific legislative or judicial mandate. By examining the manner in which the *Paramount* case was decided, enforced, and eventually forsaken by the judiciary, the close relationship between antitrust laws and the construction of empires of entertainment is further revealed. The effective vertical re-integration of production, distribution, and exhibition in the film industry offers one of the most stunning examples of the flexibility of antitrust enforcement under the Reagan Department of Justice, and the overall impact of President Reagan's regulatory philosophy on the political economy of the media industries.

This chapter will examine how and why the vertically integrated corporate structure that was once the subject of intense government scrutiny and antitrust litigation was re-established with the endorsement and assistance of President Reagan's Department of Justice. Explaining how this industrial reorganization was effected, legally as well as practically, will also necessarily incorporate a discussion of media conglomeration in the 1980s as well as the historically changing role of antitrust policies and government regulation in the film industry. It also allows for a specific focus on the film studios and their major legal battles during this time of empire formation. This particular view offers a look at their industry on the upswing. Just as broadcasters were fighting fin-syn and cable was experiencing its own renaissance, the film studios were fighting—and winning—a victory of their own: the battle to escape the restrictions of the *Paramount* consent decrees. And while this chapter is unique in that it is limited to one industry, this specific focus provides insight into the politicized nature of regulatory enforcement, and illustrates with striking clarity the impact of this dynamic on media empires.

The Evolution of the *Paramount* Decrees

The case of *U.S. v. Paramount Pictures Inc., et al.* was originally filed on July 20, 1938, and wound its way through the courts for ten years. Ultimately, the Supreme Court decided in May 1948 that the "big five" vertically integrated studios (Warner Bros., Paramount, Loew's [MGM], RKO, Fox) and "little three" studios without theater chains (Universal, Columbia, United Artists) were guilty of restraint of trade and monopolistic practices in violation of Sections 1 and 2 of the Sherman Act. The five vertically integrated majors were forced to sell off their theaters (Paramount's chain alone was approximately 1,400 single-screen theaters at its peak),[1] with divorcement of exhibition and distribution being "the general architecture of the decree" as acknowledged by the court.[2] The studios that were not vertically integrated entered into a separate judgment because they did not own exhibition outlets. The result was a series of consent decrees that restructured the film industry and signaled the end of an era for the Hollywood majors.[3]

The specific language of the *Paramount* decision would ultimately prove to be the key to its unraveling forty years later under President Reagan. Primarily, while the government's case urged the Supreme Court to find vertical integration illegal per se, the Court refused to do so in 1948. Instead, the ruling stated that the legality of vertical integration under the Sherman Act hinged upon (1) the purpose or intent with which it was conceived, and (2) the power that it creates and the attendant purpose or intent. Consequently, to prevent future vertical integration in the film industry, the government would have to prove that the studios were intentionally conspiring to restrain trade, suppress competition, and gain control over the industry rather than simply expanding their businesses legitimately. The future burden of interpreting, enforcing, and effectively maintaining competition in the film industry was thus placed on the shoulders of the courts. Incredibly, since court administrators considered *Paramount* to be one case, the court of Justice Edmund L. Palmieri alone presided over 500 acquisition hearings and denied petitions seeking to acquire a total of over 600 theaters, all by 1980.[4]

Due to the prompt "surrender" and negotiations with the court on the part of Paramount and RKO, they received more favorable terms than the other "big 5" companies. Consequently, there is no stipulation in the actual *Paramount* decree that prohibits Paramount studios from owning theaters or participating in exhibition and thus, ironically, RKO and Paramount were actually free to acquire theaters in the future without first consulting the court. So, instead of uniformly barring all studio distributors from owning theaters, the decrees only explicitly prohibited three studios—Warner Bros., Fox, and Loew's/MGM—from venturing into exhibition in the future without prior court approval. Accordingly, the court would scrutinize every theater that these three companies bought, built, or sold for many years thereafter.[5]

The courts made a notable early exception in the case of Stanley Warner Corp., the divested exhibition branch of Warner Bros. The company was granted temporary permission (not reported officially but noted by Judge Palmieri) to engage in production and distribution of widescreen Cinerama films during the mid-to-late 1950s.[6] Cinerama was a process that utilized three synchronized 35mm projectors to show dramatically blown-up films on a curved screen and Stanley Warner Corp. argued that they needed to be able to produce these experimental films in order to have enough product to show in their specially outfitted theaters. Therefore, a brief exception was granted for the reunion of production and exhibition interests.

Yet, it wasn't until 1963 that the consent decrees began to erode on the books. At this time, National General Corp., born of the theater chain divested by Twentieth Century–Fox, was granted temporary reentry into the business of distribution and production for six years.[7] The decision was granted on the condition that National General compete for its own films on an individual basis, without any favorable treatment by/for its own theaters. The court had "hopes of increasing the amount of quality motion pictures available for exhibition" when allowing National General to expand.[8] The industry's slumping revenues and a dearth of product in the marketplace contributed to this decision, which represented the first turnaround in the vigilant spirit of *Paramount*'s regulation.

No significant output resulted, however. Historian Michael Conant has noted that National General distributed only six films from 1963 to 1969, two of which the company produced.[9] The modification was further extended twice in 1969, with its most notable arrangement being a nine-picture worldwide distribution contract for First Artists films—three each featuring Paul Newman, Sidney Poitier, and Barbra Streisand.[10] Even though the court granted National General's requests, it stressed in the opinion that "the principle of distributor-exhibitor divorcement can neither be surrendered nor eroded" and that this temporary waiver was only of an "experimental nature" and not a "blueprint" for future decisions.[11]

Thus, the beginning of *Paramount*'s end is more appropriately traced to February 27, 1980. This is the date marking the court approval for one of the original defendants (and a much more powerful industry player than National General) to vertically integrate once again. It was only President Reagan's second month in office when Loew's Corporation (former parent of MGM) and Loew's Theaters obtained limited relief from their consent decrees and gained permission to reenter production/distribution.

Vertical integration of film studios was so significant at this time because of the importance that a film's initial domestic theatrical run has traditionally held for its ultimate success. As Thomas Schatz has argued, the film industry has historically remained focused on the domestic box office because of its role in establishing the film commodity that generates revenues down the line. It is still the U.S. theatrical release "which serves as the 'launch site' for its franchise development, establishing its value in all other media markets."[12] Even *Variety* has called first-run exhibition "the bell-tone that resonates across the entire spectrum of supplemental markets."[13] If a film flopped at the box office, home video orders, television value, and all other ancillary sales usually suffered as well. Conversely, a big opening weekend and profitable first run could predict a hit in other formats. Success at the theater is the yardstick by which a film was judged when assessing its future value in the home video, television syndication, and cable markets. There is much debate about whether or not the domestic theatrical performance still carries the same weight in the digital era, but there was no question about its primary importance in the 1980s. Consequently, controlling that window was critical for the studios.

Loew's had petitioned the court for total relief from its consent decree in order to reenter the distribution business, stating that the decree had become irrelevant, outdated, redundant (in light of existing antitrust laws), and anticompetitive.[14] Attorneys for the exhibitors noted that Loew's owned only 123 theaters at the time, which accounted for less than 1 percent of the theaters in the United States and just over 1 percent of the box office receipts. They argued that it was unreasonable that Loew's was still barred from entering distribution and production, yet firms that were not subject to the terms of *Paramount* operated six times the number of theaters that Loew's did (United Artists had 690 screens and General Cinema had 760 screens).[15]

Interestingly, Paramount, Warner Bros., Universal, Columbia, United Artists, Fox, and MGM all filed comments in opposition to vacating the Loew's decree.[16] Warner Bros. and Universal urged the court to maintain the restrictions on Loew's, arguing that dismantling the decrees as requested "would violate basic antitrust policies and public interest considerations and lead to re-creation of conditions that led to the order for divorcement in the first place."[17] Essentially, their memorandum was opposed to the petitions by Loew's and also to those simultaneously filed by RKO Stanley-Warner Theaters and Mann Theaters (which were subject to the restrictions of Fox's decree) because they feared that other large theater chains would quickly follow this path, creating an imbalance of power and shutting them out of a newly integrated industry. Additionally, the major studios subsequently filed motions requesting for all decrees related to *Paramount* to be similarly abandoned if the Loews decree was indeed vacated.

While the court refused to go as far as permanently abandoning and terminating the decrees as Loew's had requested, they did nevertheless allow Loew's theaters to reenter into production and distribution, with some significant restrictions. After months of negotiation, Loew's finally accepted the government's terms, which dictated that the company could produce and distribute films but could not exhibit its own films or films in which it had a financial interest. Loew's was also bound in its capacity as a distributor by conditions that were almost identical to those in the original *Paramount* decrees (such as restraints against block booking). The court's rationale for making the adjustments was that current marketplace conditions provided for the preservation of a competitive industrial climate, even in the face of these changes.

Essentially, this decision was the outset of the *Paramount* decrees shifting from a regulatory statute to a protective blanket under which the studios would hide when splurging on theaters in the late 1980s. Loew's received the first substantive modification to the original decrees, but the change actually had more of an impact on the industry at large than it did for Loew's itself; at this point, all of the studios began to back off from their barrage of petitions. They realized that it was preferable to maintain the illusion of regulation and keep the decrees in place, rather than spend the time and resources fighting the courts—especially once government enforcement and regulation were no longer a real threat.

That threat of enforcement was actually removed not long after Ronald Reagan was in office. In 1980, the Justice Department undertook a massive project to review all consent decrees that were more than ten years old.[18] The idea was to eliminate those decrees that were no longer relevant or necessary in the current marketplace as deemed by the Department of Justice. President Reagan's first assistant attorney general of antitrust, William Baxter, saw the *Paramount* decrees as falling into that unnecessary category. According to longtime Department of Justice attorney Bernard Hollander, Baxter "hated regulatory decrees, he hated long lasting decrees, and he sure didn't like *Paramount* or the [broadcast] network cases or any of the others that were regulatory and, in the case of the *Paramount* decrees, perpetual."[19] The Antitrust Division had also laid out a new set of merger guidelines that were extremely lenient, and tolerant of behavior that would have previously been under suspicion for restraint of trade.[20] Further, during this period the staff of the Antitrust Division was reduced by 50 percent, leaving the office a mere skeleton of itself, forced to drastically alter its enforcement priorities.[21] By the summer of 1983, the DOJ announced that it was in the "final stages" of reviewing the *Paramount* consent decrees, and they expected to close their investigation soon. However, the case remained open for another eighteen months.

Then came a remarkable announcement: in February 1985 the Justice Department declared that while it would not formally terminate the *Paramount* decrees, it would support such motions in cases where the action was "in the public interest."[22] The reason given was that Reagan's second antitrust chief, J. Paul McGrath, was unwilling to expend the resources necessary to terminate the decrees in the judicial system. The message was clear that McGrath, like Baxter, no longer viewed the decrees as relevant or necessary. This approach was certainly in line with the administration's laissez-faire approach to mergers and acquisitions, and the overall spirit of supply-side "Reaganomics." Effectively, this statement dissolved the authority of the decrees, if not legally then practically; by appearing amenable to their eventual dissolution and removing the looming menace of any government lawsuit, the Department of Justice eliminated the most compelling reason to comply with the *Paramount* consent decrees.

It was at this point that the essence of *Paramount* was quietly transformed from an iron fist wielded by the federal government into a façade embraced by the studios; that façade of regulation effectively and simultaneously solidified their power while keeping potential government scrutiny at bay. Consequently, the continued existence of the *Paramount* decrees after 1985 gave the appearance that the film industry was still being actively regulated by the Justice Department, when, in practice, the DOJ was actually supporting the film industry's bid for complete autonomy.

Initially, exhibitors were publicly rejoicing over this announcement; the National Association of Theater Owners (NATO) told the press that they were delighted with the decision to keep the decrees in place. However, they were also well aware that at the time, the nine largest distributors (Paramount, Warner Bros., Columbia, Universal, Disney/Buena Vista, Twentieth Century–Fox, Orion, Tri-Star, and MGM/UA) still accounted for about 90 percent of the box office receipts.[23] The majors were well poised to take advantage of the Justice Department's increasingly permissive attitude. Thus, what appeared on the surface to be cause for celebration for theater owners should have instead sounded the alarms.

At the same time, however, exhibitors were working to expand their own holdings. RKO-Century Warner Theaters chain doubled its percentage of screens in Manhattan's first-run marketplace, and according to *Variety*, for the first time, only two companies—RKO/C5 and Loew's Theaters—would have control of more than 50 percent of revenues generated in New York City.[24] It seems exhibitors quickly realized they were in a precarious position. Less than a month after their initial reaction, NATO charged the major distributors with creating "a competitive imbalance in the marketplace in their favor which threatens the continued viable existence of exhibitors."[25] The group established a special panel that essentially sought to "knock down the majors a few pegs . . . and diminish the oligopolistic powers of the distributors."[26] Yet, nothing substantial would come of this initiative by the exhibitors, and their competitive situation would soon worsen.

Also during this period, Congress was considering the Merger Modernization Act of 1986.[27] In February, the Justice Department presented several major amendments to the antitrust laws on behalf of the Reagan administration. These bills were much more aggressive than traditional shifts in antitrust policies, which usually adopt a course of "incremental change and gradual evolution."[28] The proposed Merger Modernization Act was one of a series of revisions to antitrust policy put forth by the government that would have loosened restrictions on corporations and industrial concentration. It would have altered the key language of section 7 of the Clayton Act, making the test for illegality much more narrow and specific (and therefore more difficult to prove) and also codifying many of the revised Merger Guidelines set forth by the DOJ in 1984.[29] Extensive hearings were held but the initiative was not enacted. However, the impetus and debate behind its inception were emblematic of the shift in Washington regarding mergers and antitrust policy—one reflecting a definitive trend toward weakening enforcement procedures. It should be noted that there was also a counterproposal, the Antitrust Improvement Act of 1986, introduced by Senator Howard Metzenbaum (D-Ohio), chairman of the Senate Antitrust Subcommittee. The Metzenbaum Bill, as it became known, attempted to slow some of the deregulatory momentum. The bill ran counter to the zeitgeist in Washington—it would have made several significant changes to strengthen antitrust law as opposed to weaken it—and so Metzenbaum's alternative did not pass.

In the meantime, both Warners and Loew's continued to press on in search of legally sanctioned relief from their decrees. The studios needed a successful challenge to *Paramount* in court. A legal security blanket, no matter how small, would help to solidify the tentative gains they were making in this arena. Such a victory would also provide some measure of reassurance and confidence during the appeals process.

The studios' first substantial triumph in court came when Warners won provisional approval to acquire an ownership interest in theaters on August 27, 1986. They were interested in acquiring theaters from several chains and petitioned the court for permission to purchase theaters without prior judicial consent. They also proposed to maintain their exhibition business and management separately. Judge Palmieri granted the motion, but it is important to note that his decision did not go so far as to completely dismantle Warners' decree. What he did was allow—with significant restrictions—Warners' request to modify their original consent judgment that was delivered in 1951.

The new stipulations authorized the company to purchase theaters on an interim basis without having to obtain prior court approval, provided that they were held separately from distribution and dealt with at arm's length.[30] Thus, Warners was granted reentry into exhibition/theater ownership after thirty-five years of being barred from such activity, creating the first significant crack in the foundation of the decrees themselves. The result of this modification would eventually be the joint partnership established six months later between Warners and Gulf + Western (parent company of Paramount), in which the companies would co-own 119 theaters with 469 screens (see details later in this chapter). Warners also entertained short-lived talks to take over General Cinema's theater and lucrative Pepsi-Cola bottling operations, but nothing ever developed from those plans.

The next blow to *Paramount* would come shortly thereafter, when the newly formed Tri-Star Pictures moved to acquire Loew's. By this time, Loew's was a 300-screen circuit operating some of Manhattan's most prestigious movie houses, along with other theaters in the Northeast, Ohio, Indiana, Florida, and Texas.[31] Tri-Star was bound by the Loew's decrees once they purchased the theater company in late 1986. Because Loew's failed to win total relief from their decrees with their petition in 1980, Tri-Star would be prohibited from exhibiting its own films in Loew's theaters and was subject to the restrictions in the original consent decrees signed by Loew's. The first action Tri-Star took on this matter was to apply to the courts for interim relief in November 1986. Initially, Tri-Star wanted to be able to exhibit their films in Loew's theaters during the impending lucrative holiday release period. They also wanted to be free of *Paramount*'s injunctions in future dealings with exhibitors other than Loew's.[32] This temporary relief was granted and Loew's and Tri-Star persevered in search of permanent relief from both the *Paramount* consent decree and from the 1980 court order.[33]

Subsequently, a hearing was held in March 1987 and interested parties were invited to submit opinions to the court, as was now customary in such proceedings. Loew's was also ordered to publish notices of its motion and an invitation for comments in the *Wall Street Journal* and weekly *Variety*. Interestingly, the DOJ strongly supported Tri-Star's petition and the Antitrust Division even went so far as to state that it believed "competition in distribution or exhibition would not be unreasonably restrained, even if Tri-Star and Loew's dealt exclusively with one another."[34] This statement is a bold indication of how far the government was willing to stretch the interpretation of antitrust laws when allowing for mergers and policing *Paramount* during this period. As one antitrust analyst noted, "This is an interesting observation for the government to have made, since that question was not even before the court."[35] Still, the Department of Justice publicly maintained that there had been "neither a moratorium nor a letdown of enforcement of the *Paramount* consent decrees," despite the various modifications being made and the massive reentry of distributors into exhibition (to be discussed later).[36]

A brief was filed on the part of independent exhibitors, claiming that Tri-Star/Loew's were asking "permission to bring back the good old days of unbridled vertical integration . . . which led to the *Paramount* decrees in the first place."[37] The independents accused the DOJ of "shifting their stance on the [consent] decrees with each new administration."[38] Essentially, these exhibitors were correct. This is exactly how the *Paramount* consent decrees—and consent decrees in nearly every industry—have been enforced: subject to political interpretations of antitrust law. Accordingly, the parameters and subtleties of the ruling in the *Paramount* case (and the legal foundations upon which it has been built) have allowed for changes in prevailing political ideology and marketplace conditions to dictate the trajectory of the case in court.

Ultimately, Judge Palmieri relented to the massive political pressure that was building in Washington. He heeded the words of the Justice Department and the forceful pull of Chicago School ideals that were now gripping the government, granting Tri-Star's request and vacating Loew's decree on June 18, 1987. Thus, Tri-Star and Loew's were the first companies to gain full exemption and legal relief from the *Paramount* decrees. When Judge Palmieri signed this order, he also began to nail the lid on the coffin of the 1948 *Paramount* decision. The consent decrees would remain, but were now largely stripped of their power; they existed in name but no longer exerted any true regulatory muscle.

Here again, the strain between the Chicago School approach embraced by the Reagan administration and the populist interpretation of antitrust law that still dominated Palmieri's court is apparent. The main argument of the Chicago School is that efficiency should be the only goal of the Sherman Act, and this efficiency will only develop when the market is left alone; antitrust enforcement merely interferes with that process, according to this philosophy.[39] Consequently, the DOJ under President Reagan became less involved with enforcing the terms of *Paramount*. Palmieri, on the other hand, was still proceeding according to the populist-oriented mission of the original case. Consequently, the government was sending mixed messages when it came to studios purchasing theaters; on one hand, the judiciary was continuing to wave red flags, and on the other, the executive branch was giving the studios the green light.

Nevertheless, the new neoliberal political order carried the day. The regulatory changes ushered in by the Reagan administration ultimately led to open season on exhibition outlets, and the certain, albeit unceremonious death of the *Paramount* consent decrees. The shifting antitrust philosophy and the resulting manner in which the consent decrees were (re)interpreted by the Reagan administration during the 1980s resulted in the film industry's return to a vertically integrated corporate structure.

Theater Purchases

The year 1986 was undeniably a watershed, noted in *Variety* as a moment of "revolutionary realignment," when the industry returned to "the origins of its pre-TV growth and prosperity in the most massive marriage of distribution and exhibition since the 1948 *Paramount* decrees forced the majors to sell off their theater circuits."[40] *Variety* also underscored the powerful implications of these purchases in a front-page story, asserting that these buyouts were drawing the battle lines "in a long-range industry restructuring [that] ultimately will determine which films play on the nation's screens."[41] This period of unprecedented theater acquisitions resulted in 4,357 screens eventually changing hands for $1.62 billion.[42] Major studios acquired almost 20 percent of the country's theaters (which comprised over 50 percent of the "showcase screens," or those that consistently quadrupled the national average in box-office revenues). The studios emerged owning more than 3,500 of the 22,000 screens in the United States—or, according to historian Thomas Guback, about the same percentage as the five vertically integrated majors had operated before the *Paramount* decrees in 1945.[43]

The first producer to jump into the exhibition business in the 1980s was Columbia. Columbia Pictures began by acquiring a 30 percent stake in the Walter Reade Theaters (eleven prime screens in Manhattan) in December 1981. Coca-Cola (the company that bought Columbia in 1982) added to their shares in 1983 to bring the ownership interest up to 41.7 percent. In January 1986, Reade officially became a wholly owned subsidiary of Coke after Coca-Cola bought all remaining shares in the company, spending a total of $24 million on the circuit.[44] However, it was not technically reentry into exhibition for Columbia, nor was their action prohibited by the *Paramount* decrees, since the studio had never owned theaters in the first place. It was, nonetheless, the first step by a major distributor into theater ownership in over thirty years.

It was the bold move by MCA (parent company of Universal) in May 1986 that truly began the industry stampede to purchase exhibition outlets. MCA's acquisition of 50 percent interest in Cineplex Odeon and its then-1,176 screens/395 sites in North America for $159 million was the significant purchase that set the tone for the end of the 1980s.[45] While neither MCA nor Universal had any prior restriction on acquiring theaters—Universal was one of the "little three" studios that did not sign any consent decree—Cineplex was the largest theater chain in North America in terms of revenue and total seats, and Universal was the largest movie production studio in the United States.

Furthermore, Cineplex was initiating a massive takeover splurge of its own, going from 1,068 screens in January 1986 at the time of the MCA buy to 1,510 screens just eight months later.[46] Once CEO Garth Drabinsky purchased the Plitt circuits in late 1985—a $135 million deal for 607 new screens—Cineplex Odeon was significantly larger than any of its competitors, including General Cinema, United Artists, and AMC.[47] General Cinema was the nation's largest exhibitor chain (as well as the largest independent bottler of Pepsi-Cola products) and an early pioneer of shopping mall cinemas. AMC was also busy initiating its own series of takeovers at this time, growing to 1,336 screens in twenty-seven states.

Cineplex and its Plitt Theaters Group subsidiary went about acquiring numerous lucrative chains during the year, including the Septum (48 screens), Essaness (41 screens), Neighborhood Theaters Inc. (76 screens), RKO Century (130 screens), and Sterling Recreation Organization (100 screens plus license agreements for 30 other screens), as well as the Circle Theaters and the lease for the prestigious Carnegie Hall Cinema in New York City.

One reason behind this tremendous expansion was the freedom that companies like Cineplex enjoyed from being uninvolved in *Paramount* in any way. The consent decrees forced other chains, such as the remaining theater subsidiaries of ABC (Paramount) and Loew's, to consult with the government every time they wanted to make an acquisition. Not so for Cineplex or the long-established independent companies, such as General Cinema and AMC, which all consequently had an upper hand when embarking on expansion projects. They spread into new neighborhoods, new arenas such as shopping malls, and, beginning in the 1960s, revisited areas and markets that had not seen new theaters built since the Great Depression.

Consequently, the magnitude of the MCA acquisition sent a clear signal: the Justice Department was adhering to the hands-off approach put forth by the Reagan administration. As *Variety* put it, after MCA's Cineplex buy in 1986, "a cry was heard: 'Everybody, into the pool!'"[48] As a result, the initial rush to dive in and purchase exhibition outlets resulted in the following studio/distributor acquisitions by 1988:[49]

- Columbia began a series of takeovers that included the New York City Walter Reade Organization (11 screens).[50]
- Tri-Star (one-third owned by Columbia) then purchased the Loew's theater chain (300 screens, later growing to 470 screens) for $300 million in December 1986, USA Cinemas (317 screens) in 1988 for $165 million, and Music Makers Theaters (65 screens).
- Gulf + Western (Paramount) already controlled the Famous Players circuit in Canada (469 screens). Shortly after the MCA deal, G+W bought the Trans-Lux theaters (24 screens) for $15 million in July 1986, the expanding Mann chain (360 screens) for $220 million in October 1986, and Festival Enterprises (101 screens) for $50 million in December 1986.[51] These were ultimately consolidated into what became known as Cinamerica Theaters, L.P., once Warners purchased their 50 percent stake in February 1987.
- Warner Bros. officially became partners with Gulf + Western in theater exhibition in February 1987 when their parent company, Warner Communications, Inc., bought a 50 percent interest in Paramount's 472 Cinamerica (Mann + Festival + Trans-Lux) screens for $150 million.[52] The Justice Department consented to the acquisition on December 16, 1987, and Judge Palmieri gave his permission one year later in December 1988.
- In July 1986 Cannon bought the 425-screen Commonwealth theater chain (sixth largest in the United States) for $25 million, adding to its 587 screens in Europe.

Suddenly, everything old was new again and the theater holdings of the studios were looking strikingly similar to the way they did forty years earlier. Meanwhile, Paramount was the leader at the box office, with 22 percent of the market share in 1986 and 20 percent in 1987.[53] NATO announced that the record number of screens in the United States had reached 22,721 by late 1987.[54] Further, it was estimated that a dozen companies controlled about 45 percent of all movie screens in North America.[55] Integrated circuits (those owned by companies already engaged in production/distribution) now accounted for 10 percent of the nation's screens, as opposed to *zero* in 1980.[56] All the while, leading chains such as AMC and Cineplex were building or acquiring hundreds of screens and the antitrust division at the Justice Department was reportedly "unconcerned" with the takeovers and events.

The Cannon purchase of Commonwealth was an interesting and compli-cated one that actually put them in bed with Warner Bros. The maverick mini-major was run by Yoram Globus and Menahem Golan, and was Hollywood's largest independent film studio in the early 1980s after going public in 1979. The company was greatly overextended, reporting heavy losses, selling off key assets, and actively searching for a buyer to relieve them of their deal to purchase the Commonwealth chain. Warner Bros. came to their rescue in the form of a $75 million bailout (in exchange for rights and assets at bargain base-ment prices) in December 1986, just five months after the Cannon acquisition of Thorn EMI Screen Entertainment. Cannon also had to sell off their 900-film library for $94.4 million in cash and stock (much less than initially expected) to Weintraub Entertainment Group.[57]

Meanwhile, Warners was very busy with complicated acquisitions of their own. According to court documents, Warners and Paramount together comprised approximately 30 percent of the national market in distribution at the time of their proposed deal.[58] With the joint Cinamerica venture, they would also own about 2 percent of the total number of screens in the country (approximately 22,000 in 1987).[59] As noted earlier, the companies obtained court approval to explore their opportunities in joint ownership of exhibition chains six months prior to their announcement in February 1987. Also in accordance with the terms of their *Paramount* consent decree, Warners had to notify the Department of Justice of its intended purchases.

The studio notified the DOJ of the plan in early 1987, and after nearly a year-long investigation, the Justice Department decided *not* to challenge Warners' acquisition of ownership stake in Cinamerica. The DOJ also blessed the deal when they concluded that the Warners acquisition of 50 percent interest in Gulf + Western's theater chains (a 470-screen domestic network) did not warrant an antitrust lawsuit or present a significant problem of access to raise a problem under antitrust laws. Fred Haynes, an official in the antitrust division, justified the deal by pointing out that "both Warners and Gulf and Western were subject to theater licensing mandates of the 1948 *Paramount* Consent Decrees."[60]

One year later in December 1988, Warner Communications Inc. was granted legal permission by Judge Palmieri to retain its acquired 50 percent stake in Gulf + Western/Paramount's U.S. theater business. After a year of deliberation over filings from Gulf + Western and WCI, arguments from interested parties, and the DOJ statement, Palmieri agreed to the deal, under the conditions that Cinamerica interests would be "held separately" from all other WCI holdings and have no relationship to Warner Bros. studios.

Warners was actually petitioning for relief from *all* court-enforced supervi-sion and limitations on the expansion and management of Cinamerica, but Palmieri steadfastly refused. He determined that Warners did not require "sweeping and permanent" exemptions from the consent decrees, nor a "day to day hand" in the Cinamerica operations; thus, expansion would be granted, but with supervision and enforced separation by the court. In his forty-one-page decision issued December 12, 1988, Judge Palmieri also unleashed a vitriolic critique of the film industry's growing disrespect for the *Paramount* decrees. He noted that there was a "climate of non-compliance with the heart of the consent judgments—that films be licensed theater by theater, solely on the merits and without discrimination."[61] Ironically, this same decision in which Palmieri lashed out at the industry was also the one in which he allowed the Warner Bros.–Paramount deal to go through.

In his opinion, Palmieri denounced federal authorities for creating "a lamentable state of affairs" in their failure to effectively police the business dealings between the film studios and exhibitors. He pointed to a report by the Justice Department, which determined that most industry practices did not appear to violate antitrust laws, and then used the same statistics to conclude that there indeed was evidence of exclusive alliances, domination by a few top firms, and a lingering cause for concern. He also added that this situation, in which distributors and exhibitors have appeared to divide up local markets, "raises troubling and serious questions as to the vigor with which the antitrust laws are being enforced."[62] Effectively, Palmieri was criticizing the executive branch and regulators for not bringing enough vigilance to the oversight of this case and noting his displeasure in the opinion, should the case be brought for appeal in the future (which it was). His comments also illustrate the political and ideological tension between the longtime bench overseeing the case and the current administration—primarily stemming from their sharply differing perspectives and interpretation of the nature of antitrust.

Maurice Silverman, an attorney who had represented the government for many years in the *Paramount* case, had switched sides and was now arguing for Warners as a special counsel. Silverman emphasized that the industry had changed significantly since 1948, especially in light of the numerous "aftermarkets," as cable television and video were referred to at the time. These expanding windows of exhibition gave producer/distributors more incentive to get their films out as quickly and widely as possible, according to Warners' argument. Less market concentration, fewer barriers to entry, and little ability for Cinamerica to restrain competition and drive out its rivals were the other chief reasons that the company gave for seeking permanent relief from its decree. Warners also complained that many powerful independent theater circuits had sprung up since the consent decrees were written and they simply wanted to compete on an equal footing with companies who were not subject to the same restrictions.[63]

The court did not agree. Judge Palmieri complained that there still appeared to be "continued anticompetitive behavior by exhibitors and distributors in this industry."[64] In addition, he noted that "much of Warner's argument derives from theoretical speculations about human behavior which the court finds unpersuasive. . . . Suffice it to say that this industry has shown a proclivity for anti-competitive behavior when given the opportunity and that there is (as yet unspecified) evidence of a climate of non-compliance with this court's consent judgments. We do not believe that the mere existence of the antitrust laws and the presence in the industry of parties with adverse interests is enough to permit us to sit back and allow the dismantling of the consent judgments."[65] Palmieri would thus succinctly explain his denial and reference industry history at the same time by stating, "Warner cannot do by indirection what it cannot do directly."[66] Translation: the studios were still not to be trusted. Consequently, sweeping and permanent exemptions from the consent judgments would not be granted at this time.

Palmieri also pointed out in his decision that the heart of Cinamerica was the Mann chain, which owned and operated over 350 screens, including 9 of the 17 in the vitally important Westwood area of Los Angeles. The court's opinion added that many consider Westwood, along with the Upper East Side of Manhattan, to be the most important market in the country. "A successful run in Westwood," Palmieri noted, "often precedes a successful nationwide release and the videocassette, cable, foreign, and television profits which ensue."[67] The makeup of this audience—film industry members, avid filmgoers, and prominent critics—made Westwood an absolutely vital market and one that Palmieri did not want manipulated.

Thus, quality was more important than quantity in this decision, and while Cinamerica represented only about 2–3 percent of the nation's then 22,000 screens, the locations of those screens were among the most significant and desirable markets in the United States. This is quite similar to the ownership patterns of the major studios at the time of the original *Paramount* case—while the vertically integrated majors owned only 15–20 percent of the country's theaters, these screens were among the nation's most important and profitable, accounting for approximately 90 percent of the first-run market. Accordingly, Palmieri perceived a familiar "temptation for abuse of market power," resulting from the concentration and integration of exhibition with distribution. Palmieri also noted that the court did not have adequate information on which to base a long-range decision. Therefore, he scheduled a review of Warner and Cinamerica's bidding and licensing practices for the following year because, as the court noted, "the potential for abuse is so great."[68] Warners appealed the decision.

The significant gap between the court's attitude and that of the DOJ is evidence of Palmieri's alliance to populist interpretations and the competing, expanding influence of Chicago School economic principles on the Department of Justice and Reagan administration officials. Palmieri and populist views of antitrust legislation held that such laws are designed to protect smaller companies from being exploited or pushed out by the largest firms in an industry. This view considers vertical integration a dangerous form of industrial organization that should be regulated by government in order to prevent anticompetitive conditions. The Chicago School, on the other hand, is much more tolerant and lenient of such strategies, especially if they promote economic efficiency.

Throughout these much-heralded announcements of studio-distributors snapping up exhibition chains, Cineplex and MCA/Universal took especially great care to present themselves as separate entities, maintaining that they would build a "Chinese Wall" between theater holdings and production-distribution.[69] MCA spokesmen immediately noted that the "need to maintain 'arm's length' distance economically between distribution and exhibition is understood and respected."[70] Cineplex CEO Garth Drabinsky vigorously maintained that Cineplex Odeon and Universal distribution executives would continue to work separately in determining film scheduling and bookings.

Drabinsky's attempt to minimize his presence at this time was a bit ironic, considering that he was already acquiring quite a reputation for flamboyance and self-promotion. His relentless style in business dealings often made him unpopular among the studio crowd, and his determined expansion of multiplex cinemas (which he is credited with having pioneered with Nat Taylor, although the first one was actually built by AMC) drew fire from many corners. USA Cinema owner A. Alan Friedberg, in a representative display of ill-will toward Cineplex and Drabinsky, stated to the press that Drabinsky was "someone who purports to have reinvented the wheel [and who claims] thousands of people are going to come back to the theaters because he is putting butter on the popcorn."[71]

He did more than put butter ("100 percent farmers' butter!") on the popcorn, however. Drabinsky made his reputation by introducing gourmet concessions such as espresso drinks and fresh-baked goods, decorating extravagantly, and, most importantly, aggressively and creatively establishing the multiplex trend. After launching Cineplex in 1979 with an eighteen-screen complex in a Toronto shopping center, Drabinsky shot quickly to the top of the theater exhibition business. Within two years, he had opened another 111 screens in Canada; by 1984, he took over Odeon, one of his largest rivals (the other being Gulf + Western–owned Famous Players). By 1987, Cineplex had doubled in size and Drabinsky estimated that the chain grossed about $800 million per year.[72] The Plitt acquisition alone nearly tripled the number of Cineplex screens and provided the company with their major entrance into U.S. territory, shortly after which Cineplex became the second-largest exhibitor in North America.[73] Drabinsky was allowed to continue his buying spree even after the MCA deal (or because of it, as MCA had very deep pockets and Cineplex carried a staggering $685 million of long-term debt by 1988), thanks largely to the new attitude at the Justice Department.

Theater owners (long-time enemies of the studios) had a very divided public reaction to the takeovers of their business. Immediately after the first MCA acquisition of interest in Cineplex Odeon, they went so far as to adopt a resolution "expressing opposition to distributors acquiring and operating motion picture theaters" at the National Association of Theater Owners board meeting. A *Variety* headline in early 1986 trumpeted, "NATO Wants Distribs Out of Exhibition."[74]

However, five months later, NATO changed its tune and publicly welcomed the studio-owned theaters into the fray with open arms, inviting them "to join NATO's efforts to achieve a stronger motion picture industry."[75] The decision to drop their objections to the studio splurge indicates that perhaps the theater owners realized the potential power in aligning themselves with the growing conglomerates and/or the futility of fighting the inevitable. There was also a short-lived idea to merge the MPAA and NATO in the fall of 1986, which would have considerably blurred the boundaries between studio producer-distributors and theater exhibitors, explaining the momentary cease-fire. Yet it was not long before the antagonisms reheated and exhibitors were denouncing the newcomers to their business as a breed of "interlopers, not impresarios."[76]

Immediately after the Gulf + Western/Warner Communications, Inc. buy in 1987, attorneys for the independent exhibitors began accusing the MPAA, large theater circuits, and major distributors of monopolizing access to product. "The pendulum is now swinging back to concentration of ownership as if the [*Paramount*] decrees never existed," they complained, condemning the Department of Justice's action, or lack of it, as something that has "brought on deregulation without even an announced change in policy. They claim they are all watching closely . . . it would seem they are watching the demise of the independent exhibitors."[77] These cries went largely unheard, however, amid the clamor of distributor purchases and industry reconsolidation.

In addition to the producer/distributor expansion, there were also some independent exhibitors that decided to branch out into distribution, largely as a response to the majors' encroachment on the theater sector. First, Cineplex Odeon formed an American distribution arm in the late 1980s, but the effort was a failure. The first film they distributed was the French Canadian film *The Decline of the American Empire* (1986). However, their move came at a time when Cineplex was pursuing a breach-of-contract suit against Paramount and the De Laurentis Entertainment Group, who were distributing five features in Canada that Drabinsky and Cineplex claimed were supposed to be distributed by Pan Canadian, Cineplex's distribution company. The move into distribution was also during Cineplex's major theater expansion, and as a result, Drabinsky was unable to give this project his full attention or his usual single-minded gusto;

in the first half of 1989 alone, the distribution arm lost $16.5 million and was abandoned shortly thereafter.[78]

General Cinema, the nation's largest exhibitor and a $1 billion company with assets in numerous other industries, had also attempted to enter the production/distribution end of the business in the late 1970s. This was a tremendous failure as well, with the company taking major losses in its film financing ventures until that pursuit was abandoned in 1979, the same year that General Cinema's bid to purchase 20 percent of Columbia Pictures was also rejected. The move stemmed partly from anxiety over the scarcity of pictures and the fear that "we'd get to the point where we had 1,000 theaters and nothing to put in them," according to a company executive.[79]

Viacom, one of the biggest empires of entertainment, came to prominence by merging with a film exhibitor and growing outward. In 1987, Sumner Redstone's theater chain, National Amusements, Inc., bought controlling interest of Viacom, Inc., for $3.4 billion.[80] The company would later take over Paramount Studios (1994) and CBS (1999), but at this point, the merger is significant because the top theater chain in Boston was buying a powerful television syndicator and growing cable company, not the other way around. In addition to its syndication business, Viacom owned radio and television stations, cable systems, and cable services including Showtime/The Movie Channel and MTV. While these were not traditional partners in a marriage of product and distribution/exhibition in the 1980s, this was a somewhat prophetic union that integrated theaters with television and cable holdings. Redstone was in the theater business but shrewdly began expanding his grip on the rest of the media industries. This budding conglomerate signaled early on in its development that the film industry was going to need more than just its own theaters to compete in the future.

Vertical Reintegration in Perspective

The majors' aggressive move into exhibition was stunning for several reasons. First of all, the brazen manner in which the film industry flouted the spirit (if not the legal letter) of the *Paramount* decrees seemed to depart from traditional business practices. The majors have had a long history of maintaining the appearance of self-regulation in order to keep government regulators at bay, and it seems that the sudden and flagrant disregard for such established industry protocol would only cry out for scrutiny and possible re-regulation. This action bore the stamp of companies who felt newly empowered and invulnerable, obviously stemming from their perception of the government's shift in attitude toward *Paramount* and the security that comes with a friend like Ronald Reagan in the White House.

Secondly, the prices that distributors were paying for theater circuits were inordinately expensive. The studios were paying twelve-to-fourteen-times cash-flow for the theaters, as opposed to the five-to-six-times cash-flow price that exhibitors charged one another for screens.[81] Especially in light of the box office decline and unstable industrial terrain facing the majors, taking this risk was quite bold. As previously noted, the 1980s were characterized by numerous dips and spurts, and 1985–86 was a period of nerve-wracking recession for Hollywood. Most majors had very weak years in 1985 and the industry experienced an eighteen-to-twenty-month slump. According to *Variety*, "A combination of a domestic box-office recession and overseas currency fluctuations caused 1985 world feature film rentals to American major distributors to fall by more than 12% to $1.73 billion . . . an 8-year low."[82] Even though the domestic box office shot up to $4.25 billion in 1987, it was also the beginning of a very difficult time for a number of major players in the film industry. The manic expansion that had been taking place over the previous four years was quickly stalled by the stock market crash in October and MGM/UA, Cannon, DeLaurentis Entertainment Group, New World, Vestron, and AMC all posted losses.

Further, there was new competition from cable, pay-per-view, and especially home video that was dramatically eroding the theatrical revenues. Audience numbers were stagnant and domestic exhibition was now only a small part (about 30 percent) of a film's total revenue pie, as opposed to the days when first-run was everything. Alarmist *Variety* headlines such as "Teens Leaving Theaters for Home Vid!" and "Exhib Fear about VCR Threat Renewed" illustrated the industry's mounting fears about the uncertain future of exhibition.[83] Some in the media industries thought that the majors' rush to theater ownership was largely resulting from anxiety over the unpredictable marketplace. Fox executive Tom Sherak, for example, suggested that perhaps everyone was jumping on the circuit-buying bandwagon defensively, because "their competitors were doing it."[84]

It was also openly acknowledged in the trades that the studios hoped to improve the positioning of their theatrical releases for optimum profitability in ancillary markets. Exhibition was expanding, but only at a fraction of production's rate. While the total number of theater screens had gone from 17,590 to over 23,000 during the 1980s, this increase represented only 31.5 percent, hardly in keeping with the tremendous boom in production. While only 233 films were released in 1980, that number had more than doubled by 1983, when there were 495 films released, and hit an all-time high the following year with 536 releases.[85] These numbers were largely due to re-releases in the first half of the 1980s, until production stepped up significantly to meet demand pressures in 1986 and remained at 400 films or above until 1989.[86]

Consequently, the rental split began to shift in favor of the exhibitor, and theater owners were beginning to pull films after the second weekend in order to make room for the newer releases.[87] The window of theatrical opportunity was also shrinking due to the mounting pressure and growing importance of ancillary markets such as cable and home video. This put more importance on a film's opening weekend and less time for word of mouth to build. In turn, a frantic increase in advertising expenditures began. The average cost to market a film in 1980 was $3.5 million; that figure had doubled by 1988. Overall, the decade saw a 120 percent increase in average advertising costs (especially important, as the number of releases skyrocketed as well).

Also, as noted in *Variety*, a safe haven for showing one's own product (particularly titles that might not be strong enough to merit good bookings at arm's length) was not the only benefit to getting back into the exhibition business. Theater ownership could also provide "a very important bargaining chip in obtaining playtime at theaters owned by a fellow distributor/exhibitor, especially on a regional basis."[88] With the blockbuster strategy of ultrawide release patterns, this access to exhibition space was now critical and becoming more precious. It was also suggested that entering the exhibition business was perhaps a strategy for distributors to gain some control over play dates, and thus lower their advertising budgets.[89]

The parent companies of the studios were gradually expanding, spreading their risk out over many different sectors of the media landscape by the early 1990s. MCA/Universal, for example, was continuing to build its cable holdings with an interest in the USA network and February 1986 purchase of New Jersey cable superstation WOR for $387 million.[90] MCA also owned home video distribution for its own films and produced cable programming that could be shown on its networks. Warner Communications, Inc., produced and distributed television programming in addition to being part owner of six stations at the time. Additionally, Warner owned the nation's third largest cable system, co-owned The Movie Channel, and had significant interest in MTV and Nickelodeon, which were distributed by its cable system.

In 1989, Warner Bros. finally did win the court-sanctioned relief it had been seeking for so many years. On August 3, 1989, the Second Circuit U.S. Court of Appeals granted Warners permission to own and operate theaters without the restrictions imposed by Palmieri's court. The company was now free to own and operate the Cinamerica theaters without restrictions in its partnership with MCA/Paramount. The government actually joined Warners in its appeal, changing its longstanding public position, siding *with* the studio and arguing that Warners' 50 percent ownership in Cinamerica would not threaten competition. The government reiterated that there is nothing inherently anti-competitive about a vertical merger, and maintained (without evidence) that "the evolution of the motion picture industry since *Paramount Pictures* makes it improbable that Warner could or would endeavor to use its exhibition assets to stifle competition."[91] The court agreed with Warners and the government attorneys, and granted Warners permission, through Cinamerica, "to compete in theatrical exhibition through the construction of new theatres and the expansion or acquisition of theatres."[92] There was no opposition to Warners's appeal and the studio was legally free to continue expanding its theater holdings without court oversight.

By 1992, when Loew's and Tri-Star won complete relief from their decrees under Judge William C. Conner (ruling on the case because Palmieri had passed away in 1989), it was clear that the restrictions of the consent decrees were no longer applicable to the contemporary motion picture industry, at least in the eyes of the courts and the Justice Department.[93] The courts and the DOJ had already indicated that they would not oppose the dismantling of the *Paramount* decrees if the studios initiated proceedings, nor would they expend their own resources to originate such action. However, as Bernard Hollander surmised, "the studios must have decided they'd rather live with a devil they knew than with one they didn't, because nobody made the motion. So it never happened."[94] As a result, the decrees remained on the books primarily because the government did not want to spend the time or money to formally dispense with them, and the studios and their parent companies were content to be "regulated" by the toothless tiger that *Paramount* had become.

The effects of vertical re-integration were felt deeply by independent producers and theaters. For instance, in 1987, there were accusations that independent producers stood less than a 50 percent chance of having their films distributed to neighborhood theaters, and eleven of the industry's largest distributors were taking in 96 percent of the domestic box office revenues.[95] This was an unqualified stranglehold enjoyed by the majors, particularly in light of the 20–25 percent market share that the independents held just fifteen years earlier.[96] Independent distributors were having a similar rough time; while their presence was increasing, they still had to contend with the growing size of the studio distributor/exhibitor that was practically eating them alive. By 1989, smaller outfits like Lorimar, Cannon, Atlantic, De Laurentiis, Vestron, Film Dallas, Island, Alive, and many other independents had gone bankrupt, reorganized, or were swallowed up by bigger companies.[97]

This struggle was taking place even as independent distributors were significantly increasing their presence in the market. There was a growing realization that bypassing the domestic theatrical market and going "straight to video," as more low-budget productions were doing, was no longer a viable option. A film needs a healthy showing in theaters to establish a presence, brand name, and garner momentum that will carry it through in all other ancillary markets. Therefore, the necessary conditions for establishing a successful first run at the box office (now largely defined in terms of a film's performance on its opening weekend) were subject to the limitations imposed by vertical integration—a cost of doing business that carries tremendous consequences. Charles Acland has suggested that the return to exhibition by the major studios made these companies "increasingly interested in the entire lifespan of a film as it moves from format to format."[98] Consequently, the concept of (integrated) distribution for a conglomerate would have to also extend outward and incorporate more formats in order for the industry to remain competitive.

It is most instructive that in this context, the *Paramount* consent decrees have remained "on the books" for over fifty years. Some regulators contend that if a consent decree has not accomplished its objective within fifteen or twenty years, it is inherently ineffective. Others point out that consent decrees any older than that are unable to accommodate the amount of transformation that inevitably takes place in any industry.[99] In any case, the tenure of *Paramount* is indeed extraordinary, and the commitment to retaining the appearance of its viability even more remarkable, particularly in light of the changes visiting the media industries during the 1980s, and those that were just around the corner.

5

1989–1992

Big Media without Frontiers

As the 1980s came to an end, deregulation was transforming the political economy of entertainment in surprising and unexpected ways. Its impact was varied, if widespread; regulators treated the film, cable, and broadcast industries all quite differently at this moment of empire construction. The film industry had just enjoyed years of deregulation and slackening antitrust enforcement, but cable would experience radically increased oversight, restrictions, and regulations by the early 1990s. At the same time, policies governing the broadcast industry were being progressively downsized. In all, when viewed from a transindustrial perspective, deregulation was a very uneven, yet relentless process that produced a halting rhythm to the convergence of media industries in the late 1980s and early 1990s.

In the meantime, ownership and business strategies were being deeply impacted by globalization. The focus and definitions of markets, audiences, and industrial identity were primarily affected and altered: "Ancillary" was no longer secondary, "domestic" was no longer primary, and "Hollywood" was no longer local or national, as studios were being bought by Japanese-, Australian-, and European-controlled companies. By 1991, foreign companies owned four of the seven major studios producing all U.S. filmed entertainment, including television programs. The combined forces of globalization and deregulation created tremendous potential upsides and possibilities for media consolidation on a scale previously unimaginable. Market concentration intensified these upsides and also sparked government regulators to take a closer look at the media industries—particularly cable, where distributors and content producers were merging at a rapid pace.

This chapter interrogates the roles played by globalization, deregulation, and market concentration in transforming media industries during a particularly intense four-year period, beginning with the birth of the world's largest entertainment conglomerate and ending with the death of one of its key visionaries, the re-regulation of cable, and the election of a new president. Each one of these forces had its corresponding villain in trade press and industry narratives—and while globalization and deregulation were intertwined at this moment, so were cable companies, the concept of "big media," and foreign investors. As a result, unpacking the many competing versions of this history embedded in the dominant narratives put forth by industry and government sources requires a consideration of multiple perspectives, and a vigilant attention to their points of contradiction. Therefore, to truly understand this particular period, we need to recognize which players were functioning as villains—for the government, the press, and the various media industries—and how those characterizations were leveraged to affect the deregulatory process.

Through that process, new relationships between media industries were enacted. The regulatory and industrial implications of the Time-Warner merger and the second major wave of 1980s conglomeration played major roles in reinventing these relationships. Combined with the impact of the 1992 Cable Act and the progressive deregulation in broadcast, a new model for media conglomeration was born—one that was focused more on cable properties with every passing year. The emerging model would offer only a preview of what was on the horizon for empires of entertainment, however. For the time being, film, cable, and print resided together under a vertically and horizontally integrated corporate structure. Broadcast would not join them until 1995. Nevertheless, in 1989, the media industries began preparing for the next century.

Cable's Kingdom

Political transformation and conflict unfolded on a staggering scale at the end of the 1980s and often served as catalysts for technological and industrial advances in the now-mature cable industry. As monumental geopolitical events unraveled—student protests in China led to the Tiananmen Square massacre in the summer of 1989, the Berlin Wall fell in November that same year, the United States began bombing Baghdad in January 1991, the Soviet Union collapsed eight months later—the world watched it all happen on cable, or more specifically, CNN. The network's live reporting of the first Gulf War was a first for cable, for broadcast journalism, and for media coverage of a global conflict, elevating the industry and setting the standard for how the audience would "watch war" in the twenty-first century. As CNN's chief executive characterized it, "We're the only network with our own foreign policy."[1]

CNN's contribution to the spread of information across the globe was so significant that Ted Turner was named *Time* magazine's "Person of the Year" in 1991. (It should be noted that *Time* owned 20 percent of Turner Broadcasting at the time of this award.) Turner was honored "for influencing the dynamic of events and turning viewers in 150 counties into instant witnesses of history."[2] He had essentially brought Marshall McLuhan's "global village" to life with the help of the twenty-four-hour news network, a fact McLuhan himself had reportedly acknowledged to Turner (at a cable convention, no less). For this and his many other accomplishments with CNN and cable news, Turner was praised for demonstrating "that politics can be planetary, that ordinary people can take a deep interest in events remote from them in every way—and can respond to reportage in global rather than purely nationalistic terms."[3]

On the domestic front, there was a rising tide of concern over the growth of consolidated power in cable television and the resulting impact on consumers. Rates were going up and subscribers were getting restless as President George H. W. Bush took office in January 1989. In June, President Bush named Alfred Sikes the new FCC chairman. Sikes's tenure, which lasted until 1993, was a contentious one; the Missouri Republican was viewed as stubborn and resistant to compromise, often offending Congress and losing its support. His time at the FCC saw the further deregulation of broadcast and the simultaneous re-regulation of cable. While the cable industry did manage to escape new legislation during Sikes's first year, the political momentum and social outcry against cable's "robber barons" quickly grew too powerful to be denied. By the end of 1992, the industry would come up against a Congress determined to scale back the concentration, monopolization of markets, and astronomical profits to which the cable companies had become accustomed. The public had seen enough of their empire building.

By the end of the 1980s, cable had experienced explosive growth. Basic cable households had more than doubled between 1980 and 1985 (from 17.5 million to 35.4 million), and then grew nearly another 50 percent to reach almost 51 million subscribers in 1990. This would slowly increase for another ten years, but the most dramatic change in the subscriber base occurred during the 1980s.[4] Cable's cultural cachet was rising along with its audience numbers, as major league sports started migrating to ESPN, cable journalism and entertainment programming were finding prestigious critical awards and acclaim, and by 1990, more than half of all households in the United States were wired for cable television.[5]

Cable's annual revenues were also growing exponentially, reaching $15.4 billion by 1989—more than six times the $2.5 billion that the industry started out with as the decade began.[6] Revenues from both subscribers and advertisers were part of this picture—as cable reached even more television homes, advertising dollars quickly followed, representing a steadily increasing piece of cable's expanding pie. Advertising was a mere 2 percent of revenue in 1980; after rising about 1 percent each year, it accounted for about 11 percent of cable's total earnings by 1990.[7]

As channel capacity increased, the number of offerings had also swelled—almost doubling from 1981 (thirty-four) to 1987 (sixty-five).[8] By 1990 there were seventy channels available.[9] Nearly thirty new services were launched between 1985 and 1992 alone, including the Discovery Channel, TNT, the Cartoon Network, and CNBC.[10] Cable schedules became more than merely syndicated broadcast reruns; channels began to gradually develop original series and programming, moving toward the model of narrowcasting and specialty channels that would expand during the mid-1990s.[11]

This period of prosperity and growth, particularly in the mid-to-late 1980s, was mainly characterized by increasing consolidation, within and between the various sectors of the industry. Merger activity was especially pronounced between cable channels and distributors (systems/MSOs). The unrestrained ability for cable companies, particularly MSOs, to vertically and horizontally integrate created tremendous concentration in the industry by mid-decade. There were very few limitations on the size of cable systems, and no limits on distributors (MSOs and local systems alike) that prevented them from owning programming services (cable channels). Consequently, by 1989, MSOs had ownership stakes in seven of the nine national pay cable channels and twenty of the fifty-two national basic channels, including twelve of the top twenty.[12] In 1990, cable operators owned half of the seventy channels in existence.[13] The distinction between those who were supplying the programming and those distributing it was fading fast.

Operators that had moved into ownership of the channels were able to create favorable price and carriage arrangements for their own properties and negotiate much less desirable terms for their competitors. They chose the quantity, type, and configuration of services they would carry, as well as their prices. Most programmers were thus at the mercy of the larger MSOs for their survival and very unhappy about the consolidated power of their distributors. A systemic hostility was brewing. That tension, amid the skyrocketing cable prices and increasingly unhappy consumers, led to growing pressure to (re)regulate cable, and the issue finally entered the radar of Congress and the FCC. These conflicts between independent programmers, MSOs, subscribers, and policymakers reached a critical mass in the late 1980s and ultimately led to a series of government reports, hearings, and recommendations aimed at exploring concentration and vertical/horizontal integration in the industry.

The first study of interest was conducted by the National Telecommunications and Information Administration (NTIA), a bureau of the U.S. Department of Commerce and the president's principal advisor on telecommunications and information policy issues.[14] The resulting 1988 report, "Current Policy Issues and Recommendations," indicated concern over rising ownership concentration levels in cable and declared that the government would seek to develop policies that encouraged greater competition "throughout the 'video market,' *among* potentially competitive services as well as *within* a given service."[15] Though largely exploratory, the study served as one of the first official acknowledgments that consolidation was taking place within and across the various sectors of the cable industry, and that it warranted government attention.

The report determined that the FCC should initiate an inquiry to evaluate the effects of the growing concentration in cable ownership and the disparity in regulatory oversight between the broadcast and cable industries. The NTIA concluded that treating the two differently, in terms of policing concentration and concerns about diversity, no longer made sense. "It is necessary," the report declared, "to reconcile the ownership limitations placed on broadcasters with the lack of such limitations on cable systems."[16] Accordingly, one of the NTIA recommendations sought to further deregulate broadcast by eliminating the network/cable cross-ownership rule. This ban on broadcasters owning cable systems was initially devised in 1970 because the FCC reasoned that a co-owned cable system could be used to "enhance the competitive position of the broadcast owner in competition with other broadcasters," meaning that ownership of the cable system could allow the network to undermine or prevent the carriage of competitors' networks over their cable wires.[17]

This rationale grew out of the early perception and treatment—and in fact, the very *definition*—of cable as initially a mere complement or additional distribution technology for broadcast as opposed to its direct competition.[18] However, as the cable industry evolved, it became a source of original programming and eventually represented true competition for the networks. The recommendation to eliminate the network/cable cross-ownership rule was based on the growing significance of cable in the video market, the simultaneous waning dominance of the broadcast networks, and the recognition that previous definitions of the cable-broadcast relationship were outmoded. With the challenge to network power brought on by cable's growing popularity, the government concluded that broadcast would be less able to exploit cross-ownership in the name of reducing competition than previously thought possible. In fact, they determined that the networks were over-policed and that the regulatory crosshairs should be retrained on the cable industry instead.

It is important to note that the telecommunications companies had been prohibited from entering the cable market as well since 1970.[19] They were subject to their own cross-ownership rules, preventing them from offering cable services to subscribers in their telephone service areas. The "cable-telco" cross-ownership ban was issued by the FCC but later codified by Congress with the 1984 Cable Act. Although the FCC recommended lifting this ban in 1988, as did the NTIA report, the rules remained in place for the time being due to congressional inaction.[20] The question of whether to permit the phone companies to enter the cable market by transmitting television and other video services over their phone lines on a common carrier basis (the concept was known as "video dial-tone" at the time) occupied a large part of the early hearings.

As a new presidential administration and congressional session began in 1989, the momentum for structural change in the cable industry remained high. Senate hearings were held again in June to explore diversity and concentration in media ownership.[21] They were guided by questions such as, "Has the media market become too concentrated? Are new rules required? Should old rules be changed?"[22] Testimony was divided among champions of cable, broadcasting, the Hollywood studios, and independent producers/stations as well as media scholars, consumer groups, and even the phone companies. Rather than achieve a consensus, the hearings put the many anxieties and tensions fueling these groups on very public display. Each industry carefully testified about the holdings of the others as grossly concentrated and stifling competition, while painting a picture of themselves as veritable nonprofit organizations. If there was a common villain, however, it was undeniably cable; the industry's astonishing growth was the most aggressive and threatening to the rest of the media industries at that time and the most vexing to increasingly vocal consumers.

The characterization of the cable industry as villain endured throughout the additional oversight hearings that began anew in November. This time, the focus was exclusively on cable and proved to be hostile territory for the executives who showed up, particularly MSO owners. The poster child for consolidation in cable distribution was John Malone, president and CEO of Telecommunications, Inc. (TCI), and he was clearly the chief target for the senators. TCI was the largest cable operator in the country, wiring almost 20 percent of the cable homes in America (more than twice its biggest rival, ATC) and having added over 150 cable companies to its portfolio by 1987.[23] Malone said that TCI was so aggressive in its approach to consolidating the industry because he knew from the beginning that "scale economics was going to determine who was going to survive and who wasn't." At one point, he estimated he was "probably doing a deal a day."[24] Malone bought big and bought often, devouring operators and programmers of all sizes on a multi-billion-dollar spending spree to expand TCI. At the time of the November hearings, TCI, with its various cable holdings, controlled between one-fourth and one-third of the nation's cable subscribers . The company also had significant interests in programming services (including Turner Broadcast System, The Discovery Channel, Black Entertainment Television, Home Sports Entertainment, American Movie Classics, QVC) satellite companies, and movie theaters all over the globe.[25]

Senator Al Gore and Malone had a publicly acknowledged animosity for one another, with Gore once famously referring to Malone as "Darth Vader" in an open condemnation of TCIs business practices. Malone was well known for an "all business" demeanor and for having an uncanny ability to successfully engineer exceedingly complex deals. Gore had just introduced a bill to re-regulate cable—one of a dozen that attempted to deal with the growing concentration and consolidation of the industry—and he hit Malone hard on all counts in the questioning. At one point Gore was interrogating him about horizontal and vertical integration strategies, and asked Malone, "Do you think that your size and power have made your company arrogant and heavy-handed?" In the combative spirit that had come to characterize their relationship, Malone replied, "I don't beat my wife, either."[26] The rest of the questioning was open season on cable, depicting the industry—MSOs in general and TCI in particular—as the enemy of rural communities, broadcast networks, their own subscribers, independent networks, the satellite dish industry, marketplace competition, and even the telcos, which were not yet allowed into the cable business but were desperately trying to get a foot in the door. "You know, we really are not bad guys," Malone maintained in his testimony. And he added, despite all appearances to the contrary, "We really are not trying to build an empire."[27]

TCI and the rest of the MSOs managed to escape these hearings without new regulatory constraints leveled on their business, but the war was far from over. As scrutiny increased, the industry continued to consolidate: in 1991, vertically integrated operators controlled about 60 percent of all homes with cable access (or approximately 2,300 cable systems). These operators owned roughly one-third of the total national and regional program services available at the time.[28] Broadcasters, satellite companies, and now the regional telcos (the "Baby Bells") were joining in the fray, lobbying Congress and trying to get the FCC to enact stricter regulations on the cable industry.

As momentum for these regulations grew, Malone knew that TCI was being watched particularly closely. During the hearings, he had even acknowledged that the government could be more active in regulating his business (completely surprising Senator Gore by saying as much). The writing seemed to be on the wall: cable would face government re-regulation to clean up some of the mess created in 1984. To avoid what looked like impending congressional intervention in his own company, Malone launched a preemptive breakup of TCI in 1991. He spun off most of its programming properties into a new company, Liberty Media Corporation. In one of Malone's deals full of his trademark complexity, he wound up as the chairman of Liberty (content) and the president of TCI (distribution). The government was placated . . . for the moment.

Almost single-handedly, John Malone was able to illustrate the growing importance of the cable industry to the modern entertainment company's blueprint. The broadcast networks wanted to expand into this arena, but they were prevented from owning any distribution interests. Film studios, however, were not subject to any such restrictions and began to invest more substantively in cable properties. In fact, as cable was being investigated for its level of concentration, the film industry was somehow managing to stay off the antitrust radar, even though the major studios alone effectively controlled the theatrical film market, the videocassette market, produced most of syndicated and network prime-time programming and television, and were moving steadily into cable as well. Ultimately, Time and Warner would merge all of these elements into the media empire that would set the pace for the new millennium.

Big Media

Just as the congressional hearings on media ownership ended in June, the proposed merger between Time, Inc. and Warner Communications, Inc. (WCI) heated up. After two years of negotiations, the two media giants were finally on the verge of creating the new gold standard for vertically and horizontally integrated entertainment companies with an unprecedented merger that would unite film, broadcast, cable, publishing, music, video, retail, and other ancillary markets under one conglomerate insignia.[29] At the same time that talks were reaching a boiling point, Warner's *Batman* opened on 2,200 screens, presenting the world with a shining example of how to combine your corporate media holdings into wildly popular, synergistic entertainment. It was a virtual shrine to the WCI portfolio and the art of cross-promotion, boasting everything from a DC Comics character to one of their best-selling recording artists within the film, and spawning an endless parade of novelizations, soundtracks, merchandise, and media properties around the character.[30] As Tom Schatz has discussed, Time-Warner began to rewrite the way Hollywood did business and *Batman* provided the vision for a developing conglomerate aesthetic, one in which a film's narrative would be designed to capitalize on all potential revenue streams and corporate holdings.[31]

Their proposed blueprint for the modern global media conglomerate became the new paradigm that all others emulated within the next decade. The union of Time's publishing empire (which included *Time*, *Life*, *People*, *Fortune*, and *Sports Illustrated*) with Warner Bros.'s studio and production capacity created synergistic strategies for developing and marketing properties, particularly big-budget spectacles in wide release. The potential for combining a film studio and print holdings were the most publicly understood and widely covered by the press. Much less discussed but equally as significant were the ramifications the merger had for cable, in terms of industry consolidation as well as the importance of cable holdings to the profile of modern entertainment empires.

In fact, both Time and Warner had been busy integrating cable programming and distribution assets into their portfolios for decades.[32] Time owned cable systems since the 1960s and programming services since the 1970s, when they invested with Charles Dolan. Dolan was an early cable entrepreneur and owner of the first underground urban cable system in America: Sterling Manhattan Cable in lower Manhattan. Time had an ownership stake in Sterling Manhattan and also backed Dolan's Green Channel in 1970—a premium channel that cost cable subscribers extra, but delivered commercial-free, uncut feature films and sports. The Green Channel was eventually renamed Home Box Office on November 8, 1972, and less than a year later, Time took it over entirely.[33] Time also participated in the 1987 MSO-led bailout of Ted Turner and owned 14 percent of Turner Broadcasting from that deal. Additionally, Time owned the premium cable network Cinemax (which HBO started in 1980) and also controlled ATC (American Television and Communications Corp.), the second-largest cable company in the United States.

Warner was also extremely active in the cable industry. The company held a stake in Turner Broadcasting (WTBS, TNT, and CNN) and owned Warner Cable Communications, Inc., the fifth-largest cable system in the country.[34] By 1990, Time Warner would have an ownership stake in a massive array of successful cable properties, including Turner Broadcast Systems (CNN, WTBS, TNT), BET, E! Entertainment Television, Court TV, The Comedy Channel, HBO, Cinemax, Movietime, and various regional systems in addition to what became Time Warner Cable—the second-largest cable distributor after TCI, with systems in thirty-five states.[35] Cable revenues equaled film, publishing, and music in Time-Warner's earnings, with each sector accounting for roughly 25 percent of the total for the merged company at the outset.

Talks between Time and Warner had been ongoing since 1987. The process began with Nick Nicholas, president of Time, approaching Warner's CEO Steve Ross about a joint cable venture, and ended with their decision to merge and be co-CEOs.[36] In 1989, Steve Ross was on top of a production powerhouse: Warner sold nineteen series to the "Big Three" networks for the fall schedule—almost twice as many as its next highest competitor (Columbia Pictures TV with ten series).[37] He was having a fantastic year in theaters, too, as Warner's *Batman* and *Lethal Weapon 2* represented almost 25 percent of the $2 billion summer box office returns. Ross had also been aggressively streamlining Warners throughout the decade, selling off most assets that were unrelated to film, music, cable, and publishing while still expanding the business. As Eileen Meehan has noted, WCI had transformed during the 1980s and was already "a highly concentrated and integrated media conglomerate" upon entering the merger.[38] It was also an extremely successful one.

The vision held by Ross, Nicholas, and Time's CEO J. Richard Munro (who would retire shortly after the merger) was largely propelled by an abiding faith in deregulation and the borderless media landscape it would produce. Nicholas even predicted in the months before the merger that "within a year, it will become legally permissible for cable companies and broadcasting networks to own each other. . . . [P]robably a year after that, relationships will change between broadcasting networks and production companies in television and movies. They will be permitted to own each other."[39] While he was off by a few years—cable/broadcast cross-ownership would be relaxed in 1992 (see later in this chapter) and broadcast networks would not be able to own their programming/suppliers until 1995, Nicholas was correct that these regulations would be quickly relaxed, stripped away during the next decade, and their repeal would motivate further mergers in the industry.

The deal for the merger was finally announced March 5, 1989. The public relations campaign began in earnest: the companies argued to their shareholders, to Congress, and to federal regulators that survival in the current marketplace was dependent upon this merger. Further, Time and Warner asserted that America's assured competitiveness in a global era needed companies that had the ability to transcend national borders in business, and that this merger was key to the country's future economic prosperity. "Indeed, the new foreign media giants seem to have an insatiable appetite for gobbling up media properties abroad and in the United States," Steve Ross said in hearings before Congress without a hint of irony. While making his case for the merger to the House Judiciary Committee, he continued by explaining that Time Warner would be "one company that will help tip the balance of trade in America's favor" because it would be the largest exporter of media in the country.[40] The recording industry was held up as a cautionary tale for Congress as the executives urged lawmakers to permit the merger. After all, the record business that was born and nurtured in America had been steadily eaten up by foreign acquisition of late (Sony Corp. buying CBS records, and Bertelsmann AG buying RCA records and Arista records).

On June 6, just two and a half weeks before *Batman*'s release, a major stumbling block emerged: Martin Davis, CEO of Paramount, attempted to derail the merger, launching a hostile takeover bid for Time, Inc. Paramount's $10.7 billion, $175/share offer was rather low, but it was enough to start an all-out war between the companies. The ensuing boardroom drama dominated the trade press; *Variety* characterized this "unprecedented battle of latter-day media moguls" as an epic struggle to control entertainment culture, noting that "[t]he fallout should unsettle all of show business for the foreseeable future."[41]

Paramount had been doing its own corporate restructuring since 1980. Similar to Warners, they had slowly shed various businesses that were expensive and extraneous to their focus on entertainment. By 1989, parent company Gulf + Western Industries had divested their holdings in manufacturing, financial services, agriculture, auto parts, and home furnishings, and renamed the company Paramount Communications, Inc.[42] In addition to Paramount's film and television production companies, they also owned Madison Square Garden and MSG Network, major theater chains, controlling interest in seven independent broadcast stations, and the USA Network (co-owned with MCA), among other properties. Acquiring Time, Inc. would certainly have been in accord with the corporate strategy at the time.

However, Paramount's aggressive bid did not win over public opinion or enlist many industry sympathies. This became apparent in the bitter propaganda war that followed, as Time/Warner and Paramount worked aggressively to tarnish one another's image with the help of attorneys, public relations specialists, and the media. Time and Warner also had a large roster of Hollywood's A-list publicly rooting for their merger. Among them, Steven Spielberg (a close personal friend of Steve Ross) was frequently spotted walking around Los Angeles in a WB baseball cap that summer, and George Lucas wrote a column for the *Wall Street Journal* in July supporting the Time-Warner merger. Lucas (who was distributing the *Indiana Jones* films through Paramount, including one that summer) praised the Time-Warner deal as "a combination from strength, creating a company uniquely capable of exploring new frontiers—geographical, technological, thematic and human—discovering new talent, nurturing important ideas and linking the world through new systems of delivery and distribution." He went on to attack Paramount for "contributing to the further destabilization of the entertainment industry and the U.S. economy," further claiming that Paramount's hostile bid "surely contributed to losing America's war in the global marketplace."[43]

In order to stave off the takeover, Time was forced to restructure their initial offer and propose a new deal to buy WCI outright, as opposed to the debt-free stock swap originally intended. In response, Paramount made a second, more aggressive bid for Time on June 26, but "[l]ike a homecoming queen brushing off the advances of a campus nerd," *Variety* reported that Time "contemptuously rejected" the new proposal ($12.2 billion, or $200/share), which came almost three weeks after the initial offer.[44] Significantly, Time's board also made this decision without asking for a shareholder vote—a highly unorthodox and controversial tactic employed because the board feared they would not have enough support for their desired merger with Warner to continue.[45]

Paramount sued Time to try and undo their plans, but was shut down by the courts on July 14, as were any Time shareholders who objected to the merger. The acquisition of WCI turned out to be a highly leveraged transaction after all, and one analyst noted that the decision sent a strong signal to media moguls that "short of outright chicanery, they are free to ignore shareholder sentiments in negotiating mergers and acquisitions."[46] Paramount's appeal was also denied, and Time moved ahead swiftly at the end of July to take control of Warner Communications, Inc.

Thus, after a rather rocky courtship, the merger in the summer of 1989 ultimately created the world's largest media conglomerate, with a stock market value exceeding $15 billion and annual revenues at the time of over $10 billion. Time Warner also started the decade's second wave of consolidation and take-overs, and the renewed feeding frenzy resulted in four major studios changing ownership within a year. With this union, a new paradigm for the global media conglomerate was firmly established: very large, shorn of the extraneous busi-nesses (such as funeral homes, parking lots, insurance companies) that had infused Hollywood studios with much-needed cash in the late 1960s and early 1970s, and newly focused on complementary media properties that included print, film (and home video), cable, and, to a lesser extent, music. Broadcast would have to wait five more years to be fully integrated into the recipe.

Aside from producing the archetypal media empire on a scale never before seen, Time Warner also emphasized the importance of global markets to an empire's architectural philosophy. At this time, foreign revenues were growing much faster than domestic ones, and 40 percent of Warners's revenues came from overseas as opposed to 5–6 percent of Time's.[47] The value of the international market—along with focused conglomerate expansion—was touted in the company's Annual Report in 1990: "While we share the unease over the sale of U.S. media and entertainment properties that has left Warner Bros. as one of only three American-owned major studios and the Warner Music Group as the sole American-owned record and distribution company, we think there is a better response than blaming the acquires. It is called competitiveness. The keys are vertical integration and copyright ownership, combined with international partnerships."[48] Valuing the global landscape for "international partnerships" was the first major step; embracing foreign owners was the next frontier for Hollywood studios and their expanding media empires.

Global Ownership and Audiences

While media was the third most active industry for mergers and acquisitions in the 1980s overall (over 2,000 deals at a value of $89.2 billion), it was the second most attractive industry for foreign buyers.[49] The specter of foreign ownership was especially threatening for those in the business of content production. Foreign buyers took over four major studios in the 1980s: Fox, Sony, MCA/Universal, and MGM/UA and began a veritable panic in the industry. As the decade came to a close, *Variety* assessed the takeovers and posed the question: "Europeans, Japanese, Australians—Predators or Parasites?"[50]

- Fox

  As discussed extensively in chapter 3, Twentieth Century–Fox was pur-chased by Rupert Murdoch's Australian-based News Corp. in 1985. While there was a small outcry, concentrated mainly in media circles, it was a much lower level panic than the one exhibited when Sony entered the picture. An Australian takeover of U.S. media properties did not elicit nearly the same cultural paranoia that a Japanese one did.

- Sony Columbia-Tri-Star

Globalization offered tremendous opportunities for American firms, but also created growing concerns that Asia (primarily Japan) was outdistancing the United States in technology development, manufacturing capacity, and industrial prowess. Japan's ascent as an economic powerhouse along with its vibrant currency, growing consumer base, and marketing victories across the globe posed a threat to struggling American industry. The Japanese also purchased one of America's most iconic buildings, Rockefeller Center, and by the end of the 1980s, Japan had spent nearly $100 billion on U.S. properties, leading to cries in the press of "America for Sale!" and "What Will Japan Buy Next?"[51] It was in this climate that Sony took over Columbia (which had merged with Tri-Star in December 1987) from Coca-Cola, finalizing the $6 billion deal by the end of 1989.

Aside from the extensive library (2,700 films) and successful film and television production company, Sony also acquired Loew's theater management company and their chain of over 800 theaters in the deal. They also spent an estimated billion dollars acquiring the services of Peter Guber and John Peters from Warner Bros., which remains one of the most overpriced, overhyped, and ill-advised deals in industry history. Of course, this was not the Japanese company's first foray into the U.S. entertainment industry; it had bought CBS records for about $2 billion in late 1987, which added such lucrative artists as Michael Jackson and Bruce Springsteen to their roster.

The most notable aspect of this merger, other than the nationalistic fervor it ignited in Hollywood, was the larger paradigm it presented: the merger of hardware and entertainment software in the media industries. This signaled the changing of the guard in the entertainment business and was just a precursor to what came next: the merger of software across many industries in the form of Time Warner. At this point, the industries were in search of a formula, and the debate about hardware versus software was a very prominent one. Would Sony-Columbia be the model? Or would it be more of a content-oriented future for the media industries, à la Time Warner?

- MCA/Universal

Matsushita Electric Industrial Co.—the progenitor of the VHS—was also involved in a marriage of hardware and software between Japanese and American interests, much like the Sony deal. Matsushita was Japan's largest manufacturer of consumer and industrial electronic products and owner of the Panasonic, Quasar, and Technics brands with estimated revenue of $45 billion. In December 1990, the company took over Universal (both Universal Studios and MCA Records) for $6.6 billion. Michael Ovitz, head of Creative Artists Agency, brokered this deal and Sony's, yet another similarity between the two mergers. The takeover was the largest-ever foreign acquisition of a U.S. media company, inspiring a Japanese headline in the weekly *Variety* (see figure 5.1). Along with Universal, Matsushita got 49 percent interest in Cineplex Odeon theaters, half of United Cinema International, and half of USA Network, and MCA records, Geffen records, global music labels, and a library of 2,900 films and 13,000 television shows.[52]

Of course, Sony and Matsushita's approach to owning both hardware and software is a strategy as old as the mass media itself; Edison created and owned all of the films shown on his Kinetoscope, and RCA famously produced programs for its NBC network as it developed television technology and sold more sets, creating quite an empire of entertainment on that model. Unfortunately for Matsushita-MCA, theirs was not nearly as successful a bid into hardware/software ownership as Edison's or RCA's. Ultimately, the merger failed, largely due to clashing management, failed promises on the part of Matsushita, and resentments at Universal. The company held together for four years until Universal was sold to Seagrams of Canada in April 1995.

- MGM/UA

MGM/UA was the subject of a global free-for-all, with buyers from all over the world competing for the studio and its massive library at the end of the 1980s. The company went through a dizzying array of owners and configurations during this period. In the spring of 1989, Australian company Qintex was to acquire the company from Kirk Kerkorian. Even after Rupert Murdoch attempted to buy the company first and drove the price up, Qintex made a deal but then collapsed in October, leaving MGM/UA available again. Italian financier Giancarlo Parretti (owner of Pathé) was the next buyer, spending $1.3 billion and almost immediately finding himself in serious financial trouble. To stay afloat, Parretti started selling off the library; the exclusive cable rights for the MGM/UA film library were sold back to Turner, the videocassette rights and the Cannon library went to Warner Bros., and the foreign rights to a Paris company. When Parretti defaulted on a bank note and wound up in bankruptcy court, France's Credit Lyonnais got control of the studio in 1992.

At the same time that foreign companies were taking over Hollywood studios, the international markets for American film and television were exploding. European television was being increasingly deregulated and priva-

FIGURE 5.1. *Variety* headline during Matsushita takeover of MCA

tized, and there was a move away from strictly public monopolies funded by licensing fees toward more private ownership. This particular change has been discussed by Rod Carveth as resulting from three key factors: (1) the movement in Europe toward political conservatism and free-market capitalism, (2) the proliferation of new distribution technology—satellites in particular—and the resulting loss of governmental control they introduced, and (3) the approaching formation of the EC and the unification/opening of trade markets.[53] With these developments, cable spread, governments and private companies launched satellites, and the space and demand for programming rose dramatically.

As a result, the revenue potential for the foreign market and the value of studio film and television libraries increased exponentially. Columbia's foreign sales doubled in two years, Warner Bros.' revenues in France went from $2.3 million to $30 million in five years, with similar percentage jumps in Italy.[54] By 1990, the number of channels and hours of broadcasting in Western Europe alone had nearly tripled from what was available just six years earlier, and sales of American-made programs to European stations totalled around $1 billion.[55] In addition to the products, most of the pipelines running U.S. entertainment directly into European homes were being Americanized as well: by 1992, for example, the cable industry in the U.K. was 90 percent owned by American-based companies.[56]

In response to the incursion of the United States into their media industries, the European Community had recently issued a directive for "soft quotas" in transnational television. After many years of debate, the EC accepted the Television Without Frontiers initiative, and effectively reserved a "majority proportion" of broadcast time in the twelve member states for European works. And as MPAA President Jack Valenti said, "[m]ajority means over 50 percent and that means quota and that means you got trouble in River City."[57] Of course, Television Without Frontiers met with immediate excoriation from Washington and the creative community in Hollywood. The Bush administration criticized the quota proposal as "violative of international trade agreements [e.g., GATT] and aimed at reducing a $2.5 billion trade surplus in one of the very few remaining sectors where the United States enjoys a trade surplus."[58] Congress asked: "Is it a call for television without frontiers? Or television without Americans?"[59] Opposition to this plan brought the Hollywood production community together, united by their concern for the future of the European market that had just returned $1.8 billion for film, television, and home video sales the previous year.[60]

Valenti described TWF as "a regulation that puts manacles on American television programs in EC countries," arguing that entertainment trade had little to do with culture but was instead a "hard, cold economic issue."[61] The Europeans countered that it was not just a financial matter; TWF was also about protecting national cultures.[62] Of the 105,000 hours of filmed entertainment on European television at the time, only 5,000 were produced there. The rest were largely imported from the United States. In testimony before Congress, British media magnate Robert Maxwell not only explained that this was threatening European cultural diversity, and the jobs in their entertainment industry, but he also made it clear that the Americans would have to accept the quota. "No nation should tolerate its culture being subjugated by a foreign one," he said. "Now it's our time and it is our turn. You can have us in partnership; you will not be able to grind us into the ground . . . either go for soft options or go for hard options. Yours is the choice."[63] At issue was the ability for entertainment empires to continue their distribution expansion overseas, and at this point, such expansion hinged on a regulatory definition of entertainment properties as commerce, rather than culture. Amid much discussion of cultural imperialism and regulating taste, the conceptualization of entertainment as culture won the day, the Americans lost, and Television Without Frontiers went forward with its quota.

Hollywood responded by creating new global partnerships to work around some of the restrictions. Paramount, Warner Bros., Disney, and all three broadcast networks formed alliances with European producers. Film distributors were also getting into global exhibition ownership. Charles Acland has argued that numerous transformations in screen culture at the time contributed to this trend, including the growth of the multiplex. "In effect," Acland wrote, "the exportation of the multiplex served as a beachhead for globalizing distribution."[64] Indeed, distributors were taking advantage of the increased number of screens all over the world. Warners (via Warner Bros. Theaters) and Paramount (via United Cinema Intl.) were competing for first-run multiplex sites in the U.K., Australia, West Germany, and Spain.[65] Even TCI, known for their cable properties that spanned the continental United States, had holdings in Mexico, and owned theaters in Hong Kong, Puerto Rico, and the U.K. By the early 1990s, the major studios led by Paramount, Universal/MCA, and Time Warner had invested "well over $100 million" in building modern movie theaters overseas, with the hopes of further expanding global exhibition traffic.[66]

The reaction to all of these developments was rather unbridled industrial and cultural panic over the international trafficking of media culture. The fact that foreign investors now owned more of the major Hollywood studios than Americans did was quite disturbing for the U.S. industry. During congressional hearings on the merger of Time and Warner in 1989, there was a great deal of talk about U.S. companies being "outflanked by large and aggressive Japanese and European companies" taking advantage of favorable conditions and siphoning the industrial power and creativity from America.[67] In Europe, the French minister of communications characterized satellites bringing American programs overseas as "a genuine war machine," in *Le Monde*.[68] War was in fact a common metaphor used in the discourse about the imbalance of trade in entertainment across national barriers, and militaristic rhetoric was equally popular. American executives used patriotic and even xenophobic appeals to try and protect media from foreign takeovers (panicking about an "Alien Invasion of Hollywood"), and Europeans often talked about facing "a combat for our own culture."[69] Maxwell even flat-out warned Congress, "do not blindly support this industry if it leads you to war with Europe."[70] Jack Valenti himself was in full combat mode once Television Without Frontiers had been put forth: "I came here to see whether there's peace or war," he said at the EC headquarters in Brussels. "You people just threw a grenade into our area, and the pin's pulled out."[71]

And yet, the global remained intricately connected to the construction of entertainment empires during this period. European executives still favored buying American because Hollywood TV was popular, cheaper, and came with better production values than most European shows. They also needed American programs to fill the air-time that was expanding with satellites, privatization, and the growing number of channels on the air. American producers needed the Europeans because they now relied heavily on revenues from the international marketplace to either help offset deficit financing in television production. They also used earnings from pre-sold rights to foreign video or theatrical markets to fund feature film production as costs spiraled upward. Disney even opened their first international park, EuroDisney, in April 1992.[72] Big media and the international marketplace were increasingly dependent on one another.

Global earnings for U.S. distributors during this period continued to climb. Revenue from the international box office was over a billion dollars and rising. As one analyst noted, "What Saudi Arabia is to oil, the United States is to entertainment."[73] With increasing demand and no legal mandate to enforce TWF quotas, the European market for American television was also thriving. In 1984, international syndication revenues were $500 million. By 1989, they had tripled, and by 1992, they were over \$2 billion.[74] Britain already maintained hidden quotas on television imports of 14 percent, but the enforcement of TWF was very lax outside of the U.K. and France, so American entertainment retained its gigantic presence on European TV screens. The United States remained the chief exporter to Western Europe (despite Television Without Frontiers) and continued to dominate the Latin American market as well.

Interestingly, the tension brought on by globalization, foreign takeovers, and the heightened focus on overseas markets also affected the dialogue about re-regulating television at home. As borders were being effaced by the technological developments and international trade of entertainment, they were simultaneously being reified by local, state, and federal regulatory policies, particularly in relation to cable. The demands of the global marketplace began to create a strain on regulatory paradigms and the cracks were revealed early on by the fight to repeal the Financial Interest and Syndication Rules (fin-syn). While the perils of globalization briefly distracted the film community from their domestic squabbles with television, it served to galvanize the networks in their fight against the studios and the restrictions of fin-syn. Soon, the takeover of Hollywood studios by foreign companies would be inextricably linked to the regulation of American television.

Deregulation/Re-regulation

As international markets were deregulated, and foreign companies acquired American studios, the broadcast networks began to complain that regulations put them at a disadvantage in the global marketplace. Their complaints refocused and somewhat reframed their efforts to repeal fin-syn. Indeed, the fin-syn talks turned decidedly nationalistic once four of the largest seven Hollywood production companies were taken over, with the networks' lobbying taking on renewed intensity as the Sony and MCA deals went through. Concerns about America's ability to compete, as well as the appearance that foreign companies were being protected in the marketplace in a manner that U.S. companies were not, began to significantly erode what remaining governmental support the rules had.

After all, Sony owned the rights to nine current series on American television, including hits like *Who's the Boss?* (ABC), *Designing Women* (CBS), and *Married . . . With Children* (Fox) after taking over Columbia. None of the networks were allowed to own their own programming or participate in global syndication, however, and they soon began to cry foul and point to this "foreign invasion of American television" as yet another reason that they should be allowed to take back ownership of their schedules. The networks were joined by many in Congress who saw the rules as giving competitive advantages to foreign-owned studios and eliminating American networks from opportunities to compete on a global scale. It appeared unfair that Japanese and European companies were able to compete for American air-time and profit from American audiences but the country's own networks were not extended the same privileges, either at home or abroad.[75] Already suffering tremendous market share losses (although not actual ad revenue losses), the networks also pointed to these takeovers to help sell themselves as the underdog, and their approach began to win them sympathy from Congress. They used the globalization of media industries as an argument for deregulating their own business even further.

Accordingly, as *Batman* opened on 2,194 theaters and the Time-Warner merger entered the final stages, the three broadcast networks went to battle in Washington, determined to level the global playing field a bit. As part of the aforementioned congressional hearings on media ownership, the "Big Three" network presidents faced off against Jack Valenti, independent producer Stephen Cannell, and Fox Broadcasting president Jamie Kellner to debate fin-syn. It was precipitously timed, taking place just months before a portion of the network consent decrees that paralleled the fin-syn restrictions were set to expire, in November 1990. If that were to happen, the networks would no longer legally be prevented from owning the programming on their schedules or syndicating their own shows. A very intense battle resulted, with the Hollywood studios on one side, the broadcast networks on the other, and the FCC in the middle.

This impending deadline of November 1990 inspired the creative community to organize around their opposition to the repeal of fin-syn and to publicize their position to those beyond the entertainment industry. The result was an umbrella organization opposing the networks: the Coalition to Preserve the Financial Interest and Syndication Rules. This was comprised of a rather diverse group of Hollywood studios, independent producers, station owners, guild representatives, and consumer advocates. Rejecting the notion that it was just a group of independent producers who got in bed with the major studios to trade "three East Coast masters for six West Coast ones," the group very actively touted their unorthodox constituency.[76] The coalition argued to the FCC, in editorials, and to Congress that repealing the rules would hurt competition, diversity, and independent creativity. Left unsaid in their public appeals was the fact that a repeal of the rules would also loosen their unchallenged grip on the $5 billion syndication business.

The networks, on the other hand, argued that the continuation of fin-syn would endanger "the continued health and vitality of this country's free, over-the-air broadcast system."[77] They talked of the end of the networks' buyers market and the advent of a new seller's market in a broadcast landscape that contained 380 independent stations (as opposed to the 90 when the rules were implemented) and a fourth broadcast network, as well as VCRs and cable television to siphon off their revenues. In fact, by 1986, the revenues of

American cable systems surpassed those generated by all American broadcast stations.[78]

The networks also argued that the rules were out of date, designed for another era of television. The fact that the Fox network, created long after the rules were implemented, was not even subject to fin-syn restrictions seemed to support that claim. Fox had been lobbying intensely for revisions to the rules, even though the network was exempt because of its status as an "emerging network." When Fox was established in 1986, it did not have more than the requisite fifteen hours of prime-time programming nor the affiliates to reach 75 percent of the U.S. television households that were necessary to be designated a network by FCC regulations. However, Fox did eventually plan to become a full-fledged network and did not want to be subject to the restrictions of fin-syn when that time came. The company had already received various waivers from the rules, including one in May 1990 allowing them to program more than the fifteen hours per week that defined a network without having to be hamstrung by the regulations preventing them from airing their own programming. The one-year waiver allowed them to program eighteen-and-a-half hours in prime-time with no restrictions on ownership, giving the network the ability to produce and air its own original programming, such as *The Simpsons* and *In Living Color.*

The FCC decided to side publicly with the networks. President Bush's chairman Al Sikes saw the rules as being anachronistic and unfair and the commission began deliberations and hearings of their own, revisiting the idea of repealing the rules for the first time since 1983. After much back and forth throughout the winter and spring, the commission passed a new proposal in April by a vote of three–two that would go into effect in July 1991. Those who voted against revising the rules (James Quello and Chairman Sikes) were actually against retaining them at all—which was the last thing Hollywood would want but exactly what the networks were hoping for. The new "1991 rules" made some significant changes, including redefining restrictions on network ownership and syndication to be for "prime-time" programming only, allowing the networks to now fill their prime-time schedules with 40 percent of their own productions, also allowing them to participate in foreign syndication without restrictions (previously networks could only sell their *own* programs overseas) and domestic syndication with restrictions.[79] Nobody was very happy with the compromised ruling, not even the networks. Aside from the "Big 3," the studios, the production community at large, the chairman of the FCC, and even the Bush administration were all displeased with the outcome. The networks, the Bush administration, and Chairman Sikes were hoping for much more deregulatory action and the elimination of the rules, while the coalition and the studios wanted to preserve the status quo and see the networks win far fewer concessions.

Although the new modifications were significantly beneficial for the networks, they did not get the full repeal they were waiting for. Consequently, the networks (and a large group of plaintiffs that included affiliate station groups, consumer advocates, and the Coalition to Preserve the Financial Interest and Syndication Rules) appealed to the Seventh Circuit Court of Appeals in Chicago to challenge the outcome of the 1991 FCC Order. On November 5, 1992, the court came back and rejected the FCC's ruling, calling the rules "unreasoned and unreasonable." Judge Richard A. Posner—a chief architect of the Chicago School's market-based approach to antitrust—wrote the opinion for the three-judge panel. It was scathingly critical of the FCC's decision to keep the rules in any form whatsoever, calling the compromise handed down by the FCC, among other things, inadequately argued and illogical: "Key concepts are left unexplained, key evidence is overlooked, arguments that formerly persuaded the Commission and that time has only strengthened are ignored, contradictions within and among Commission decisions are passed over in silence. The impression created is of unprincipled compromises of Rube Goldberg complexity among contending interest groups viewed merely as clamoring suppliants who have somehow to be conciliated."[80] The judges ordered the new rules "vacated" and the FCC was directed back to the drawing board for another attempt at revising fin-syn. Immediately following the court's decision, the studio-led coalition filed a formal protest against Judge Posner, charging that he was biased. The coalition revealed that the judge had worked as a consultant for CBS in 1977 and, as a law professor, filed a legal brief on behalf of the networks attacking the restrictions of the consent decrees (which basically codified the fin-syn rules). The FCC joined the coalition in the call for Posner to step down, bringing together two very unlikely bedfellows and, until now, opponents in the fin-syn war. Posner refused, however, and there was nothing left for those fighting the repeal to do. The work on revising fin-syn would continue the following year; at the moment, the networks were gaining ground. *Variety* held this compromise decision up as a diplomatic failure that stood as "a monument to Sikes' inability to forge a consensus."[81]

Another key deregulatory initiative that worked out in favor of the networks at this time was the relaxation of cross-ownership rules for cable and broadcast in June 1992. The FCC first adopted the cable/broadcast cross-owner-ship rules (CBCO) in 1970, prohibiting the combined ownership of broadcast *stations* and cable systems (which also automatically affected all networks, since they each owned a host of local stations) as well as rules preventing the ownership of broadcast *networks* and cable systems.[82] These cross-ownership rules were promulgated at the same time as fin-syn, and although they are rarely considered in relation to one another, the cross-ownership rules and fin-syn worked in tandem. Together, they enacted a very particular, secularized structure for the media industries that kept cable separate from broadcast, and broadcast separate from film studios for over two decades. Both sets of rules were designed to protect the other competitors in the marketplace from the broadcast networks. They were so successful that the broadcast networks were the weakest players in the game by the early 1990s.

In 1992, the FCC made a unanimous decision to overturn the prohibition on broadcast networks owning cable systems. Revisiting the 1970 rule was a major deregulatory action designed to give the networks new areas for expansion in the face of cable competition. The Bush administration (through a letter from the NTIA to FCC chairman Sikes) had already urged the FCC to lift the ban, arguing that it would improve the overall "economic health and stability of the television industry."[83] This, after the NTIA had previously concluded in their study from 1988 that the cross-ownership ban was no longer justified. Even the cable companies were on board. James Mooney, president of the National Cable Television Association (NCTA), allowed that eliminating the rule was "not surprising" and "reasonable" because "[t]he conditions which existed when the rule was adopted no longer apply."[84] The cable industry, however, remained adamantly opposed to any proposals for allowing telephone companies to buy into the cable business the same way.

In revising the ban on networks' owning cable systems, the commission did impose safeguards, including subscriber caps on national and local ownership, which sharply limited the networks' ability to acquire larger cable systems.[85] Ultimately, this meant that the ban was relaxed but not removed. FCC chairman Sikes, by then a rather frustrated advocate of deregulation, praised the vote. Still, there were some very complicated legal twists and turns, and it would actually be another ten years until this ban was entirely repealed. Nevertheless, this 1992 action began to undo the enforced separation of broadcast and cable ownership, and was a dramatic development for the construction of entertainment empires.

Just as broadcast was being deregulated, the cable industry was being re-regulated by the Cable Consumer Protection and Competition Act of 1992. The 1992 act was the most extensive reform of the cable industry since 1984. The main focus was on federal rate regulation, but there were provisions for everything from rate restrictions and technical standards to customer service and indecent programming. There was also the "Must-Carry" provision, which allowed local broadcasters to demand that cable operators carry their signal (or, alternatively, they could negotiate a fee for their programming in what was known as "retransmission consent").[86] This began to alter the relationship between broadcasters and cable providers and would be a longstanding source of tension between the two industries. Broadcasters now had the opportunity to extract compensation from the cable providers for their signal. As Patrick Parsons has explained, most broadcasters gave away their signal and attempted to either secure space for their fledgling cable channels (as Fox did with FX, and ABC did for ESPN2), or often they bartered for advertising time, but cash payments were not the norm in retransmission consent negotiations.[87]

Of course, the cable industry had furiously lobbied against the 1992 act and its many conditions. However, Congress was behind it, as were the broadcasters, the satellite industry, consumer groups, and even most local politicians, who wanted to negotiate new franchise fees for their cities. Still, despite the widespread public and congressional support, George H. W. Bush vetoed the bill. By a wide margin, the Democrat-controlled Congress overrode that veto (by a vote of 74–25 in the Senate, and 308–114 in the House), a first for the Bush administration. The vote was well timed for Senator Al Gore, who was Bill Clinton's vice presidential running mate and a well-known advocate of stricter regulations for the cable industry. He used his opposition to cable as a prominent campaign issue and even stopped campaigning to return to Washington and vote on the veto override. It was a major defeat for the cable industry.

The elements of the act with the most direct relevance to the issue of media conglomeration were clearly the structural regulations, specifically those that directed the FCC to establish limits on the reach and program ownership. These were *horizontal* limits imposed on the number of subscribers one company could reach with their cable systems (30 percent of the national market) and *vertical* limits on the percentage of their programming that a system was allowed to have a financial stake in (40 percent of the first seventy-five channels offered, beyond that, they could own as many as they wanted). However, as William Kunz has explained, these rules did not aggressively mitigate against further concentration for two key reasons. First, the channels held by system owners prior to the passage of the 1992 act did not count in the 40 percent limit. That meant, for example, that HBO, Cinemax, CNN, CNN Headline News, TBS, TNT, the Cartoon Network, E! Entertainment Television, and Comedy Central did not count in the 40 percent of channels that Time Warner Cable could have a financial interest in, as their investments were made prior to the passage of the act. Second, the FCC defined the market as the number of households passed by cable systems (that is, those that have access to cable, or those that *could* subscribe), not the number of households that actually did subscribe. While cable systems passed around 97 percent of all television homes at the time, just over 60 percent of television households were cable subscribers. Consequently, this allowed for much greater concentration in the cable industry, as the market was artificially inflated by the government's definition.[88] Moreover, the original cap on the number of cable homes reached by a single MSO was proposed to be 25 percent, but when regulators realized TCI already had a reach of 27 percent, they chose to raise that proposed limit to 30 percent and allow TCI's holdings to remain intact.[89] Instances of regulators following market activity (instead of the other way around) would remain commonplace, even after the modern empires of entertainment were well established.

Not surprisingly, the cable industry was very unhappy with recent events. The new regulations severely restricted their expansion and promised to cost them billions in lost revenues and compensation now required for the broadcast networks carried on their systems. Direct Broadcast Satellites (DBS) were beginning to compete with cable for subscribers, and the local phone monopolies (aka "the Baby Bells") saw chinks in the regulatory armor and started gearing up to participate in the video delivery business. The cable industry and their uncontested dominance in program delivery started to face some serious challenges at the end of 1992.

Nevertheless, John Malone of TCI did not let extensive new governmental regulations get in his way. In fact, TCI was thriving; they were the largest MSO in the country, with almost 9 million subscribers and over 15 percent of the market to themselves.[90] The company also had an ownership stake in a vast array of channels, including CNN, TBS, The Discovery Channel, TNT, The Family Channel, Headline News, QVC, BET, The Learning Channel, Home Shopping Network, Home Shopping Network II, E! Entertainment Television, the Cartoon Network, Court TV, and Encore. It was even said that Malone, because of his aggressive consolidation, ruthless business practices, and almost punitive attitude toward government regulation, was single-handedly responsible for the 1992 Cable Act.[91]

Still, he continued to push his agenda forward, and it was in the wake of the passage of the 1992 Cable Act that Malone made his famous "500 channel" promise. On December 2, 1992, in front of a massive annual gathering of thousands of cable industry representatives, Malone held a press conference to talk about an interactive, on-demand world. Despite the major struggles cable was now facing, Malone's dramatic vision of digital compression, a world with 500 channels and individualized entertainment and information options delivered to cable subscribers was quite seductive. The interactive, customized services recalled the failed Warner Amex system, QUBE, but this time they were part of an anticipated digital revolution. Malone's proclamation was greeted with mixed reviews, most notably on the front page of the *New York Times* in a headline that read "A Cable Vision (Or Nightmare): 500 Channels."[92] Nevertheless, he was working overtime to help put a new face on the cable industry—one that was less of a villain and more of a technological fairy godmother delivering entertainment fantasies beyond our wildest dreams.

At the end of this pivotal period in the development of entertainment empires, one that saw the deregulation of broadcast, the re-regulation of cable, and the dramatic incorporation of global ownership and new markets into the film industry's paradigm, there were also equally significant political developments. In November 1992, Bill Clinton was elected president. After twelve years of deregulating the entertainment industry under Republican administrations, it would actually be a Democrat who would preside over the complete and total deregulation of structural and ownership policies that allowed for the final phase in the construction of modern-day media conglomerates. Clinton and his administration's policies were not much different than those of George H. W. Bush, and in fact, the Telecommunications Act of 1996 that he signed was the biggest bonanza of deregulation the media industries had seen since the Reagan years.

The end of 1992 was truly the end of an era. In December, Joe Roth resigned as chairman of Twentieth Century–Fox and was replaced by Peter Chernin, who had made his name at the company's television network, as president of Fox Entertainment Group. Bringing over someone from television to head the entire studio was also a prescient statement about the shifting priorities of media conglomerates, as television would represent the largest part of the revenue pie for the company within four years. Chernin's tenure was also one of the longest and most remarkable in modern industry history—he had a seventeen-year run at Fox and did not step down until June 2009.

December 1992 also brought the death of Steve Ross, head of Time-Warner and a true visionary in the media industry. Ross, who took a funeral home and rent-a-car business and turned it into the world's largest media conglomerate, saw himself not only as a creator of an entertainment empire but also as a major contributor to the country's culture, economy, and social experience with that empire. When asked about the difference between himself and those who bought media properties only to flip them for a profit, he scoffed "they're not building America, I am."93 Big media and the defense of the nation in the face of globalization were forever linked in Steve Ross's mind.

The last and final phase of assembling the blueprints for the modern media conglomerate began as Bill Clinton took office in January 1993. The telecommunications industry was now in the mix as well; their lobbying against the cable monopoly had recently taken on a more urgent tone as they grew more anxious to take advantage of the deregulatory tide and start carrying video through their own wires. With their aggressively expanding presence, the drama of media empires had a brand new villain just as the third act was getting under way. As the media industries grappled with the new rules of engagement after 1992, the cable companies were furious, the broadcast networks were scrambling, and the trade papers trumpeted: "Bring on the telcos!"

6

1993–1995

The Last Mile

Taken in aggregate, the events in the years leading up to 1996 could almost give the appearance that structural convergence was a fait accompli. Looking back, the media industries of the past seemed to be careening toward the full-blown deregulation of the Telecommunications Act with purpose and intensity. Momentum had been building for greater consolidation within and across media since the early 1990s. Of course, in 1993 fin-syn still stood in the way of film studios and broadcast networks joining forces, and the cross-ownership rules (albeit relaxed) still prevented the union of broadcast networks and large cable systems. But all signs pointed to further erosion of the remaining boundaries. In the years preceding the Telecommunications Act, the final regulatory obstacles were removed, ideological consensus achieved, political will solidified, and significant deals struck. By 1996, the political landscape was no longer hostile to common ownership of telecommunications, cable, broadcast, and film. The Telecomm Act would be the end of the road for the regulatory vision of the New Deal, and the unmistakable triumph of the Chicago School.

On this road, however, the final push, or the "last mile," to borrow an industry term, was a dramatic one.[1] Prior to the passage of the Telecommunications Act, the media industries saw an unprecedented wave of major mergers, a host of significant policy changes, and the introduction of new players: the seven regional phone companies that were known as the "Baby Bells." These events and the entrance of the telcos initiated a new series of animosities that even threatened to upstage the rivalry between cable and broadcast companies. As the FCC tried to navigate these perennial battles—going so far as to publicly urge an end to the "holy war"[2] that had long pitted cable companies against broadcasters—the commission had to manage a new set of competing and conflicting interests. In the process, the body designed to regulate broadcast and telecommunications helped to re-envision and re-engineer what those industries could be, what their constituencies would look like, what competition would consist of, and what the role of cables and telephone wires would be in stringing together even grander empires of entertainment.

Negotiating Globalization

The question of how best to strategically position and police industry in light of globalization's influence occupied policymakers, legislators, and media moguls even after the debates that surrounded the Time Warner and Sony-Columbia mergers at the end of the 1980s. The government largely advocated for regulatory agencies and lawmakers to maintain a deregulatory posture, arguing that fewer constraints on media firms would allow the industry to be more competitive in the global market. Accordingly, in January 1993, the NTIA/Department of Commerce released a 360-page report entitled *Globalization of the Mass Media*. Initially, the document went only to certain members of Congress and government agencies. It was a concentrated discussion of media regulations and policies as they related to the international economics of entertainment. The report examined globalization trends, various policies, and their histories, and presented findings and recommendations for the future regulation of media industries doing business in a global marketplace.

Overwhelmingly, the NTIA recommended eliminating regulatory barriers separating media, mainly by eliminating cross-ownership (cable-telco, network-cable, and broadcast station–cable) and other multiple ownership rules to increase efficiency and competitiveness in media industries. The report was a neoliberal manifesto of sorts, arguing that "the United States cannot afford to be complacent" about the global market, advocating in turn for policymakers to "adapt in order to promote the development of international mass media markets that are open and competitive—the type of markets in which U.S. firms historically prosper."[3] The report touted efficiencies and benefits of horizontal and vertical integration and saw greater consolidation as promoting enhanced competitiveness in media industries. *Variety* noted that some Washington insiders saw this report "as a last-gasp effort by the Bush administration to influence telecommunications policy."[4]

Throughout the year, the growth and dramatic opportunities in the global market continued to drive media industries and their empires in search of more inroads overseas. The Uruguay Round of the GATT (General Agreement on Tariffs and Trade)[5] had been ongoing for six years, and the issues being negotiated were of interest to all producers and distributors of entertainment. Key issues for media industries—tariffs and market access—were a sticking point because of major differences between the European Community and the United States. Europe was especially resistant to further incursion of U.S. media companies and productions into their cultural landscape and very protective of their subsidies for national productions. Some in the EC advocated for a "cultural specificity" clause allowing nations to determine how they would deal with issues such as subsidies and import quotas based on their own cultural policies. Despite this and various other attempts at compromise, France in particular remained insistent that the film and television industries be wholly exempt from GATT, that there be a "cultural exception." This exemption would effectively exclude "culture" from the current trade negotiations and allow European countries to uphold more stringent import quotas and tariffs on entertainment products. The issue inspired a great deal of hyperbolic and alarmist rhetoric, with French foreign minister Alain Juppe even accusing France's EC partners of subjecting his country to "intellectual terrorism"[6] by trying to force a December 15 deadline for the new treaty.

France's position was that only complete exclusion of audiovisual matters from GATT would allow for the proper enforcement of their cultural policy directives, such as Television Without Frontiers. This particular initiative was designed to limit imports and protect European-produced programming from being overrun by foreign (read: American) media—but still was not fully complied with anywhere in Europe five years after being established. On the other hand, Jack Valenti and the MPAA were pushing extremely hard for there to be *no* cultural exemptions so that the multinational agreement could further pry open foreign markets and keep the trade balance working heavily in America's favor. President Clinton pledged he would not leave the entertainment industry out of GATT. After all, audiovisual materials were (and still remain) the United States's second-largest export after aerospace equipment, and the sales of American films, TV shows, and videocassettes to the EC were at $3.7 billion per year, while the United States imported only $300 million of European audiovisual goods.[7] Further, the average film earned more than half of its box-office overseas and American television shows accounted for between 25 percent and 30 percent of European schedules. Foreign markets were serious business and the MPAA and its constituents were extremely busy lobbying against the cultural exception. The aggressive nature of their appeals, along with the larger GATT debates, had the added effect of "waking up" many previously apathetic or neutral Europeans to the troubling extent of American domination taking place in their media markets.

The battle over GATT became so heated that even major directors were dragged into it, taking pot shots at one another across the Atlantic. In October, Martin Scorsese and Steven Spielberg issued a press release about the European effort to exclude culture from GATT, criticizing the impact it would have and the quotas it would uphold. Scorsese argued that closing the borders would not guarantee a rise in creativity or more audience interest in local product. "National voices and diversities must be encouraged and protected," he said, "but not at the expense of other filmmakers."[8] In response, a group of European directors including Pedro Almodóvar, Bernardo Bertolucci, and Wim Wenders wrote an open letter that ran in *Daily Variety* as a full-page ad on October 29, 1993 (see figure 6.1). In the letter, Almodovar and the rest criticized Spielberg and Scorsese for their statements defending the U.S. position on GATT, saying these comments threatened to erase the bond forged between the United States and Europe at the Venice festival a month earlier (where Scorsese's *The Age of Innocence* and Spielberg's *Jurassic Park* screened—and won prizes). The Europeans said that the Americans were misinformed, that in fact "the demands of the MPAA for open borders will result in the complete annihilation of the European film industry."[9] After all, they pointed out, European films reach 1 percent of the American public and U.S. productions are covering more than 80 percent of European screens.[10] The GATT negotiations produced a unique moment when creative labor and industry debates were focused on regulatory politics and their many implications for the media industries, and these exchanges between American, Spanish, Italian, and German directors had the politics of globalization playing out across the pages of the U.S. trade papers.

Still, on the surface, it looked as if the business of entertainment might be GATT-proof. Film studios, cable companies, and broadcast networks alike were continuing to buy foreign media properties and expand their empires overseas. At the time of the negotiations, in Europe alone:

- *TCI* invested hundreds of millions in cable programming networks and systems in Britain, Norway, Sweden, Hungary, Ireland, and France. They were also one of the largest programming suppliers in Europe
- *Disney* recently opened EuroDisney and had production deals with the broadcast networks in France, German, Italy, and Spain[11]
- *Warner Bros.* was preparing to build multiplexes in the Netherlands as part of an international consortium
- *NBC* was in the process of buying a controlling stake in Super Channel, a pan-European cable network, and *Cap Cities/ABC* invested in a Scandinavian satellite company.
- Time Warner's *HBO* recently created a new pay-TV service in Turkey in partnership with Canal Plus, adding to their German television holdings, British production and distribution interests, Scandinavian pay-cable investments, and Eastern European television channels.[12] HBO was intensely focused on Hungary's media landscape in the wake of communism's collapse, and HBO Hungary was the company's first European channel. The company was so aggressive in staking its claim in the newly freed market, it was argued that HBO "wrote its own media law . . . [and] transformed Hungary's cable television business in its own image."[13] HBO Poland and Czech Republic soon followed.

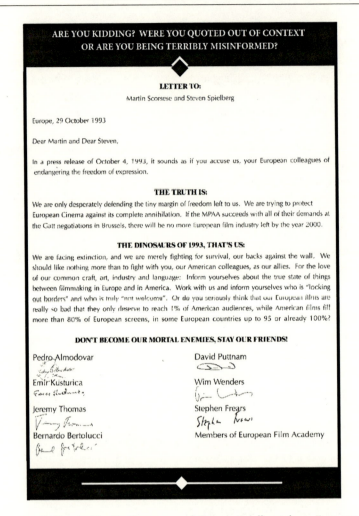

FIGURE 6.1. Letter to Martin Scorsese and Steven Spielberg from European film directors as seen in *Daily Variety*, October 29, 1993.

In the end, however, President Clinton, Jack Valenti, and the producers and distributors represented by the MPAA lost the GATT fight. No cultural exception was included per se, but in December 1993 the 117-nation accord decided to keep audiovisual materials out of the new rules altogether.[14] As a result of this exclusion, the terms would remain the same for American imports, and the United States could not insert more liberalized rules of trade for their cultural products. The U.S. production community was quite dejected over the loss, Valenti was furious, and the Europeans celebrated a major victory of, as they saw it, the triumph of "culture over commerce."[15] In fact, in many ways it was just that: it was a triumph of European rhetoric and discourse about film and television and other media products (as indigenous culture that must be cultivated and protected) over American conceptualizations of those products (as commerce and a market-driven commodity that should extend as far as the audience that will buy it). Still, America retained a formidable presence in the European media markets and continued to advance their audiovisual empires overseas, despite the diplomatic disagreements and quotas that remained intact.

New Wires versus Old Empires

As threats of international quotas loomed, another menacing force—particularly as viewed by the cable industry—prepared to enter the media business: the "Baby Bells." When AT&T lost its antitrust case in 1982 and the Department of Justice forced it to divest its local operations, seven independent Regional Bell Operating Companies were formed, also known as the "Baby Bells."[16] They were specifically prohibited from providing cable services (technically information services) by the terms of their consent decree.[17] This particular rule against cross-ownership—the cable-telco cross-ownership ban—was actually instituted more than a decade earlier with the FCC's rule in 1970.[18] It was originally created in order to protect the budding cable industry from the telephone companies who were eager to expand their business to include cable television carriage using the infrastructure they already had built. The ban was subsequently codified in the Cable Communications Policy Act of 1984 with Congress also banning the telephone companies from delivering any video programming in their local service areas. In all, there were regulatory agency rules, consent decree provisions, and legislative mandates against telephone companies in the cable business, all enacted between 1970 and 1984.

The telephone companies were therefore unable to control or provide video content, despite their tremendous desire to get a foothold in the cable television business. And even though FCC commissioner Ervin Duggan had once joked that the cable companies had nothing to fear from the telcos because telecomm's stuffy executives still "slept in their pajamas," the cable companies still viewed the Baby Bells as a tremendous potential threat to their industry, pajamas or no.[19] A fierce rivalry raged on between the two, despite regulations and laws preventing the Baby Bells from encroaching on cable's territory. The economic power and value of cable did not even come close to that of telecommunications: the total revenue for cable in the mid-1990s was $26 billion; for telephony, it was $200 billion.[20] They each had something of value that the other lacked: while cable had more bandwidth on their coaxial lines, the phone companies had vast amounts of capital and expertise in point-to-point communication that the cable companies did not. Yet, telecommunications remained on the outside of the entertainment industry looking in.

The FCC had already recommended that Congress do away with the cable-telco cross-ownership ban in 1988 and President Reagan's Department of Justice had also recommended fewer restrictions on telephone companies. Although Congress did not act on that right away, U.S. . District Court Judge Harold Greene made major changes when, in July 1991, he ordered the lifting of restrictions in the AT&T consent decree that had prohibited phone companies from providing cable services (also known as information services). Greene was the presiding judge in the AT&T case after being assigned to it his first day on the bench in 1978. He subsequently was in charge of administering the AT&T consent decrees or what became known as the MFJ (Modified Final Judgment). Greene's decision was naturally appealed by the cable industry, and the appeals court later affirmed Greene's order: the Baby Bells were now free to provide cable service or "video dial tone," as it was then called, outside their local area.[21] The concept of video dial tone was envisioned by FCC Chairman Sikes when he was at the NTIA under President Reagan; it was a transitory step, allowing telephone companies a foot in the door of the cable business, but not quite all the way into ownership. Cable historian Patrick Parsons has argued that the concept of video dial tone was "old wine in new bottles," drawing on previous cable policy proposals and allowing phone companies to act as conduits and lease their wires/capacity to third-party program providers.[22] It basically allowed the telephone companies to act as a common carrier for cable programming and deliver someone else's content to the subscriber over their wires. Thus, the telcos were not controlling or owning the content, they were merely transporting it. The FCC also formally authorized a video dial tone plan in 1992, and the telcos were able to act as common carriers of cable programming.[23]

This common carrier status became a key element in the Baby Bells' bid to end the congressional ban on cable-telco cross-ownership that was enshrined in the 1984 Cable Act. The Cable Act put the longstanding FCC's cross-ownership rules on the law books and it was the only thing still standing in the way of the telephone companies and their dreams of owning cable systems. Common carrier status was one thing, but ownership was what they wanted. The fact that the FCC was supportive of repealing the cross-ownership rules now that cable had grown into a powerful and mature industry was favorable for the Baby Bells. After all, the six largest cable operators (TCI, Liberty Media Corp, Time Warner, Inc., Viacom, Cablevision Systems Corp., and Comcast Corp.) held more than seventy investments in cable programming ventures and served over 25 million subscribers, nearly half of the nation's total. Together these cable operators earned more than $3 billion in 1992.[24] Clearly, cable was no longer vulnerable and in need of protection from telecommunications. At the same time, House Telecommunications Subcommittee Chair Ed Markey was being lobbied to hold hearings on allowing the telephone companies into the cable business. It seemed that the political will might finally be on the telcos' side.

This was the moment that the Baby Bells decided to take their case to the courts. Interestingly, they argued that the ban on cable ownership was in violation of their First Amendment rights. Suing the U.S. government, the FCC, and the U.S. attorney general, they claimed "common carriers may be required to carry freight for others . . . but that does not mean they may constitutionally be barred from carrying expressive freight for themselves."[25] Thus began a series of court decisions, starting with federal district courts in 1993 and moving on to appeals courts. Various Baby Bells won relief in their own areas, beginning with Bell Atlantic and US West, and these decisions collectively chipped away at the 1984 Cable Act. Ultimately, the issue went all the way to the Supreme Court in 1995, where it remained until Congress changed all of the rules with the 1996 Telecommunications Act.

In the meantime, John Malone tried to expand his own empire into new territory. On October 13, 1993, Malone announced a $33 billion merger with Bell Atlantic—a deal that combined a phone company, a cable MSO, and holdings in major production studios and programming services. The annual cash flow of Bell Atlantic was about $5 billion (on $13 billion in sales)—the same as the entire domestic theatrical market.[26] The Baby Bell was *three times* the size of TCI, and TCI was the biggest player in the cable business. This deal combined the most aggressive companies in both telecommunications and cable television, and it would have been the largest corporate merger in history to date. It also represented the beginnings of a détente between the two industries. The merger was characterized in *Fortune* as "an information-age coupling—more effect than cause, more a defense than an offense, and having to do more with things coming together than falling apart."[27] Ultimately, such a vaunted arrangement was not to be; the FCC announced their second round of cuts for cable rates, forcing the industry to take a 7 percent hit, and the very next day, the merger was off. The FCC's rules were going to "erase close to $1 billion from TCI's cash flow"[28] and decrease the company's value so much that Bell Atlantic tried to renegotiate their price. When TCI refused, the deal was over.

Some industry observers believed that it was more the clash of corporate or industry cultures instead of the rate rollback that led to the demise of the deal. After all, the fine print on the FCC ruling allowed cable systems new ways to pass along costs to subscribers, and to hike rates in ways that would eliminate most of the losses incurred from the FCC's cut.[29] Still, the cable industry was fuming over their rate cuts, the telcos remained in limbo, and another planned merger between SBC and Cox Cable would also be scrapped—collateral damage in the war over the much-anticipated union of cable and telecommunications. This particular piece of convergence would have to wait two more years.

Fin-Syn Repeal: A Drama in Five Acts

While the efforts of the Baby Bells to expand their own empires into entertainment were stalled for the time being, another major wall was coming down: the one separating common ownership of film studios and television networks.[30] Thanks to the growing momentum to repeal the Financial Interest and Syndication Rules, this element of the convergence blueprint was on the verge of falling into place. Some constraints against the networks were already relaxed in 1991 with the FCC's newly revised fin-syn rules, leaving ABC, CBS, and NBC free to produce 40 percent of their prime-time programming and retain their financial interests and syndication rights in those productions (with some restrictions). However, the networks were still barred from participating in first-run syndication. Even with the 1991 rules, the Hollywood studios' power and dominance in television program production was largely preserved. Nevertheless, the broadcast networks were in a better position with respect to fin-syn and program ownership than they had been in two decades. As previously mentioned in chapter 5, the networks appealed to the courts to vacate the 1991 rules. The ruling from the Seventh Circuit Court of Appeals at the end of 1992 sent the matter back to the FCC for reconsideration with a blistering criticism of the commission's reasoning for preserving the rules at all.[31] Judge Posner's harshly worded opinion may have inspired the FCC to shift their thinking and align themselves more closely with the networks; after all, there were more votes on the commission in 1991 to revise fin-syn than to drop it altogether, and that changed after this ruling.

It was quite apparent that the true beneficiaries of fin-syn, which was originally intended to protect independent producers, were the major Hollywood studios—most of which were foreign-owned at this point. According to *Variety*, since the regulations were adopted in 1970, the share of independently produced programs had fallen dramatically, from 55 percent to 26 percent, while the percentage of prime-time productions by major studios increased from 43.5 to 62.8 in the same period.[32] Clearly, the rules had been a tremendous boon to the major studios, which created an increasingly hostile marketplace for the independents to do business. As Mara Einstein determined, by 1995, the top independent producers only accounted for 10 percent of prime-time production, with the major studios (Warner Bros., Paramount, Universal, Columbia, Disney/Touchstone, and Fox) and the broadcast networks accounting for the rest.[33]

In April 1993, the FCC came out again on the side of the networks; they delivered a newly amended and revised set of rules that allowed the networks to negotiate for an ownership stake in all programs on their schedule and produce as much of their own programming as they wanted.[34] There were still restrictions on syndication but this decision practically eliminated the rules and allowed the broadcast networks to stock their own prime-time schedules with programming entirely produced "in house" for the first time in over twenty years. The few remaining restrictions on the networks were set to expire in November 1995. This was not good news for the major film studios, as they saw their iron grip on the television production and syndication business essentially coming to an end.

Fox supplied prime-time series to all networks, including *LA Law* (NBC), *Picket Fences* (CBS), *NYPD Blue* (ABC), and *The Simpsons* (Fox). Fox was also able to distribute all of these programs in syndication. The network programmed eighteen-and-a-half prime-time hours a week, after being given an exception by the FCC in 1990 to go beyond fifteen hours without having to be regulated as a "network." In the 1993 revision, Fox managed to remain an exception and the studio-based network got another free pass from the FCC. With this exception, Fox was allowed to expand to the twenty-two prime-time hours that the Big Three were programming because of its status as an "emerging network." In light of Fox's market power and the network's unique advantages of being integrated with a film studio, the special exceptions from the FCC seemed particularly unfair to the rest of the broadcasters. Even Judge Posner, looking back, said that the exemption seemed "arbitrary" given Fox's remarkable growth and role as a producer of many prime-time programs.[35]

The networks could not begin celebrating quite yet, though. After the FCC's rules were modified and set to expire, the matter of court-mandated antitrust restrictions still remained. ABC, CBS, and NBC were under constraints from a lawsuit filed by the Department of Justice and settled with consent decrees in 1978/1980.[36] These terms paralleled and essentially codified the fin-syn rules. Consequently, the three networks petitioned the court to remove them after the FCC made the revisions to fin-syn in 1993.[37] The Antitrust division of the Department of Justice came out publicly in support of removing the consent decrees and also wrote to the judge overseeing the case in support of the networks' petition.[38] In November 1993, Judge Manuel Real granted the networks' motion and lifted the consent decrees, clearing the way for the networks to conduct any and all business in the programming arena—including producing/owning their prime-time schedules and participating in the domestic syndication market (first-run and off-network)—by November 1995.

Incredibly, the networks were *still* fighting the decision and they petitioned the Seventh Circuit Court of Appeals to throw out the 1993 rules and eliminate fin-syn altogether and immediately, without having to wait two more years.[39] Judge Posner refused, saying that what remained was not "unduly burdensome," as they were set to expire in November 1995. In his opinion, Posner wrote that he thought the networks' true concern might be that the final review of the rules before the scheduled expiration would not go their way after all, that "the Commission (three of whose five members were new since the decision came under review) may change its mind about deregulating the television program market." That would not go over well with the court, Posner indicated, saying "if it does so, it had better have an excellent, a compelling reason. The three original networks are even weaker today than they were in March of last year when the decision to deregulate was made, and no doubt they will be weaker still next year when the new proceeding is to commence."[40] The court was firmly on their side, even if Posner would not deregulate the networks earlier than scheduled.

The pro-fin-syn coterie of film studios and independent producers/broadcasters continued lobbying the FCC to keep the rules in place. At this point, Reed Hundt was the chairman of the FCC. He had been a high school pal of Al Gore's, and Gore was responsible for him being picked to head the commission in 1993. Hundt was in favor of letting the rules expire, and it seemed that at least two more commissioners would be as well, giving the networks the three votes they needed. Hundt was to conduct a review six months before the November expiration of the rules to ensure that the decision was still good policy. Things looked on track, and *Variety* even noted in a headline that the rules were "prepared for burial."[41]

In September 1995, the undertaker came early. The FCC decided unanimously, two months before the rules were set to expire, that there was no justification to keep them until November. As a result, fin-syn was officially repealed on September 21, 1995, and the drama's five acts were complete: Enactment (1970), First Repeal Attempt (1983), First Revision (1991), Second Revision (1993), Final Repeal (1995). What's more, a twenty-five-year battle over television programming and finance was over, and a new era in structural convergence was about to begin. The broadcast networks were now free to produce and syndicate their own programming. They were newly empowered players in the media landscape, and could now own production companies, syndication businesses, and even the programming that they scheduled.

The networks were also allowed to broadcast as much in-house programming as they wanted and they could retain the lucrative syndication rights as well. The percentage of programming produced in-house by the networks has steadily climbed ever since the repeal of fin-syn. In 1995, the networks owned approximately 40 percent of their schedules on average. By the start of the 2000 season, however, CBS, for example, had an interest in or owned outright 68 percent of its prime-time schedule, including ten weekly entertainment series. Fox owned 71 percent of its prime-time lineup.[42] NBC produced seven shows, all airing on their own network.[43] This trend would continue, and in 2009, twenty-two out of the thirty-two new shows were produced and owned by the network on which they aired.[44]

More importantly, film studios and broadcast networks could now have common ownership. With this change in policy, the final phase in empire building had officially begun. The build-up to the fin-syn repeal and the eventual termination of the rules set into motion four extremely significant mergers, each one re-imagining the media conglomerate in a slightly different way and carrying their own unique implications for empires of entertainment.

Paramount-Viacom 1993

While the FCC was still deliberating about the repeal of fin-syn, there were rumblings and rumors about more mergers and consolidation in the media industries. In September 1993, a major takeover was announced: Viacom's parent company National Amusements would be buying Paramount Communications for $8.2 billion. This merger would combine one of cable's largest content providers and the biggest library of syndicated television with a massive film library, over 2,000 movie screens, radio and television stations, theme parks, and the Paramount film production and distribution assets. National Amusements had an interesting lineage that was intricately connected to the history of media regulation, a history that would ultimately come full circle at the end of the twentieth century. It began as an East Coast (drive-in) theater chain during the Depression. When expanding, National Amusements purchased some of Paramount's divested theaters after the consent decrees created a new landscape of independent exhibitors. Viacom itself began as a syndicator, which was spun off by CBS in 1971 when fin-syn forced the networks out of the syndication business. The two companies merged when Sumner Redstone's National Amusements bought a majority stake in Viacom in 1987 and Redstone became Viacom's chairman. The merger brought together properties resulting from the regulation of the film industry in the 1940s and the regulation of the broadcast industry in the 1970s, among many others. The result was a formidable media empire that showed no signs of slowing down.

Paramount had been on a losing streak for some time and the studio was producing fewer, but pricier films, releasing only thirteen features in 1993. Their underperformance rendered them a target for takeover as media companies began envisioning a post-fin-syn landscape that would allow film and broadcast to cohabitate under one conglomerate roof. Before Viacom was able to seal the deal, however, QVC, led by Barry Diller, launched a hostile bid for the studio. Diller (who had been chairman of Paramount for ten years before moving over to Fox in 1984) was willing to pay $8.5 billion for his old studio, and Viacom's price was just under $8 billion at the time due to stock values. It was good business: QVC was backed by TCI and Comcast, and combining those cable assets with all of Paramount's programming would have greatly elevated QVC's place in the market. But it was also personal with Diller—he had left Paramount (it was widely understood that he was pushed out) because of the current chairman and CEO, Martin Davis. Taking over the studio would have been an especially sweet way to return. A vigorous bidding war ensued, and after five months of heated back and forth with Diller and QVC, Redstone and Viacom ultimately emerged victorious. Their $9.85 billion bid for the studio was roughly $1.35 billion higher than their original offer before the bidding war.[45] Viacom officially took control in March 1994 and the second-largest media conglomerate in the world (after Time Warner) was born, creating an empire of entertainment that combined film, cable, broadcast, radio, content libraries, publishing, live entertainment, and theaters. The deal was completed in July and wound up closer to $10 billion. Even with that inflated price tag, Redstone called the merger "an act of destiny."[46]

One big factor in Viacom's triumph over QVC was Blockbuster—or, more accurately put, Viacom's takeover of Blockbuster. The video chain was a huge cash cow—at the time, it was the world's largest video retailer with 3,600 video stores in forty states and nine countries, 500 music stores, concert venues, and over $2 billion in annual sales that could help Viacom with its debt load.[47] Moreover, the home video market was the industry's chief revenue source at this point, and the video store business was three times what the theater business was in North America.[48] It seemed the tail was outrunning the dog, and if you were a content provider, the time to get into the video business was sooner rather than later. Blockbuster was practically untouchable in this market—they owned almost 25 percent of all video stores and generated more revenues than their next 550 competitors combined.[49]

Viacom proposed the merger in January 1994 for $8.4 billion and talks went through a series up ups and downs; Viacom's stock took a nosedive during the QVC battle but the rebound over the summer started negotiations once again. After ten months, the deal was finally done for $7.6 billion. The merger was announced in October 1994, just after the Paramount takeover was complete. It was an unlikely chain of events that shed some light on the shifting valuation of various media industries in the mid-1990s. As media scholar Frederick Wasser wrote, "A film institution had been bought with the cash flow of a video rental business."[50] What's more, it was bought by a cable colossus with a parent company that began life as a chain of movie theaters.

This new entity was a giant in film and television programming. Blockbuster's subsidiary Worldvision already owned Spelling TV and Republic Pictures, a supplier of TV movies with a vast library.[51] Along with Worldvision, Paramount, and Viacom's massive library of film (over 8,500 titles) and television series (including *Cheers*, *Roseanne*, *The Cosby Show*, and *I Love Lucy*), the company's network series and syndication holdings were larger than any other company's. In addition to Paramount, Blockbuster, and Viacom's syndication library, the assets after the merger also included:

- 2,020 theater screens (National Amusement Inc. owned 800 theaters in the U.S. and U.K., Paramount owned the Famous Players chain in Canada, 50 percent of the Cinamerica chain, and hundreds of screens around the world in their joint venture, United Cinemas International)
- Nine cable networks (Showtime, The Movie Channel, Comedy Central, Nickelodeon, MTV, VH-1, Flix, Nick at Nite, and MTV Europe along with USA Network, which was co-owned by Paramount and MCA, and the Madison Square Garden Network)
- Twelve TV stations (three NBC affiliates, two CBS affiliates, four independent stations, and three Fox affiliates)
- Fourteen radio stations
- Viacom Cable with over a million subscribers
- Five theme parks, Madison Square Garden, the New York Knicks, and the New York Rangers
- Simon & Schuster[52]

Viacom was now a producer/distributor of film, broadcast television, cable series, and publications, as well as the proud owner of thousands of theaters and video stores. Synergies abounded, and it was just two years before MTV's *Beavis and Butt-head* had their own Paramount feature film—*Beavis and Butt-head Do America*—in wide release, while the company was funneling product from MTV to Simon & Schuster, or from Paramount to Showtime. There were strategic opportunities around every corner for Viacom, between cable and film, broadcast and syndicated library holdings, content providers and theme parks and publishing. The company was also in very good financial health, allowing Redstone to brag that Viacom was "Time Warner without the debt."[53]

Mostly, Viacom was an empire built on a devotion to content. It did not have the pipelines that Time Warner did, but Viacom had more content for those pipelines than anyone else. Redstone was counting on subscribers everywhere demanding their MTV and he stayed focused on Viacom's strengths in software/programming. Redstone also continued to capitalize on the increased regulation constraining the film and broadcast industries, and this "cable company" would continue to expand across media boundaries, ultimately buying the very broadcast network (CBS) that originally spun it off. Before that cycle was complete, however, Redstone would do his part to further blend the film and television industries by delivering one of two studio-based broadcast networks created expressly for the post fin-syn media landscape.

UPN and The WB—Film and Broadcast Unite!

Despite speculation that one or the other would back out of their plan, the year 1995 began with two brand-new broadcast networks developed in anticipation of a full fin-syn repeal. The FCC's modifications in April 1993, plus the lifting of the consent decrees in November, allowed the studios that were producing some of television's most popular shows (*Friends, E.R., Frasier*) to create and program their own networks. Time Warner's WB network aired its first two hours of original prime-time programming on January 11, 1995. Paramount's UPN debuted five days later with a two-hour premiere of *Star Trek: Voyager* (and finished first in their time slot!), followed by original prime-time hours the next day.[54] The WB would continue with only a Wednesday night schedule while it got off the ground, and UPN had two nights of programming a week to start.

Echoes of the doubts that greeted the Fox network in 1986 were everywhere in the trade press. Indeed, the last time a film studio decided to start a broadcast network, nobody thought it would work then, either. Time Warner and Viacom were hoping that industry observers would be wrong again. However, the state of the broadcast industry was even more precarious than it had been when Fox arrived on the scene. Cable had reached a 65 percent penetration rate in 1995 (as opposed to 45 percent when Fox began), the dial was more crowded and competitive than it was ten years earlier, and networks were increasingly niche-oriented, specialized for particular and narrow demographics.[55] Further, there were far fewer independent stations available to support these networks than were available when Fox was looking for affiliates.[56] It was not an ideal environment for one new broadcast network, let alone two. One trade report even viewed Michigan J. Frog, the Warner Bros. cartoon star and new mascot for the WB, as an ominous symbol. "The frog, faithful cartoon viewers will recall, sang for only one person: The construction worker who had the misfortune of finding him. Every time the guy tried to cash in on the frog's talents," the story cautioned, "it would only croak, driving its owner into bankruptcy and insanity."[57]

Aside from the widespread skepticism, there were many other similarities and parallels drawn between Fox and the studio-based fledgling networks. The WB, for instance, had hired many of the same personnel that got Fox off the ground, Jamie Kellner (Fox's first president) and chief programmer Garth Ancier among them. Fox started with *In Living Color*, an enormously popular show with Keenan and Damon Wayans, and the WB had their younger siblings starring in *The Wayans Brothers*, one of the network's first new programs. The "netlets" as they were called also primarily targeted younger viewers, just as Fox had done when it started.[58] Both Fox and Paramount counted quite a few broadcast stations among their holdings, given Murdoch's purchase of Metromedia in 1986 (just before the launch of the Fox network) and the Paramount Stations Group, which had been under full control of the studio since 1991. In many ways, the three studio-based networks were very similarly positioned.

The affiliates were mainly independent stations along with some cable channels. UPN reached roughly 80 percent of the country but had to rely on "secondary affiliates" that also broadcast other networks' shows in order to find their audience. Key for the WB was its largest affiliate, the Tribune Broadcasting's WGN. The Chicago Superstation, a hybrid which was a broadcast station also on cable and in 25 percent of U.S. homes at the time, helped the WB to reach approximately the same size audience as UPN when it started.[59] The importance of WGN's cable audience to the WB, plus the fact that the network planned to have Time Warner's cable operators create local channels for them in smaller markets, made cable critical to the WB's success. Even in a deal for a broadcast network brought to life by a film studio, cable was omnipresent, underscoring how significant the industry had become to all empires of entertainment. In fact, it represented 40 percent of all Time Warner's revenues in 1995, up from 25 percent when the companies merged.[60] Acknowledging the powerful place cable occupied in the Time Warner media landscape, WB chief Jamie Kellner explained, "The cable industry plays a role in the next network. To not address that in a business plan is a mistake."[61]

It was largely understood that for these companies, launching the networks was also part of a strategy to produce, program, and syndicate their own shows after the repeal of fin-syn. Both parent companies were major players in television production (and syndication). Warner Brothers Television was the top television supplier for the last nine straight years and was producing twenty shows across all networks, and Paramount was responsible for twelve programs on the air.[62] Now, Warner Bros. and Paramount would have their own network and a guaranteed outlet for their product, reminiscent of the vertically integrated studio system in Hollywood's golden era. Robert Daly, former CEO of Warner Bros., even admitted, "I never would have started The WB if the financial interest rules were not repealed. . . . I knew that eventually it would be harder and harder to get shows on the network that they didn't own a piece of or control."[63]

Within the year, Warner Bros. produced six of the WB's eleven primetime shows and nearly all of its children's programming, while Paramount had a stake in four of UPN's nine nighttime shows.[64] Both networks struggled out of the gate but their affiliation with a major film studio—modeled after the precedent established by Murdoch and Fox—would prove to be an enduring hallmark of entertainment empires going forward; in fact, it was not long before a new studio-network combination would arise to command everyone's attention.

ABC/Disney

Like Viacom, Disney was focused on product as opposed to delivery systems, and they wrote the book on content creation and brand management. The "Mouse House," as *Variety* often called it, was attuned to developing intellectual property, branding, and synergy long before their competition; indeed, Disney had been cross-promoting film properties, television series, music, and theme parks, and behaving like a bona-fide media conglomerate since the mid-1950s. The company was a bit rudderless in the 1960s and 1970s, but under the leadership team of Michael Eisner, Frank Wells, and Jeffrey Katzenberg assembled in 1984, Disney was revamped and found increasing success with their theatrical releases, home video, and expanding theme parks. Eisner had been a programming executive at ABC until 1976, when he left to become president and CEO of Paramount Studios. Wells had been vice chairman of Warner Bros. Together, they brought in Katzenberg to run the studio and by 1987, the film unit was once again adding to the corporate profits.[65] Throughout the 1990s, the studio was regularly trading the yearly box office championship with Warner Bros. Their animated features had been very successful, with *The Little Mermaid* (1989), *Beauty and the Beast* (1991), and *Aladdin* (1992) all delivering the company enormous hits. Disney was also expanding beyond the Walt Disney Studios, founding Hollywood Pictures in 1989 and the accompanying Hollywood Records label in 1990, creating Hyperion Books in 1991, and buying the Mighty Ducks NHL expansion franchise in 1992.

During this expansion, Disney also bought Miramax Films in June 1993 for $80 million. This was one of the first major instances of Disney's media holdings growing by merger/acquisition as opposed to expanding their own properties further or "upsizing an established division," as Tom Schatz has noted.[66] With the Miramax deal, a funny thing happened on the way to the ABC-Disney merger: Disney and its abundant resources also helped to revitalize independent film. As Alisa Perren has argued, Miramax was able to tap into Disney's deep pockets to accelerate some of their customary business practices such as aggressive deal making, acquisitions, and bold marketing plans.[67] Once a company as large as Disney was supporting the "indie boutique," Miramax was able to lead a renaissance in the independent film world that would continue to build steam throughout the 1990s. They released films such as *The Piano* (1993), *Pulp Fiction* (1994), *Muriel's Wedding* (1995), and *The English Patient* (1996), the film that gave Miramax their first Academy Award for Best Picture. Following the Miramax purchase, Disney continued to diversify, moving further into sports (buying 25 percent of the California Angels in 1995), live entertainment and theater (*Beauty and the Beast* made its Broadway debut in 1994 and went on to gross well over $1 billion), all of which took place as *The Lion King* became one of the highest-grossing films of all time, dominating the summer box office that year. This was also the moment that overseas rentals surpassed domestic theatrical rentals for the first time; the global market was exploding and Disney product, particularly animation, traveled very well across national and international boundaries. In 1995, almost one quarter of their revenues were foreign.[68]

At the same time, Disney was experiencing a major shift in management. In April 1994, company president Frank Wells died in a tragic helicopter crash. When studio chief Jeffrey Katzenberg was not promoted by Eisner to succeed Wells, he resigned that August. Katzenberg left Disney and created Dreamworks SKG with Steven Spielberg and David Geffen in October 1995. Dreamworks was the first new film studio to emerge since the birth of RKO in 1928. Back at Disney, Eisner hired his good friend and CAA chairman Michael Ovitz to be his president and second-in-command. Ovitz had recently brokered the Sony-Colombia and Matsushita-MCA deals, and was at the height of his power. He came to Disney in October 1995 (for what would be a very brief tenure—just over one year) and presided over the quintessential marriage of film product and TV pipeline: Disney's $19 billion purchase of ABC.

This would be the first merger of the post fin-syn landscape between a film studio and broadcast network (even though it was announced in August 1995, a month before the official repeal of the rules). At the time, it was also the second-largest corporate deal ever made. Disney paid an exorbitant amount for the network—three and a half times the price that Westinghouse paid for CBS that same week, in fact. Still, the press hailed the merger as "the type of combination other media moguls dream about," and Wall Street was lauding the deal as "the benchmark for the rest of the industry."[69] The new conglomerate represented the promise of boundless synergy for a brave new Magic Kingdom. It was not the first time that Disney and ABC had joined forces. In April 1954, Disney and ABC created a new television series, *Disneyland*. The program, which showcased Disney's theme parks and short films on ABC, proved to be a tremendous success for both companies. It also ushered in a new era of cooperation and collaboration between the film and television industries.[70]

In 1995, ABC was the most profitable and highest-rated network on television, and also the majority owner of cable networks ESPN and ESPN2, and a partner in the A&E and Lifetime cable networks. ABC also owned seven daily newspapers, ten TV stations, thirty radio stations, and fed more than 200 affiliates on their television network. The Disney studio was an immense global entertainment juggernaut of its own in 1995, a $12 billion conglomerate in command of multimedia content, theme parks, publishing enterprises, a cable channel, and a brand recognized all over the globe. "Synergy" was a buzzword trotted out in practically every story printed about the merger.

The astronomical cost involved incited some skeptics to scoff at the potential for productive synergies in such an overloaded and expensive deal. Nevertheless, Eisner was repeatedly quoted as being "totally optimistic that one and one will add up to four" when discussing the cross-promotion possibilities associated with the deal.[71] "The synergies are under every rock we turn over," he beamed.[72] Vertical integration was widely promoted by entertainment executives in the trade press as their preferred strategy for the new millennium. The media industries had clearly come a long way since the days (and politics) of the *Paramount* decrees. For his part, Eisner was quite proud of the role that vertical integration played in the purchase of ABC. He also boasted of Disney's new role as its own best supplier. "The purpose of the acquisition was to protect the mouse, to ensure that no other institution could block us from getting our shows access on the networks and on cable," he explained. "At Disney, we like to control our own destiny, and we concluded that the only way not to be at the mercy of other institutions ('gatekeepers') was to assure our own access. The ABC broadcast highway now provides an open road for some outstanding new Disney shows and an avenue that will help our entire company travel successfully into the 21st century."[73]

ABC was already one of Disney's biggest customers at the time; the network was paying $81 million in license fees for *Home Improvement*, *Ellen*, and *Boy Meets World* and the rights to run Disney's movies. They were also paying an additional $9 million each year for the rights to Disney's syndicated programs.[74] The FCC did force Disney to sell off just one local ABC station, KCAL in Los Angeles; one company could not own two VHF outlets in the same market and Cap Cities already owned KABC.[75] Once that sale was finished, Disney rode the crest of the fin-syn repeal to a smooth FCC approval, and the acquisition of Capital Cities/ABC (renamed ABC, Inc.) was completed in February 1996.

This deal is of key significance to this study for several reasons, the primary one being that it established the blueprint for most media conglomerates that were formed in its wake. From this point on, the "must have" list for every entertainment empire included *both* a film studio and a broadcast network, in addition to extensive cable properties. Disney-ABC became the precursor to major mergers that would take place in 1999 (AOL Time Warner), 2000 (Viacom-CBS), and 2004 (NBC-Universal), all of which followed the model Disney established in 1995. It represented the first incarnation of a global media conglomerate that was able to incorporate holdings in and across the film, broadcast, and cable industries, thanks in part to the repeal of the Financial Interest and Syndication Rules.

This strategic merging of Disney and ABCs assets also provided another less obvious but equally interesting example of how important cable would become to an entertainment empire. A few observers speculated that Disney's purchase of the broadcast network was primarily done to capture ESPN, which was 80 percent owned by ABC. At the time of the merger, the service earned more advertising revenue ($377 million) and monthly fees from cable operators ($485 million) than any other channel.[76] (Their per-subscriber fees continue to be the highest in the industry.) That acquisition would prove to be a prescient one; soon, it would be cable holdings—not film studios and definitely not broadcast networks—keeping their parent companies afloat. Ultimately, this merger would also become an example of synergy's somewhat hollow promises, but that full realization was still a few years down the road.

Another broadcast network changed owners the same week that Disney bought ABC. The CBS-Westinghouse merger, a $5.4 billion deal, was less significant in terms of financial and industrial implications for media industries. However, it does remain a telling illustration of a trend that has impacted the entertainment landscape ever since the Reagan era: instead of regulators dictating the direction and degree to which media companies are allowed to grow, policy now follows the lead of industry and merely sanctions the status quo. With the combination of Westinghouse (a powerful station group) and CBS, the company owned fifteen stations that reached 33 percent of the country.[77] This was over the FCC limit allowing one company to own twelve stations reaching 25 percent of the country. It was expected that the rewrite of the Communications Act that Congress was undertaking in 1995 would greatly increase those limits. Nevertheless, the Telecommunications Act was not unveiled for many months, and CBS made that deal far in advance of any new limits becoming law. So while this "other" network takeover did not generate nearly as much press as the acquisition of ABC, it was in many ways equally as indicative of the many dynamics necessary for the construction of entertainment empires to continue apace.

Time Warner–Turner

Just as Disney was buying Miramax, Ted Turner made a major purchase of his own. In August 1993, Turner announced he would buy the prolific independent outfit New Line Cinema (primarily known for its low-budget genre and horror output, such as *Teenage Mutant Ninja Turtles* and *Nightmare on Elm Street*) and Castle Rock Entertainment (producer of *Seinfeld* as well as films such as *When Harry Met Sally* and *A Few Good Men*). The deal was estimated to be between $660 and $750 million, depending on stock valuation.[78] This greatly expanded Turner's own empire beyond his primary stronghold in cable, into television and feature film production and distribution. In addition to *Seinfeld*, Castle Rock was producing five-six moderate-budget films per year at the time, with plans to double their feature output. New Line was producing fifteen to twenty films and distributing about the same.

The purchase would be a boon for Turner's cable channels, generating more product to air on TNT and TBS. Turner had recently started the Cartoon Network, which he programmed with the Looney Tunes and Merrie Melodies catalogs that he acquired in his purchase of the MGM library.[79] He also bought

Hanna-Barbera Productions specifically for the Cartoon Network's schedule. His penchant for buying studios and their libraries to funnel into niche cable channels that showcased those assets also resulted in the creation of Turner Classic Movies (TCM) in 1994, which was primarily a channel devoted to the MGM and early Warner Bros. film libraries that he owned. Turner was a master craftsman of synergy and knew better than almost anyone else how to exploit his properties across media platforms in innovative ways.

Turner had many of cable's biggest players as investors in his personal empire, thanks to their 1987 cash bailout after his purchase of MGM. As a result, Turner would not be able to make the deals for New Line and Castle Rock (or almost anything else) without the approval of what then-*Variety* chief Peter Bart called "his two shadow partners"—Gerald Levin and John Malone, chairmen/CEOs of Time Warner and TCI, respectively. At the time, Time Warner had a 20 percent stake in Turner's company and three seats on his board, and TCI owned 21 percent of Turner Broadcasting System.[80] This intimate involvement between such powerhouses in cable became a focal point for regulators when Time Warner and Turner announced their intended merger on September 22, 1995—the day after the official repeal of the Financial Interest and Syndication Rules, and one month after the Disney-ABC deal became public. It seems that Turner and his company's $2.8 billion in annual revenues had become enough of a mini-empire that the biggest media conglomerate in the world wanted him to sell. Despite last-minute offers by GE, Microsoft, and Rupert Murdoch, with Murdoch rumored to have told Turner he could write his own ticket, Time Warner and Turner came to a $7.5 billion agreement after five difficult weeks of negotiations.[81]

While Time Warner was a multimedia entertainment empire, its stronghold was cable, as was Turner's. The year of the merger, $5 billion of Time Warner's $8 billion in total revenues came from cable-related properties.[82] In turn, the web of cable relationships in this merger presented Time Warner and Turner with significant hurdles. For one, it was not initially certain whether or not Malone and TCI, the largest cable company in the United States, supported the deal. This was a problem, as TCI owned 21 percent of Turner's company, along with a consortium that included Comcast and Continental Cablevision. Others in the consortium were uneasy about TCI's majority stake and interest, and what kinds of favorable treatment it would afford Malone when dealing with Time Warner properties. There were also larger, antitrust-related concerns for regulators because of the consolidation of interests represented by this deal. First, there would be a potentially anticompetitive degree of horizontal and vertical integration in cable channels and cable providers owned by the merged company. The combination of Turner and Time Warner's holdings raised red flags, as did the fact that Time Warner and TCI were the biggest cable providers in the country and chief investors in Turner's company—which was mostly cable programming services and content. By 1995, TCI was serving 25 percent of American homes with cable, and Time Warner cable was the second-largest distributor, with 15 percent of cable homes. TCI had significant holdings in nineteen cable programming services as well.[83] This merger would bring together these mighty distributors in addition to all of the content owned by Turner and Time Warner.

The FTC initially opposed the merger as it was put forth. Their concerns were mainly about the new company's market power, and the potential for anticompetitive activity, given the amount of vertical and horizontal integration. In a preliminary statement, the three FTC commissioners who were against the deal explained that this merger and its related transactions between Time Warner, Turner, and TCI "involve[s] three of the largest firms in cable programming and delivery—firms that are actual or potential competitors in many aspects of their businesses. The transaction would have merged the first and third largest cable programmers (Time Warner and Turner). At the same time, it would have further aligned the interests of TCI and Time Warner, the two largest cable distributors."[84] The commissioners also noted that the level of vertical integration in an already concentrated industry would have further increased with this merger.

A deal was made to put TCI's stock in the new company into a trust and take away Malone's voting rights (who then surprised many by giving control of his shares to Levin). In exchange, Levin and Turner would give TCI a twenty-year distribution deal at a 15 percent discount, so Malone would pay less to carry Turner channels like TNT and CNN. Further, Malone's stock swap was done at a higher exchange rate than most investors, and he wound up with about 9 percent of the new company.[85] This brought Malone on board. Turner publicly dismissed the lingering worries about whether Time and Turner's past troubles and disputes with one another would get in the way. He ascribed their differences as natural rivalries among competitors. As if to dispel all thoughts of discord between the two companies, Time Warner chairman Gerald Levin was earnestly throwing around terms of endearment like "genius," "family," "best friend," and "partner" to describe Turner, his former rival.

After a year of investigation, the FTC and Time Warner–Turner finally agreed on the terms of a consent decree, and the companies were granted permission to merge in August 1996. Most of the terms (which were quite lenient) were designed to limit the influence of TCI: the discount for TCI was removed, Malone's ownership capped at 9.2 percent, and the commission also forced Time Warner cable to offer room for a competitor to Turner's CNN on its system by 2001.[86] In the end, all of the concentration and consolidation that the FTC was concerned about went largely undisturbed in the new company. The result was an unprecedented merging of media assets spanning film, cable, broadcast, music, publishing, sports, and journalism that included:

- *Film libraries (largest in the world):* Warner Bros. films (over 4,000 titles including some from Allied Artists and Monogram); MGM (over 2,000 titles); RKO (700 titles); Hanna-Barbera, Warner Bros., MGM, Looney Tunes, and Merrie Melodies cartoons (over 7,500); and tens of thousands of television episodes from the MGM and Warner Bros. catalogs
- *Filmed entertainment/production:* Warner Bros. Studios, New Line/Fine Line, Castle Rock, Turner Pictures, Witt-Thomas Productions
- *Broadcasting:* WB Network, TBS Superstation, CNN Radio
- *Cable programming:* HBO, Cinemax, CNN, CNN Headline News, CNNfn, TNT, TBS, Turner Classic Movies, Cartoon Network, E! Entertainment TV (58 percent interest), Court TV (33.3 percent), BET (17.8 percent), 50 percent of Comedy Central, Warner Bros. Pay TV, New York 1 News, and many international ventures and HBO/CNN/TNT spin-offs in Europe, Latin America, and Asia
- *Cable systems:* Time Warner Cable (11.7 million subscribers covering 20 percent of U.S. households)
- *Music:* Warner Bros. Records, The Atlantic Group, Elektra Entertainment, Warner Music International, Time Life Music, Warner/Chappell
- *Publishing:* Time Inc. (including *Time*, *Sports Illustrated*, *People*, and *Entertainment Weekly*), DC Comics, Books-of-the-Month Club, Time Life Books, Warner Books, Little, Brown, Turner Publishing
- *Sports:* Atlanta Braves, Atlanta Hawks

There were also a wide variety of retail stores, new media ventures, video distributors, theme parks, real estate, and film theaters owned by the newly merged empire.[87] Turner seemed most pleased about the merger enhancing his ability "to squash Rupert like a bug. . . . Rupert can trot out news, and Disney can trot out cartoons. We will whip their asses," he promised reporters.[88]

While the deal for Turner was less than half the price that Disney had just paid for ABC, it brought a much larger magnitude and range of assets under the same corporate insignia and far greater potential for strategic use of vertically and horizontally integrated media properties. Time Warner films had a much larger array of proprietary windows on which to play out; studio releases could now be funneled to HBO, TNT, and TBS and then on to the WB network. Warner Bros. and New Line/Fine Line were on quite a roll at the time, with a very heavy release schedule. Warner Bros. had been releasing an average of twenty-eight films a year for the past few years. New Line was also rather prolific, with over twenty films a year, and the company had significantly increased in value since Turner bought it.[89] Turner's strategy of buying film libraries to enhance cable proved to be quite prescient, given the growing importance of cable to a conglomerate's bottom line and the holdings of the newly merged Time Warner–Turner; indeed, he now had a broadcast network, a superstation, and six wholly owned cable channels to program at will with his archives. Just as Christopher Anderson has suggested that television took on the role of film's archivist in many ways once film libraries were sold to broadcast networks in the late 1950s, Turner helped to fortify cable television as the new archivist for the film industry in the 1980s and 1990s. As feature films were disappearing from broadcast television and making more of an impact on cable schedules, Turner's philosophy for building a media company did much to preserve and enliven cinematic history, albeit on the small screen.[90] Being part of Time Warner enhanced this capability even more.

With this merger, Turner was also able to experience a new kind of power: the kind that comes with being a major media mogul—a position that had always eluded him, despite his best efforts to buy his way in. "After 33 years as a CEO of a small company, I'm tired of being little all the time. I want to see what it's like to be big for a while," he explained.[91] He would indeed get his view from the top. Turner had become the largest shareholder in the biggest empire of entertainment in the world.

The Blueprint of Empires

By the end of 1995, the transformation of media policy and structure that began in the 1980s was nearly complete. Horizontal ownership limitations were dramatically reduced for cable and broadcast; vertical limits were similarly lightened or even eliminated, as they were in the film industry. Cross-ownership restrictions (such as cable–telco, broadcast network–cable) were significantly relaxed, and the film, telecomm, and broadcast industries were free to mingle their DNA and share the same parent company after twenty-five years of legal separation. At the same time, the ideology of antitrust had become almost entirely aligned with neoliberal economic philosophy, and the primary agencies charged with regulating the media industries were chiefly guided by market-based, Chicago School principles. Regulatory concerns about diversity, localism, "the public interest," or social welfare had all but disappeared.

These converging forces and developments resulted in one of the biggest waves of consolidation the entertainment world had ever seen. In the span of two short years between 1993 and 1995, independent film giants Miramax, New Line, and Castle Rock were subsumed by global media conglomerates, half of the broadcast networks were now owned by companies with a major film studio (and cable/publishing empires), and mergers in excess of $35 billion were finalized. In addition to Paramount-Viacom, Disney-ABC, CBS-Westinghouse, and Time Warner–Turner, one more takeover helped to signal a new era: the purchase of Universal-MCA by Seagram, the Canadian liquor company. In March 1995, Seagram bought 80 percent of the company for $5.7 billion and renamed it Universal Studios. Thus began the dismantling of Matsushita's control, and the introduction of a new corporate face for Universal and its many media holdings. What's more, the takeover represented the end of Lew Wasserman's decades-long reign of power, as Matsushita decided to sell the company without even telling Wasserman, the "last mogul." With this sale, most remnants of old Hollywood were effectively gone from the media landscape. The entertainment industry had transformed into corporate empires, and even though he continued to go to work every day, Wasserman, his influence, and his era were now officially Hollywood history.

The future of entertainment belonged to new players, new wires, and new empires. A Telecommunications Deregulation Bill moved through Congress with almost no public comment, and this bill would be the finishing touch on the new paradigm of media industry infrastructure. America also had its first Republican-led Congress in forty years, and the GOP rout in the midterm elections of 1994 had the media industries poised for a revolution of their own. Democratic Representatives John Dingell (D-Mass) and Ed Markey (D-Mass), and Senator Fritz Hollings (D-SC) lost their committee and subcommittee chairmanships to Republicans.[92] This was particularly significant in the case of Markey. His chairmanship of the House Telecommunications Subcommittee was marked by a commitment to fighting media concentration and monopolies in the cable, telecommunications, and satellite industries. With a new Republican chairman, the rhetoric surrounding the Telecommunications legislation shifted from access, fairness, and reining in big media to privileging market forces and deregulation as the bill's chief values and worthy goals.

As proposed, the new bill would lift national ownership reach for TV stations from 25 percent to 35 percent, remove all limits from radio station ownership, allow broadcast networks to own cable systems, allow telephone companies to enter the cable delivery business, and permit further consolidation in local television markets. Al Gore hailed it as "a centrist bill for the 21st century" and President Clinton was on board as well, but threatened to veto anything that was excessively deregulatory.[93] Given the details and impact of the Telecommunications Act, it is hard to imagine what, if anything, could have possibly qualified a bill as being "excessively deregulatory" in this context. As it stood, the media industries at the end of 1995 were burdened by fewer regulatory constraints than ever before in history, and they were about to become even more concentrated with the passage of the Telecommunications Act. In fact, the blueprints for the new millennium empires of entertainment were just one signature away from their final form.

Conclusion

1996 and Beyond–The Political Economy of Transformation

The Telecommunications Act of 1996 was the ultimate deregulatory initiative to complete the structural convergence of the media industries that began during the 1980s. It was the first major reform of the Communications Act of 1934 and the last piece of legislation necessary to solidify the blueprint for new millennium entertainment empires. This was not an isolated, singular shining moment for convergence and deregulation as it was often characterized. It was instead the outgrowth of fifteen years' worth of dismantling regulatory structures, the ascendance of neoliberal ideological values in economic and political spheres, and the latest triumph of media oligopolies over marketplace diversity and the public interest.

The Telecommunications Act and the Politics of Convergence

The passage of the bill received scant press attention—in fact, it was barely covered by the mainstream media. When the Telecommunications Act was discussed, it was most commonly characterized as a "revolutionary" and "trans-formative" policy, and almost all coverage was entirely devoid of historical context or reformist critique. FCC chairman Reed Hundt contributed to the hyperbolic tone when he commented, "It's like the Berlin Wall of communications coming down."[1] Awash in reverential rhetoric and the unified perspective of the government, cable, and telecommunications companies, the few stories about this remarkable moment in media policy forced readers to wade all the way through, often to the last paragraph, for any hint of what consumer/advocacy groups thought about the legislation's impact on the public interest, localism, and diversity in the media.

The legislation passed with a 91–5 vote in the Senate and a 414–16 vote in the House of Representatives. As *Variety* noted, it was the type of unanimous congressional support that was generally reserved for resolutions like Apple Pie Week.[2] President Clinton signed the bill into law on February 8, 1996, and thus eradicated a host of legally imposed structural divisions between industries, allowing broadcast, cable, and telephone companies to create convergent media empires with newly expanded boundaries.[3] One legal analyst has succinctly explained that the end result of the legislation "was to wave the green flag at the convergence race . . . by reducing or eliminating ownership barriers."[4] Among the many barriers done away with by this legislation were:

- *Ownership caps on broadcast stations*
  The act eliminated the former cap of twelve broadcast stations and increased the nationwide audience reach limitation. One company could now own stations that reached up to 35 percent of the national audience, up from the limit of 25 percent established in 1985. All caps and limits on radio station ownership were also removed.
- *Broadcast network/cable system cross-ownership rules*
  Statutory restrictions on broadcast networks and cable systems owning one another (originated in 1970 and relaxed in 1992) were removed by the act; specific deals were now at the discretion of the FCC but no longer prohibited by law. This repeal had the most significant impact on the entertainment landscape in the way of empire building.
- *Cable system and telephone cross-ownership ban (cable-telco)*
  Both the FCC rule and the 1984 Cable Act statute keeping the phone companies out of video delivery were repealed by the act, which meant that cable systems and telephone companies could now own one another. The Baby Bells had been lobbying for legal relief from the AT&T consent decree since 1984 in order to gain access to the video market; with the Telecommunications Act, they finally got it. The Baby Bells were now allowed to operate as information providers and were no longer restricted to just telecommunications. The purchase of a cable system in the telephone carrier's local area was still prohibited, however.[5]

The net effect of the Telecommunications Act in terms of media ownership was that one company could now own significantly more broadcast stations than ever before, and cable systems were legally permitted to combine with broadcast networks and phone companies. While the bill was initially built on promises of cross-industry competition that was supposed to create more choices, and better rates and services for consumers, none of that came to pass. Instead, prices went up, service went down, concentration increased and as a result, media markets were less competitive. As the chairman and CEO of Comcast Brian Roberts noted ten years after the Telecomm Act was passed, "most of the competition that the 1996 Act generated took place before the FCC and the courts, not in the marketplace."[6]

Another important component of the Telecomm Act for the construction of media empires was the directive for the FCC to begin conducting Biennial Regulatory Reviews and modify or repeal those rules no longer deemed to be "necessary in the public interest." This ensured a deregulatory trajectory for the commission's future, as part of their charge would be to regularly review regulations with an eye toward eliminating those that were "unnecessary." One of those rules repeatedly reviewed was the Cable/Broadcast Cross-Ownership Rule ("CBCO"), which prevented broadcast station and cable system cross-ownership. The CBCO was codified by Congress in the 1984 Cable Act and went unchanged by the Telecommunications Act. The rule essentially prohibited common ownership of a broadcast station and a cable television system in the same local market. This meant, for example, that Time Warner could not own television stations in New York City where it also owned a cable system, or that its WB network could not own affiliate stations in many major markets (like all of the other networks did) because Time Warner Cable operated there. It was designed to promote diversity of ownership and prevent cable operators from discriminating against their competitors or privileging their own properties. Fox Television stations sued the FCC over this rule and the courts ultimately ordered the FCC to repeal the ban in 2002 because the language and reasoning that preserved it in the 1996 Telecommunications Act was deemed to be "arbitrary and capricious."[7] The CBCO is no longer in effect and entertainment empires are now permitted to own broadcast stations and cable systems in the same market.

Another rule that continued to come before the FCC for review in the wake of the Telecommunications Act was the limitation on broadcast station ownership. After 1996, one company could own broadcast stations that reached up to 35 percent of U.S. television homes. Still, the broadcast networks aggressively lobbied Congress to raise the ownership ceiling even higher, painting apocalyptic portraits of their demise in the face of cable competition. In June 2003, the FCC announced that it would modify five of the six major ownership restrictions for broadcast including the ownership limits; FCC chairman Michael Powell proposed raising those limits so that one company could own stations reaching 45 percent of American televisions.[8]

This was another major change to go largely unreported by the mainstream media. However, in a stunning turn of events, media reform activists began getting the word out, the public became engaged with this issue, and the ensuing uproar basically stopped the FCC in its tracks. The last half of 2003 was an unprecedented time for media policy, as the FCC ruling and the campaign to reverse it became part of civic debate. Suddenly, the politics of regulating media had found its way into public discourse. The opposition to the

FCC's policy change was remarkably unified and widespread, and, many have commented, it might have been the first time that the National Organization for Women and the National Rifle Association were standing together on the same side of an issue. Still, despite hundreds of thousands of comments, 99 percent of which opposed further media consolidation, the FCC was still moving ahead with their plans to further relax broadcast ownership limits.[9]

Engaged citizens and activist groups managed to change those plans a bit, however. In a major blow to Chairman Powell, a federal appeals court issued an emergency order blocking the ownership rules from taking effect as scheduled. Shortly thereafter, Congress introduced a resolution to nullify the new rules at the same time that a Senate committee voted to block their passage. Media policy finally arrived on the front page of the *New York Times*, which featured the language of the amended bill. President George W. Bush tried to step in on behalf of his FCC chairman and threatened to veto efforts to roll back the reforms, but instead a "compromise" was announced on Thanksgiving in which the station ownership cap would be increased to 39 percent—just over what Viacom and News Corporation already owned. Thus, instead of policing the broadcast industry on behalf of consumers or monitoring the size of media conglomerates, the FCC merely changed their rules to accommodate the largest station owners in the business and legalized the status quo.

While the events surrounding the "uprising of 2003," as Robert McChesney has called it, did not necessarily effect any structural changes that would have lasting impact on the size or scope of future entertainment empires, they did provide critical insight into the regulatory environment in which this growth would occur.[10] Chiefly, these events demonstrated the FCC's primary concern for private interests (those of media conglomerates) and at the same time, the agency's overwhelming disdain for the public interest. This was also evident in the way the FCC disregarded the hundreds of thousands of citizen complaints during the rulemaking process, and even more so in the comments of Chairman Michael Powell. One speech to the American Bar Association was particularly revealing about Powell's unflinching contempt for the public: "The night after I was sworn in, I waited for a visit from the angel of the public interest. I waited all night, but she did not come. And, in fact, five months into this job, I still have had no divine awakening and no one has issued me my public interest crystal ball. But I am here, an enlightened wise man without a clue."[11] During public hearings, protestors showed up wearing angel wings to remind him of this statement, hoping to deliver his divine awakening. Of course, that awakening never arrived. The ownership rules remain in limbo at the time of this writing, after being sent back to the FCC for another rewrite when the Supreme Court decided not to get involved in 2005.

Post-1996 Mergers

After the Telecommunications Act, several major mergers shifted the terrain in the entertainment landscape significantly. Incredibly, every deal took place within existing legal boundaries. The groundwork had been laid between 1980 and 1996, and nothing that happened in the construction of media empires after the Telecomm Act required changes in law or policy. Instead, everything that followed merely capitalized on the massive transformation already enacted by almost two decades of media industry deregulation.

The first merger of note was the union between Viacom and CBS in 1999. It was actually a reunion, as Viacom started life as a syndication house/programming library spawned by CBS in 1970 to comply with the fin-syn rules. Viacom proceeded to expand into a major media company with film, cable, and broadcast holdings over the next few decades; after this long, steady diet of acquisitions (which included the classic program libraries of ABC and NBC), the once-small syndicator made a $35 billion deal to buy its former parent company, CBS. With that, 55,000 hours of early television and 180 different series became part of the CBS programming arsenal. While this was certainly a promising marriage of cable, film, broadcasting, and other media assets, just six short years later Viacom CEO Sumner Redstone announced, "the age of the conglomerate is over."[12] He then proceeded to split the company in two, with one half focusing on its cable properties that included MTV, VH1, and Nickelodeon as well as the Paramount studios, the other half structured around Viacom's broadcast holdings with the centerpiece being the CBS network, along with Infinity Broadcasting and dozens of television and radio stations. While the age of the conglomerate was hardly over, the age of Viacom-CBS as one publicly traded company certainly came to an end. The declining value of its broadcasting properties dragged the company's stock price down, and the company has since continued to operate as two separate entities, both under the control of Redstone. This was one instance in which the anticipated synergies between broadcast, film, and cable properties did not pan out.

The disappointment of the Viacom CBS deal was nothing compared to the disastrous "merger of the millennium" between AOL and Time Warner the following year. This deal, which had the world's largest Internet service provider buying the world's biggest entertainment company, dwarfed all others; it was the largest in history and was touted as the transformative merger of the Internet era, bringing "new media" and "old media" together at last. AOL paid roughly $164 billion for the vast Time Warner empire in 2000, creating a $350 billion company that executives insisted was "a merger of equals" and one that would be the industrial paradigm for the digital age.[13] Unfortunately for them, the breathtaking plunge in stock price, culture clashes between the two companies, a corporate accounting scandal, and falling revenues and subscriber numbers at the Internet division severely undermined earlier fantasies and projections for the merger. By the conglomerate's second birthday, four books about the deal as fiasco were already in the works and in September 2003, Time-Warner voted to remove AOL from the company's name.[14] Just one month shy of their first decade together, Time-Warner spun off AOL in December 2009. After nine years and a loss in stock value of over $300 billion (or 86 percent of the company's original value), the unceremonious sale quietly dismantled what is unquestionably regarded as one of the least successful mergers in history.[15]

Three years after AOL Time-Warner was announced, and right in the middle of the FCC's media ownership public flap, another combination consolidated the media landscape even further: NBC's parent company General Electric Co. announced it was purchasing 80 percent of Vivendi Universal for $3.8 billion, merging Universal Studios, cable TV networks, and amusement parks with NBC, and also bringing together the buyer and seller of the most successful franchise in television history, *Law & Order*. This alone made for sound strategy, as the three *L&O* shows brought in more than $1 billion in advertising revenue in 2004 and NBC was poised to make almost one-third of its prime-time profits from the franchise.[16] NBC would have much rather just put the licensing fees back into its own pocket. NBC beat several other potential suitors for the Universal entertainment businesses, including Viacom, Liberty Media Corp., MGM, and Comcast. The new company brought together the NBC television network/stations and its cable channels CNBC, MSNBC, and Bravo and Spanish-language broadcaster Telemundo with Universal studios, several amusement parks, and the USA, Sci-Fi, and Trio cable channels.

Thus, in the decade that followed the Telecommunications Act, consolidation in the media industries was still prevalent and on the rise but not in need of any new legal or policy changes to proceed apace. The two broadcast networks not connected to a film studio (CBS and NBC) were finally merged with film studios; companies were able to own a greater percentage of broadcast stations along with their respective networks; even the two fledgling studio-based networks, UPN and the WB, wound up combining forces in 2007 to create a new network: the CW. This entity was half-owned by CBS and half-owned by Time Warner, so the broadcast networks that remained were in the same hands, but there was one less player in the business. While the political and regulatory climate allowed for this concentration to take place, these new millennium deals were, on the whole, largely considered failures. Viacom and CBS were divorced (albeit amicably) in 2006, while AOL Time-Warner's downward spiral remains the cautionary tale for all future media mergers. The one combination that wasn't a disaster was NBC Universal, but rumors of its takeover (sell-off by GE) were rampant in industry circles. Viacom and Time-Warner did not do much for the public image of media empires, but NBC Universal remained somewhat attractive, thanks largely to its cable properties.

Comcast-NBC and the Revenge of Cable

In 2009, the media landscape experienced a new game-changing deal. It was the first of its kind, and it serves as a particularly fitting conclusion to this history of media industries and deregulation. When Comcast, the nation's largest cable operator, announced in December 2009 that it would be buying a majority stake in NBC Universal, it was a stunning display of all that had gone right for cable over the last thirty years.[17] As America's largest cable system wiring 25 percent of the nation's homes, it would be the first cable operator to take over a major film studio, a broadcast network, and a host of successful cable channels. Comcast already had practice running an empire of its own; the company had amassed the traditional holdings of media conglomerates such as cable systems, cable channels, film production (as a partner in the consortium owning MGM), sports teams, and Internet delivery, and they had also updated what the modern entertainment empire's portfolio should have: web publishing, TV on demand (cable and Internet-based), social networking sites, and new-generation wireless technologies. Yet the company had never cracked the market of major content producers or broadcast network owner-ship, even after the 1996 act repealed the restriction.

Comcast had certainly been in the hunt before, attempting to buy Universal in 2004 and Disney in 2005. In both cases, Comcast saw attractive cable properties when they looked at these conglomerates, but in both cases their bid was unsuccessful. Recognizing that "dumb pipes" and wires represent the past and not the future of media industries, Comcast CEO Brian Roberts was interested in acquiring more programming services, which were extremely lucrative. After all, neither the NBC network nor Universal studios were the most profitable component of NBC Universal at the time of the proposed merger with Comcast. The network lost over $500 million in 2009.[18] Instead it is cable—USA, Syfy, Bravo—that remains the prize jewel of NBC Universal. In the years just before the merger, president and CEO of NBC Universal, Jeff Zucker, repeatedly celebrated cable as the strongest component of the company, saying that the core cable networks represented over 75 percent of the company's profits.[19] When the merger was announced, Roberts proudly proclaimed that 82 percent of the new NBCU would be cable programming channels.[20]

While this was interesting news to casual observers of the media indus-tries, it was not surprising to those who have studied modern entertainment conglomerates. Looking at the history of mergers and acquisitions as well as annual balance sheets and annual reports, it is clear that these companies have primarily been in the television business for decades, and it is actually the television properties—and lately the cable holdings—that have kept everything else, including film, afloat. In fact, thanks largely to the decades-long trajectory of deregulating media industries, particularly cable, most of these companies have evolved into giant television companies that also have holdings in film and publishing.

This is borne out in annual reports, in which the revenue breakdowns differ from conglomerate to conglomerate, but interestingly, "film" does not rate its own category in any of them. It is usually combined with television production in the catch-all "filmed entertainment" category. For the industry that produces the blockbusters and tentpoles ("event" films with the highest production and marketing budgets that are expected to bring the studios' biggest financial rewards),[21] this is a rather undignified accounting. The definition varies by company, but "filmed entertainment" can include everything from theatrical film, television production, home video, electronic delivery, television licensing, and even consumer products. Often, the film properties generate the bulk of attention and cultural cache for empires of entertainment, but digging a bit further reveals that it is actually television—or more accurately, cable—that is generating the lion's share of revenue.

Time Warner, for example, has a long history as a cable company. Both Time and Warner were heavily invested in cable since the 1970s and when the two companies merged, cable earnings were equal to filmed entertainment, publishing, and music, with each sector accounting for roughly a quarter of the company's profile on the annual report.

In 1996, publishing and music had both dropped to about 15 percent of the company's earnings, filmed entertainment dropped to about 20 percent, and

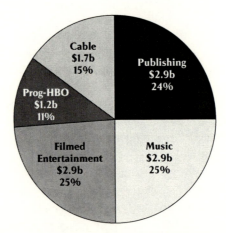

FIGURE 7.1. Time Warner 1990

Information used to generate all charts comes from numerous Annual Reports and SEC filings for Time (1988–1989), Time-Warner (1987–1997, 2008), Disney (1987–1995, 2008), News Corp. (1988, 1991–1996, 2008), Viacom (1987–1996, 2008) and GE (2008–2009).

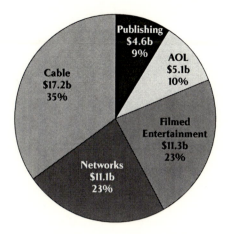

FIGURE 7.2. Time Warner 2008

cable jumped to about 40 percent. By 2008, cable revenues alone were over one-third of the company's income, filmed entertainment had dropped to about one-quarter of Time Warner's revenue (this was down 13 percent from the year before, despite the fact that 2008 saw the release of *The Dark Knight*), networks (broadcast and cable) were also about one-quarter, and publishing/AOL made up the rest. Theatrical film (as a subcategory of "filmed entertainment") represented only 3 percent of Time Warner's revenue this year.[22]

News Corporation's empire was originally built on publishing, and that sector earned four times what television and filmed entertainment did for

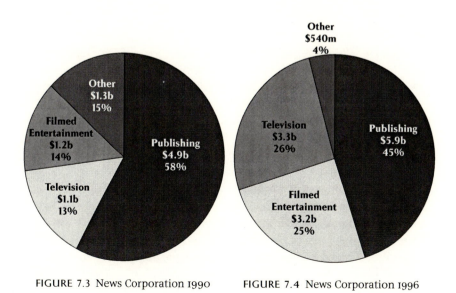

FIGURE 7.3 News Corporation 1990   FIGURE 7.4 News Corporation 1996

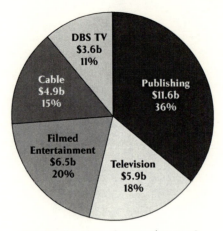

FIGURE 7.5 News Corporation 2008

the company in 1990, generating almost 60 percent of the annual income. In 1996, it was still 25 percent more than both film and television. By 2008, the newspapers and publishing shrunk to just over one-third; cable, broadcast, and satellite were about 44 percent; and filmed entertainment (representing both film and television) was at 20 percent. Thanks to the economic crisis in 2008 and the slump in advertising revenue for newspapers and broadcast, Rupert Murdoch announced that in 2009, cable generated 50 percent of his company's operating income.[23]

Disney is an interesting case, as an empire built mainly on intellectual property and software as opposed to the pipelines and/or station holdings that have been a mainstay for companies like News Corp. and Time Warner. In 1996, once the company owned ESPN and ABC, the categories of measurement on Disney's annual report were theme parks and resorts (20 percent), broadcasting (29 percent), and creative content, a category even more vague and ill-defined than filmed entertainment, which accounted for half of the company's revenue. By 2008, there was a new category for media networks (which consisted of one-third broadcast and two-thirds cable properties) that represented 40 percent of the income, while parks and resorts represented 31 percent and studio entertainment and consumer products brought in the remaining 7 percent of Disney's $37.8 billion that year.

While CEO Sumner Redstone's empire began with a few local film theaters and expanded into a major national theater chain, he has taken it quite a distance from that core business since the late 1980s. Filmed entertainment represents 40 percent of Viacom's 2008 revenues, and, broken down further, it is revealed that theatrical entertainment is only 11 percent of the yearly pie; the rest of the filmed entertainment revenues come from home entertainment,

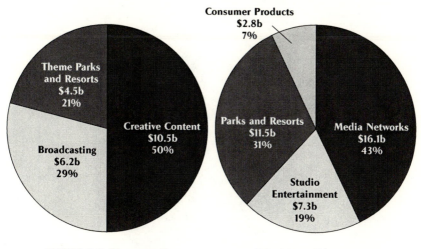

FIGURE 7.6 Disney 1996   FIGURE 7.7 Disney 2008

licensing, advertising, affiliate fees, and other ancillary earnings. The remaining 60 percent of annual revenue comes from media networks, or, more specifically, the company's major stronghold: cable television. Viacom's channels currently include MTV, VH1, Nickelodeon, TVL and BET, Spike TV, CMT, Comedy Central, and Logo.

As part of GE, the whole of NBC Universal represented a mere 9 percent of the company's annual $183 billion revenue. The entertainment unit was only mentioned five times in GE's 112-page annual report in 2008. If the proposed merger goes through with Comcast, NBCU would be more integral to the new company's overall success. At present, a vast majority of the company's revenue (77 percent) is from infrastructure and delivery systems already belonging to Comcast—cable, Internet, and phone subscriptions. The rest will come from cable programming (8 percent), broadcast properties (7 percent), movies and theme parks (7 percent), and Telemundo—the broadcast/cable hybrid Spanish-language network (1 percent).[24] While all modern empires of entertainment are heavily committed to television, Comcast–NBC Universal would be especially invested—top (content) to bottom (cable wires)—in the medium in general and in cable specifically. The company will be the first one with a name derived from cable, broadcast, and film companies, and the first to see a cable system take full advantage of the policies introduced by the 1996 Telecommunications Act to buy a broadcast network. It is, in many respects, a perfect incarnation of the new millennium entertainment empire, one that embodies the recent history of deregulating media industries in its very formation.

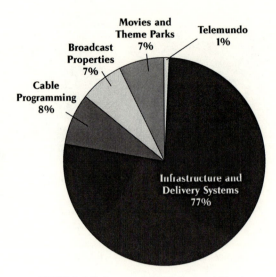

FIGURE 7.8 Proposed NBCU-Comcast Merger

Culture and Commerce

In addition to a media landscape dominated largely by six vertically and horizontally integrated entertainment conglomerates, the structural convergence that took place during this time and especially after the Telecommunications Act of 1996 also engendered an acute regulatory crisis. This perfect storm of political and industrial developments that set the stage for largely unregulated growth emanating from the cable sector ultimately combined different industries and sites of engagement with policy in ways that regulators were—and still are—unprepared for. With continuing innovation in the marketplace and blurred boundaries between media and markets, the standards and philosophical underpinnings of regulation have grown increasingly out of touch with industrial practice. Converging entertainment, information, and communication industries are being regulated by policies designed for a different era. Meanwhile, the technologies, markets, and regulatory principles for these industries are no longer distinct enough to accommodate separate paradigms.

In *Technologies of Freedom* (1983), Ithiel de Sola Pool wrote presciently about the regulatory disconnect precipitated by technological development and media convergence. He saw the mere mapping of policy from old technologies to new as often inappropriate, and as the genesis of regulatory crises. He decried the manner in which "the telegraph was analogized to railroads, the telephone to the telegraph, and cable television to broadcasting."[25] Explaining how technological advances were outpacing policy's ability to stay current, de Sola Pool noted that "Convergence of modes is upsetting the trifurcated system developed over the past two hundred years, and questions that had seemed to be settled centuries ago are being reopened."[26] His forward-thinking critique of the disconnect between policy and industry practice applies today more than ever, and legal scholars have echoed his concerns about what that means for ownership concentration ever since. Particularly in the wake of the 1996 Telecommunications Act, it has been argued that because of new technologies and legislation stimulating media consolidation, "applying existing antitrust law to the multimedia industry moves beyond the realm of 'exceptionally difficult' to the level of nearly impossible."[27]

The consolidation and vertical integration of content and delivery systems along with the arrival of Internet television, broadband, and satellite have brought even more daunting challenges for Congress and regulatory bodies. New delivery platforms and the convergence of distribution technologies have rendered the language and objects of regulation inadequate at best, and media industries have long outgrown the dimensions and arbiters of current policy. As a result, commercial demands and the mythology of the "free market" are privileged over responsibility to the public interest, localism, and diversity, or the "marketplace of ideas."

The mission for regulating empires of entertainment moving forward is twofold: update policy goals so that they are capable of addressing media industries as they exist and function today; and expand the paradigm to accommodate cultural concerns alongside those of economics and the law. Justice Oliver Wendell Holmes once said, "the law is not the place for the artist or poet."[28] In fact, it is perhaps the most *important* place for creative thinkers at this moment, as their perspective is necessary to help position legal issues and their ramifications as matters of culture. The challenge for cultural critics and policy scholars is to link ownership limits and spectrum allocation to the quality of public information, national collective cultural expression, and the strength of a functioning democracy. It is our duty as citizens, consumers, and educators to cultivate awareness about the dynamics of regulatory practice, political discourse, and the nexus of technological and institutional convergence that will shape the future of entertainment empires and the vitality of our media. It is my hope that, at the very least, artists, poets, lawyers, economists, media scholars, and an educated, engaged public will all be involved in that endeavor.

NOTES

INTRODUCTION

1. Quoted in Ken Auletta, *Media Man* (New York: W. W. Norton, 2004), 63.

2. At this writing, those companies are Time Warner, News Corp., Disney, NBC Universal (which is currently in the process of merging with the cable giant, Comcast), Viacom, and Sony.

3. See Ted Turner, "My Beef with Big Media," *Washington Post*, April 7, 2004, http://www.washingtonmonthly.com/features/2004/0407.turner.html (accessed May 31, 2010).

4. Testimony of Jack Valenti, Senate Committee on Commerce, Science, and Transportation, Hearings on Media Ownership: Diversity and Concentration, 101st Cong., 101–357, June 22, 1989, 617.

5. Henry Jenkins, "Convergence? I Diverge," *Technology Review* (June 2001): 93, http://www.technologyreview.com/Biztech/12434/page1/ (accessed July 13, 2008).

6. Justin Wyatt, *High Concept: Movies and Marketing in Hollywood* (Austin: University of Texas Press, 1994), 70.

7. Thomas Schatz, "The Return of the Hollywood Studio System," in *Conglomerates and the Media*, ed. Erik Barnouw (New York: The New Press, 1997), 84.

8. Tino Balio, "'A Major Presence in All of the World's Important Markets,'" in *Contemporary Hollywood Cinema*, ed. Steve Neale and Murray Smith (New York: Routledge, 1998), 61.

9. Quoted in Keith Conrad, "Media Mergers: First Step in a New Shift of Antitrust Analysis?" *Federal Communications Law Journal* 49, no. 675 (April 1997): 4.

10. Primarily a business term, "synergy" was also incorporated as a marketing strategy, development mantra, and ultimately became part of the popular lexicon once the phrase found its way into the trades and popular press by the end of the decade.

11. For a study of Reagan's career in entertainment, see Stephen Vaughn, *Ronald Reagan in Hollywood* (New York: Cambridge University Press, 1994).

12. The ceremony this year was postponed one day because of the assassination attempt on President Reagan on March 30, 1981. He appeared in a pre-taped message the following day.

13. Stephen Prince, *A New Pot of Gold: Hollywood Under the Electronic Rainbow, 1980–1989*, vol. 10 (Berkeley: University of California Press, 2000), 89.

14. Prominent works of note include Herbert Schiller, *Culture, Inc.: The Corporate Takeover of Public Expression* (New York: Oxford University Press, 1991), Ben Bagdikian, *The Media Monopoly* (Boston: Beacon Press, 1983); Eli Noam, *Media Ownership and Concentration in America* (New York: Oxford University Press, 2008); Robert Horwitz, *The Irony of*

Regulatory Reform (New York: Oxford University Press, 1989); and Robert W. McChesney, *The Problem of the Media* (New York: Monthly Review Press, 2004), among many others, as well as his work with Free Press www.freeepress.org.

15. In addition to the works above, see Thomas Streeter, *Selling the Air* (Chicago: University of Chicago Press, 1996); Lawrence Lessig, *Free Culture* (New York: Penguin Press, 2004); Mara Einstein, *Media Diversity* (Hillsdale, NJ: Lawrence Erlbaum Associates, 2004); Horwitz, *Irony of Regulatory Reform*; and the formative work by Don R. Le Duc, *Cable Television and the FCC* (Philadelphia: Temple University Press, 1973); as well as more recent articles such as Andrew Calabrese, "Stealth Regulation: Moral Meltdown and Political Radicalism at the FCC," *New Media and Society* 6 (1) (2004): 18–25; and Jonathan Handel, "Uneasy Lies the Head that Wears the Crown: Why Content's Kingdom Is Slipping Away," *Vanderbilt Journal of Entertainment and Technology Law* 11:3 (2009): 597–636.

16. For example, see Michele Hilmes, *Hollywood and Broadcasting: From Radio to Cable* (Urbana: University of Illinois Press, 1990); William M. Kunz, *Culture Conglomerates* (Oxford: Rowman & Littlefield, 2007); Frederick Wasser, *Veni, Vidi, Video* (Austin: University of Texas Press, 2001); Benjamin Compaine and Douglas Gomery, *Who Owns the Media?* (London: Lawrence Erlbaum Associates, 2000) and various articles by Gomery, including "Failed Opportunities: The Integration of the U.S. Motion Picture and Television Industries," *Quarterly Review of Film Studies* (Summer 1984): 219–227.

17. Michele Hilmes, "Nailing Mercury: The Problem of Media Industry Historiography," in *Media Industries: History, Theory, Method*, Jennifer Holt and Alisa Perren, eds. (Malden: Blackwell, 2009), 27.

18. Notable examples include McChesney, *The Problem of the Media*; Patricia Aufderheide, *The Daily Planet* (Minneapolis: University of Minnesota Press, 2000); Toby Miller et al., *Global Hollywood 2* (London: BFI, 2008); and Chon Noriega, *Shot in America* (Minneapolis: University of Minnesota Press, 2000).

19. Conrad, "Media Mergers," 7.

20. Robert Bork, *The Antitrust Paradox* (New York: The Free Press, 1993), 10. Bork is most well known by the general public for his 1987 failed nomination for Supreme Court justice. He is also a noteworthy antitrust scholar and one of the architects of modern merger policy. His main arguments focused on how regulatory policies were detrimental to consumers and he was very influential in and among the "Chicago School" circle of policy theorists.

21. Herbert Hovenkamp, "Antitrust Policy after Chicago," *Michigan Law Review* 84 (November 1985): 1.

22. Charles R. Geisst, *Monopolies in America* (New York: Oxford University Press, 2000), 43.

23. U.S. Department of Justice: Antitrust Division, Text of Sherman Antitrust Act 15, U.S.C., http://www.usdoj.gov/atr/foia/divisionmanual/ch2.htm#a1 (accessed July 27, 2008).

24. Congress passed the Celler-Kefauver Amendment to the Clayton Act in 1950, which strengthened the restrictions on mergers and acquisitions and gave the government more power to prevent anticompetitive behavior.

25. Herbert Hovenkamp, *The Antitrust Enterprise: Principle and Execution* (Cambridge, MA: Harvard University Press, 2005), 36.

26. Robert Pitofsky, interviewed in *Fair Fight in the Marketplace*, American Antitrust Institute video, 2006.

27. President Reagan's Remarks to Representatives of the Future Farmers of America,

July 28, 1988. http://www.reagan.utexas.edu/archives/speeches/1988/072888c.htm. Accessed June 27, 2010.

28. There are notable exceptions to this generalized approach, such as the market-specific regulatory guidelines for airlines, telecommunications (public utilities), and intellectual property.

29. See Hovenkamp, "Antitrust Policy after Chicago," 213–284; and Conrad, "Media Mergers," 11.

30. Neoliberalism also dominated UK policymaking at this time, and Prime Minister Margaret Thatcher was President Reagan's staunch ally in promoting this economic philosophy around the world. She famously coined the acronym TINA (There Is No Alternative) as a slogan when advocating for neoliberal models of national growth and development. These policy prescriptions (primarily directed at Latin American economies) and their attendant promises for growth, bolstered by the support of the World Bank and International Monetary Fund, became known as "The Washington Consensus."

31. Conrad, "Media Mergers," 10.

32. Robert Pitofsky, "Introduction: Setting the Stage," in *How the Chicago School Overshot the Mark*, ed. Robert Pitofsky (New York: Oxford University Press, 2008), 5.

33. Eleanor M. Fox and Lawrence A. Sullivan, "Antitrust—Retrospective and Prospective: Where Are We Coming From? Where Are We Going?" *New York University Law Review* 62 (November 1987): 7.

34. Numerous regulatory mechanisms for broadcast and cable television that also fell by the wayside during this era are not discussed at length here because they relate primarily to content as opposed to the book's focus on structure. They include the Fairness Doctrine, regulations on advertising as it related to children's programming and political candidates, and the erosion of public access requirements for cable TV.

35. Robert McChesney, "Global Media, Neoliberalism, and Imperialism," *Monthly Review* 52, no. 10, http://www.monthlyreview.org/301rwm.htm (accessed August 17, 2008).

36. For the most extensive historical look at the relationship between the film and television industries, see Michele Hilmes, *Hollywood and Broadcasting: From Radio to Cable* (Chicago: University of Illinois Press, 1990). Also see Christopher Anderson, *Hollywood TV* (Austin: University of Texas Press, 1994) and Gomery, "Failed Opportunities: The Integration of the U.S. Motion Picture and Television Industries."

37. Kraig G. Fox, "Paramount Revisited: The Resurgence of Vertical Integration in the Motion Picture Industry," *Hofstra Law Review* 21 (Winter 1992): 7.

38. Geisst, *Monopolies in America*, 285.

39. Streeter, *Selling the Air*, 142.

40. Horwitz, *Irony of Regulatory Reform*, 6.

41. Ibid.

42. See Robert E. Litan and Carl Shapiro, "Antitrust Policy During the Clinton Administration," in *American Economic Policy in the 1990s*, ed. J. Frankel and P. Orszag (Cambridge, MA: The MIT Press, 2002), 435–485.

43. Patricia Aufderheide, *Communications Policy and the Public Interest* (New York: The Guilford Press, 1999), 9.

44. Jon M. Garon, "Media & Monopoly in the Information Age: Slowing the Convergence at the Marketplace of Ideas," *Cardozo Arts & Entertainment Law Journal* 17 (1999): 539.

45. See Kunz, *Culture Conglomerates*, 186–190. Also see David Waterman and Andrew A. Weiss, *Vertical Integration in Cable Television* (Cambridge, MA: The MIT Press, 1997).

46. Transcript, Paul F. Kagan interview, The Cable Center, Oral History Collection, October 1999, http://www.cablecenter.org/education/library/oralHistoryDetails.cfm?id=128 (accessed July 27, 2008).

47. MPAA, *1999 U.S. Economic Review.*

48. "2008 Cable Show: Cable @60: The 1980s," *MultiChannel News*, May 16, 2008, http://www.multichannel.com/article/CA6561707.html (accessed July 30, 2008).

49. The Satellite News Channel was a joint venture with Westinghouse Broadcasting's Group W.

50. Thomas Schatz, "The New Hollywood," *Film Theory Goes to the Movies*, ed. Jim Collins, Hilary Radner, and Ava Preacher Collins (New York: Routledge, 1993), 9.

51. For a more comprehensive overview of United Artists during this period, see Steven Bach, *Final Cut: Dreams and Disaster in the Making of "Heaven's Gate"* (New York: William Morrow, 1985).

52. Standard & Poor's *Industry Surveys* 1985, L18.

53. Harold Vogel, *Entertainment Industry Economics*, 4th ed. (New York: Cambridge University Press, 1998), 83.

54. Tino Balio, "Adjusting to the New Global Economy: Hollywood in the 1990s," in *Film Policy: International, National and Regional Perspectives*, ed. Albert Moran (New York: Routledge, 1996), 23.

55. MPAA, *1999 U.S. Economic Review.*

56. Carl Bernstein, "The Leisure Empire," *Time*, December 24, 1990, http://www.time.com/time/magazine/article/0,9171,972035,00.html (accessed August 10, 2008).

57. R. Craig Endicott, "Media Feast Fuels Growth," *Advertising Age*, June 30, 1986, S-2.

58. Schatz, "The Return of the Hollywood Studio System," 85.

59. NBC remained on the outside the longest, becoming part of Universal in 2004.

60. Reed E. Hundt, "The Hard Road Ahead: An Agenda for the FCC in 1997," speech delivered December 26, 1996, excerpted in Patricia Aufderheide, *Communications Policy and the Public Interest*, 284.

CHAPTER 1　　　1980–1983: FILM VS. CABLE

1. See Sloan Commission on Cable Communications, *On the Cable: The Television of Abundance* (New York: McGraw-Hill, 1971).

2. Ibid., 1, 47, 167.

3. The Cabinet Committee on Cable Communications, *Cable: Report to the President* (Washington, D.C., 1974), 13.

4. Ibid.

5. Ibid., 63.

6. Ibid., 17.

7. This is due to the *Paramount* consent decrees and the Financial Interest and Syndication Rules, both of which are discussed at length in chapters 4 and 2, respectively.

8. Quoted in Connie Bruck, *Master of the Game* (New York: Simon & Schuster, 1994), 72.

9. Jill Hills, *Telecommunications and Empire* (Chicago: University of Illinois Press, 2007), 6.

10. Sharon Strover, "United States: Cable Television," in *The Encyclopedia of Television*, vol. 3, ed. Horace Newcomb (Chicago: Fitzroy-Dearborn, 1997), 1724.

11. See *Home Box Office v. Federal Communications Commission*, 567 F. 2d (D.C. Cir. 1977). Cert. denied, 434 U.S. 829 (1977).

12. Tony Schwartz, "FCC Battleground: Deregulation of TV," *New York Times*, October 22, 1980, D1.

13. National Cable & Telecommunications Association, Statistics: Basic Cable Subscribers, http://www.ncta.com/Statistic/Statistic/BasicSubs.aspx (accessed August 3, 2008).

14. These figures all from *U.S. v Columbia Pictures Industries, Inc.; Getty Oil Company; MCA, Inc.; Paramount Pictures Corporation*; and *Twentieth Century–Fox Film Corporation* and *Premiere*, 80 Civ 4438, S.D.N.Y., Opinion Filed December 31, 1980, 2, Department of Justice Files.

15. Viacom Annual Report, 1982.

16. For more interesting background on the Warner Star Channel and its roots as the Gridtronics movie network, see Megan Mullen, *The Rise of Cable Programming in the United States* (Austin: University of Texas Press, 2003), 105–106.

17. Tony Schwartz, "Warner Amex: Cable's Winner," *New York Times*, November 21, 1980, D1.

18. Quoted in Tony Schwartz, "TV Notebook," *New York Times*, January 7, 1981, C19.

19. Harold Vogel, *Entertainment Industry Economics*, 4th ed. (New York: Cambridge University Press, 1998), 325, see n. 17.

20. Tom Nicholson, Janet Huck, and Peter McAlevey, "HBO versus the Studios," *Newsweek*, November 15, 1982, 83.

21. Ken Auletta, *The Highwaymen* (New York: Harcourt, Brace, 1998), 105.

22. George Mair, *Inside HBO* (New York: Dodd, Mead, 1988), 103.

23. For an insightful discussion of this dynamic, see Thomas Whiteside, "Cable I," *New Yorker*, May 20, 1985, 76–82. Whiteside's three-part article in the "Onward and Upward with the Arts" series contains a wealth of early cable history.

24. Ibid., 76.

25. Michele Hilmes, "Pay Television: Breaking the Broadcast Bottleneck," in *Hollywood in the Age of Television*, ed. Tino Balio (Boston: Unwin-Hyman, 1990), 302.

26. Larry Kramer, "Movie Industry Files Complaint on Cable T.V.," *Washington Post*, November 30, 1977, D11; and Michelle Hilmes, *Hollywood and Broadcasting: From Radio to Cable* (Chicago: University of Illinois Press, 1990), 174.

27. Nicholson, Huck, and McAlevey, "HBO versus the Studios," 83.

28. Ibid.

29. Memorandum from Richard H. Frank dated December 12, 1978, and cited in *U.S. v. Columbia Pictures Industries, Inc., et al.*, n. 13.

30. Robert Lindsey, "Home Box Office Moves in on Hollywood," *New York Times*, June 12, 1983, 34.

31. Nicholson, Huck, and McAlevey, "HBO versus the Studios," 83.

32. Sandra Salmans, "Hollywood Takes On HBO," *New York Times*, February 2, 1983, D1.

33. *U.S. v. Columbia Pictures Industries, Inc., et al.*, 12.

34. Ibid., 15.

35. Getty had an 85 percent interest in the all-sports cable network in 1980.

36. Mair, *Inside HBO*, 48.

37. *U.S. v. Columbia Pictures Industries, Inc., et al.*, 15.

38. David A. Cook, *Lost Illusions: American Cinema in the Shadow of Watergate and Vietnam, 1970–1979* (Berkeley: University of California Press, 2000), 415.

39. *U.S. v. Columbia Pictures Industries, Inc., et al.*, 1.

40. Stephen Prince, *A New Pot of Gold: Hollywood Under the Electronic Rainbow, 1980–1987* (Berkeley: University of California Press, 2002), 29.

41. *U.S. v. Columbia Pictures Industries, Inc., et al.*, 9.

42. These films were *The Empire Strikes Back* ($223 million) and *9 to 5* ($103.3 million)—Fox; *Stir Crazy* ($101.3 million)—Columbia; *Airplane* ($83.4 million), *Ordinary People* ($52.3 million and winner of Academy Award for Best Picture), and *Popeye* ($50 million)—Paramount; *Coal Miner's Daughter* ($79.9 million), *Smokey and the Bandit II* ($60.5 million), and *The Blues Brothers* ($54.2 million)—Universal.

43. Lionel S. Sobel, "Justice Department Opposition to Showtime/Movie Channel Merger Raises Questions about Tri-Star Pictures and other HBO Deals," *Entertainment Law Reporter* 5, no. 2 (July 1983), www.lexisnexis.com (accessed August 4, 2009).

44. *U.S. v. Columbia Pictures Industries, Inc., et al.*

45. Ibid.

46. Ibid., 19.

47. Ibid., 39.

48. Ibid., 40, 45.

49. Ibid., 19.

50. Ibid., 21.

51. Also according to the December 31, 1980, opinion, ATC owned 78 cable systems and owned a partial stake in 25 more, which gave the company control over more than 100 cable systems that had 1.2 million subscribers (see page 21).

52. *U.S. v. Columbia Pictures Industries, Inc., et al.*, 21.

53. Ibid., 25–26.

54. Ibid., 26.

55. Mullen, *The Rise of Cable Programming in the United States*, 109.

56. Clearances were periods of time that—upon the studios' insistence—had to elapse between the exhibition of a film in two different theaters in the same area. This practice (among others) was found to be illegal by the Supreme Court.

57. *U.S. v. Columbia Pictures Industries, Inc., et al.*, 32–33.

58. Hilmes, *Hollywood and Broadcasting*, 180.

59. *U.S. v. Columbia Pictures Industries, Inc., Getty Oil Company, MCA, Inc., Paramount Pictures Corporation*, and *Twentieth Century-Fox Film Corporation*, 80 Civ. 4438, S.D.N.Y. Stipulation and Order of Dismissal, Filed February 11, 1982.

60. MPAA *1996 U.S. Economic Review.*

61. Lawrence White, "Antitrust and Video Markets: The Merger of Showtime and the Movie Channel as a Case Study," in *Video Media Competition*, ed. Eli M. Noam (New York: Columbia University Press, 1985), 340.

62. *U.S. v. Columbia Pictures Industries, Inc., et al.*, 12.

63. Tony Schwartz, "HBO: Success Brings Criticism," *New York Times*, September 15, 1982, C1.

64. Salmans, "Hollywood Takes On HBO," D1.

65. Figures from Sally Bedell Smith, "U.S. Will Fight Pay-TV Merger by Film Studios," *New York Times*, June 11, 1983, 1.

66. Mair, *Inside HBO*, 103.

67. These guidelines rely on what is known as the Hirfindahl-Hirschman Index (HHI) which is calculated by adding together the squared market shares of each company in an industry. The government sets limits that delineate an industry as "fairly concentrated," "highly concentrated," etc. that are based on various factors specific to that particular market.

68. Department of Justice, Antitrust Division, "Merger Guidelines," June 30, 1982, 47 FR 28493, www.lexisnexis.com (accessed December 29, 2009).

69. White, "Antitrust and Video Markets," 346.

70. *U.S. v. Columbia Pictures Industries, Inc., et al.*, 21.

71. Sobel, "Justice Department Opposition to Showtime," www.lexisnexis.com.

72. Ibid.

73. Department of Justice, Antitrust Division, "Merger Guidelines," June 30, 1982.

74. Smith, "U.S. Will Fight Pay-TV Merger by Film Studios," 1.

75. Tony Schwartz, "Hollywood Debates HBO Role in Film Financing," *New York Times*, July 7, 1982, C19.

76. Department of Justice Press Release, Friday August 12, 1983, AT 202–633–2016, page 2.

77. Department of Justice Memos dated October 14, October 17, and November 10, 1983, File # 60–211037–65.

78. The three companies were partners until 1987, when Time withdrew, leaving MCA and Paramount co-owners of the channel.

79. Figures from "The 1980s: A Reference Guide to Motion Pictures, Television, VCR and Cable," *The Velvet Light Trap* 27 (Spring 1991): 78–79.

80. Viacom Annual Report 1983, 2–3.

81. Salmans, "Hollywood Takes On HBO," D1.

82. Lindsey, "Home Box Office Moves in on Hollywood," 38.

83. Hilmes, "Pay Television: Breaking the Broadcast Bottleneck," 308.

84. Douglas Gomery, "Corporate Ownership and Control in the Contemporary US Film Industry," *Screen* 25, nos. 4-5 (July–October 1984): 61.

85. Vogel, *Entertainment Industry Economics*, 60.

86. Gomery, "Corporate Ownership and Control in the Contemporary US Film Industry," 67.

87. Stratford P. Sherman, "Coming Soon: Hollywood's Epic Shakeout," *Fortune*, April 30, 1984, 204+.

88. "Making the Most of Those Films in the Vault," *Business Week*, April 13, 1981, 147.

CHAPTER 2   1983–1985: BROADCAST AND THE BLUEPRINTS OF EMPIRES

1. The other majors at the time were Paramount, Universal, 20th Century–Fox, Columbia,

Warner Bros., MGM/UA, and (barely) Disney. Orion was the smallest of the big players, then considered a "mini-major."

2. Sandra Salmans, "Hollywood Takes On HBO," *New York Times*, February 2, 1983, D1.

3. "Debt Offerings Provide Look at Financial Workings," *Broadcasting* 107 (Oct 29, 1984): 55.

4. Stephen Prince, *A New Pot of Gold: Hollywood Under the Electronic Rainbow* (Berkeley: University of California Press, 2002), 31.

5. Sandra Salmans, "Tri-Star's Bid for Movie Stardom," *New York Times*, May 13, 1984, C1.

6. Ibid.

7. The original deal was structured to charge HBO approximately 30 percent of a film's cost in exchange for exclusive rights to show it on the pay-cable channel. However, that was renegotiated by late 1986 so that HBO began paying significantly less for these exclusive rights in 1987.

8. Robert Lindsey, "Home Box Office Moves in on Hollywood," *New York Times,* June 12, 1983, 32.

9. Thomas Whiteside, "Cable I," *The New Yorker*, May 20, 1985, 78.

10. Lionel S. Sobel, "Justice Department Opposition to Showtime/Movie Channel Merger Raises Questions about Tri-Star Pictures and other HBO Deals," *Entertainment Law Reporter* 5:2, July, 1983, www.lexisnexis.com.

11. Department of Justice Press Release, September 14, 1983, AT # 202–633–2016.

12. Ibid.

13. Ibid.

14. Tom Girard, "Pay TV Hasn't Hurt Growth of Theatrical B.O.," *Variety*, March 16, 1983, 1.

15. Stratford P. Sherman, "Coming Soon: Hollywood's Epic Shakeout," *Fortune*, April 30, 1984, 204+.

16. Lindsey, "Home Box Office Moves in on Hollywood," 31.

17. Jack Loftus, "Sales Miscues Spell CBS Blues," *Variety*, May 18, 1983, 1.

18. Prince, *A New Pot of Gold*, 52.

19. Aljean Harmetz, "Now Lawyers are Hollywood Superstars," *New York Times*, January 11, 1987, C1.

20. "Tying up Films on Cable," *The Economist*, July 30, 1983, 73.

21. *Star Wars*, as an astonishing comparison, opened in thirty-two theaters in May 1977. It took a month for the release to expand to 100 theaters. More relevant comparisons can be made with such films as *Raiders of the Lost Ark* (1981), which opened on 1,078 screens, *E.T.* (1982) on 1,101, *Bladerunner* (1982) on 1,295, *Return of the Jedi* (1983) on 1,002, and *Beverly Hills Cop* (1984) opened on just over 1,500 screens.

22. Although the film had a successful showing at the box office, it was not especially profitable for the studio because of all the money Tri-Star spent on production and marketing.

23. Ronald Grover, "Movies! Theaters! Cable! How Tri-Star Is Shaking up Tinseltown," *Business Week*, November 17, 1986, 140.

24. Prince, *A New Pot of Gold*, 31.

25. Kathryn Harris, "Tri-Star Looks for Hits on Road to Big Time," *Los Angeles Times*, July 5, 1987, D1.

26. Grover, "Movies! Theaters! Cable!," 140.

27. Harris, "Tri-Star Looks for Hits on Road to Big Time," D1.

28. Ibid.

29. Ronald Grover, "How *Ishtar* put Columbia on the Road to Merger," *Business Week*, November 30, 1987, 75.

30. Vincent left Coke shortly thereafter and became the commissioner of Major League Baseball in 1989.

31. Puttnam was fired immediately after Coke's September 1, 1987, announcement of the entertainment division's spin-off.

32. Ronald Grover, "At Columbia, Things Might Go Better with Tri-Star," *Business Week*, November 30, 1987, 74.

33. Ibid.

34. The price of this deal would go up significantly, as Sony took on more debt and also acquired the services of Peter Guber and John Peters from Warner Bros. In the end, the price tag was said to be closer to $6 billion.

35. The Radio Act also established a government agency—the Federal Radio Commission (FRC)—to allocate spectrum space and handle licensing based on these principles. The FRC evolved into the Federal Communications Commission (FCC) with the passage of the 1934 Communications Act.

36. See Erwin G. Krasnow and Jack N. Goodman, "The 'Public Interest' Standard: The Search for the Holy Grail," *Federal Communications Law Journal* 50 (1998): 605; and Philip M. Napoli, *Foundations of Communication Policy* (Creskill, NJ: Hampton Press, Inc., 2001), chap. 4, "The Public Interest."

37. Patricia Aufderheide, *Communications Policy and the Public Interest: The Telecommunications Act of 1996* (New York: Guilford Press, 1999), 13.

38. Ben Bagdikian, *The Media Monopoly*, 5th ed. (Boston: Beacon Press, 1997), xxxiii. For other historical and theoretical perspectives on the loss of the "public" in the public interest, see, for example, the work of Robert W. McChesney, including *The Problem of the Media* (New York: Monthly Review Press, 2004); Thomas Streeter, *Selling the Air* (Chicago: University of Chicago Press, 1996); Robert Britt Horwitz, *The Irony of Regulatory Reform* (New York: Oxford University Press, 1989); and Aufderheide, *Communications Policy and the Public Interest*.

39. Horwitz, *The Irony of Regulatory Reform*, 21.

40. Mark Hertsgaard, *On Bended Knee: The Press and the Reagan Presidency* (New York: Farrar Straus Giroux, 1988), 180.

41. "The Bittersweet Chairmanship of Mark S. Fowler," *Broadcasting*, February 18, 1985, 42.

42. Merrill Brown, "FCC Chief Tells Cable Meeting He'll Scrap the Rules," *Washington Post*, June 1, 1981, 3.

43. John Wilke, Mark Vamos, and Mark Maremont, "Has the FCC Gone Too Far?" *Business Week*, August 5, 1985, 48.

44. Mark S. Fowler and Daniel L. Brenner, "A Marketplace Approach to Broadcast Regulation," *Texas Law Review* 60, no. 2 (1981–1982): 209–210.

45. Ibid.

46. Rushworth M. Kidder, "FCC's Fowler: Free Market 'Ideologue' or Free-Speech Champion?" *Christian Science Monitor*, May 20, 1985, 1.

47. Caroline E. Mayer, "FCC Chief's Fears," *Washington Post*, February 6, 1983, K6.

48. "The Bittersweet Chairmanship of Mark S. Fowler," 1.

49. Hertsgaard, *On Bended Knee*, 181.

50. The newly established "12–12–12" law additionally contributed to the substantial increase in advertising ratings and station prices, as these perceived values skyrocketed along with demand.

51. Alex Ben Block, *Outfoxed* (New York: St. Martin's Press, 1990), 125.

52. Wilke, Vamos, and Maremont, "Has the FCC Gone Too Far?" 48.

53. J. Fred MacDonald, *One Nation Under Television* (Chicago: Nelson-Hall, 1990), 186.

54. Jack Loftus, "Nets Lose FCC Compromise," *Variety*, August 10, 1983, 1+.

55. Comments of the Staff of the Bureau of Economics of the Federal Trade Commission before the Federal Communications Commission, in re Review of the Prime Time Access Rule, MM Docket No. *94–123*, March *7, 1995.* http://www.ftc.gov/be/v950003.shtm.

56. MacDonald, *One Nation Under Television*, 181.

57. Kathryn Harris, "Lights! Camera! Regulation!" *Fortune*, September 4, 1995, 86.

58. Mara Einstein, *Media Diversity: Economics, Ownership, and the FCC* (Hillsdale, NJ: Lawrence Erlbaum Associates, 2004), 77.

59. Quoted in Stephen H. Klitzman, "More than a Fight Between the Very Rich and the Very Wealthy: The Impact of the Internet on the Media Consolidation and Ownership Debate," *CommLaw Conspectus* 15, no. 2 (2007): 616.

60. "The Lobbyists," *Broadcasting*, February 25, 1985.

61. Hugh Sidey, "The Presidency: The Troika That Worked," *Time*, June 3, 1985, http://www.time.com/time/magazine/article/0,9171,957794,00.html (accessed August 13, 2010).

62. Correspondence from Jack Valenti to Edwin Meese, James Baker, and Michael Deaver, June 14, 1982, Reagan Presidential Library Files.

63. Correspondence from Jack Valenti to Mark Fowler, June 1, 1982, Reagan Presidential Library Files.

64. "The Lobbyists," *Broadcasting*, February 25, 1985.

65. Ibid.

66. "Down to the Wire on Fin-Syn," *Broadcasting*, October 24, 1983, 27.

67. Memo from Chris DeMuth, Office of Policy Development, January 26, 1983, Folder 189128 OFOA 858, Reagan Presidential Library Files.

68. Correspondence from Governor Pete Wilson to President Ronald Reagan, September 28, 1983, Folder 189128 OFOA 858, Reagan Presidential Library Files.

69. Correspondence from Charlton Heston to Ronald Reagan, September 14, 1983, Folder 189128 OFOA 858, Reagan Presidential Library Files.

70. Author interview with Jack Valenti, March 30, 2000, Washington, D.C.

71. Merrill Brown, "FCC Chief Called to Oval Office," *Washington Post*, October 4, 1983, D7.

72. Memorandum to John D. Dingell, Chairman of Committee on Energy and Commerce from Subcommittee on Oversight and Investigations Staff, February 3, 1984, page 12, Reagan Presidential Library Files.

73. Ibid., 5–6.

74. Statement of Senator Pete Wilson, "Competition in Television Production Act," Senate

Committee on Commerce, Science, and Transportation Hearings, Subcommittee on Communications, November 2 and 4, 1983, S. Hearing 98–583, 9.

75. Author interview with Jack Valenti.

76. Reagan had been a client of MCA since 1940. As SAG president, he was able to help MCA tighten its tentacles around Hollywood talent. This eventually ended with the Supreme Court's 1962 decision forcing MCA out of the talent business after they bought Universal. In the meantime, MCA had helped Reagan rise above the ranks of B-movie actors to become a more prominent screen presence through numerous TV appearances and character roles.

77. Einstein, *Media Diversity*, 88.

78. I am marking the beginning of this regulatory posture at the FCC's first major ruling on cable policy, the *Carter Mountain Transmission Corp.* case of 1962. This ruling favored the needs and concerns of local broadcasters over CATV. Also of note is the FCC's *First Report and Order,* which was adopted in 1965 and again placed the needs of the broadcast industry ahead of the developing cable medium.

79. There were some exceptions to this policy—the prohibition was for stations and systems *within* the same market, so those broadcast entities that wanted to own cable systems outside of their own markets were permitted to do so. See National Telecommunications and Information Administration (NTIA), *Video Program Distribution and Cable Television: Current Policy Issues and Recommendations.* NTIA Report 88–233, June 1988, 61.

80. Ted Turner, with Bill Burke, *Call Me Ted* (New York: Grand Central Publishing, 2008), 200.

81. Nick Davatzes Interview, Cable Center Oral History Archive, http://www.cablecenter. org/education/library/oralHistoryDetails.cfm?id=76 (accessed May 12, 2009).

82. For more discussion of this merger, see Raymond E. Joslin Interview, Cable Center Oral History Archive, http://www.cablecenter.org/education/library/oralHistoryDetails. cfm?id=127 (accessed May 12, 2009).

83. National Telecommunications and Information Administration, *Video Program Distribution and Cable Television: Current Policy Issues and Recommendations*, 70.

84. There were actually only three-hour original programming segments that were presented four times daily.

85. Gerald Clarke and Peter Ainslie, "Cable's Cultural Crapshoot," *Time*, October 26, 1981, http://www.time.com/time/printout/0,8816,925022,00.html (accessed May 12, 2009).

86. Tony Schwartz, "CBS Cable Starts Cultural TV Service Tonight," *New York Times*, October 12, 1981, C17.

87. Frank Lipsius, "CBS Cable Casualty," *Financial Times*, September 28, 1982, 13.

88. See Joslin Interview and John J. O'Connor, "TV View; What Lies Ahead for Cultural Programming," *New York Times*, December 12, 1982, http://www.nytimes.com/1982/12/12/arts/tv-view-what-lies-ahead-for-cultural-programming.html?&pagewanted=all (accessed May 12, 2009).

89. This was also the same year that Disney cancelled the *Walt Disney* show on CBS (which had run for twenty-nine years on various networks, with numerous names). It is said that the reason for canceling the show was the fear that it would compete with the newly launched Disney Channel on cable. While the panic over "cannibalizing revenue

streams" is usually discussed in the era of Internet distribution, the cancellation of *Walt Disney* demonstrates that this industry fear goes back to the time when cable was ascending at the expense of broadcast. See James Stewart, *Disney War* (New York: Simon & Schuster, 2005), 76–77.

CHAPTER 3   1984-1986: OUTSIDERS MOVING IN–

MURDOCH AND TURNER

1. Neil Chenoweth, *Virtual Murdoch: Reality Wars on the Information Superhighway* (London: Secker & Warburg, 2001), 40; and "Rupert Murdoch and the Art of War," *New York Magazine*, December 23, 2009, http://nymag.com/daily/intel/2009/12/murdochs_ rivalries.html (accessed December 28, 2009).

2. Patrick R. Parsons and Robert M. Frieden, *The Cable and Satellite Television Industries* (Boston: Allyn & Bacon, 1998), 48.

3. When broadcast licenses were first being issued, the FCC barred any individual or organization convicted of monopolistic practices from owning one. While no formal declaration was ever issued, the film studios were still in the throes of the *Paramount* case and Warner Bros.—which had intended to construct its own network—had its application suspended in 1948 because of the "freeze." Subsequently, the major studios were forced to watch as the radio networks solidified their position and power in the broadcast industry over the next four years. For more on this issue, see Michele Hilmes, *Hollywood and Broadcasting: From Radio to Cable* (Chicago: University of Illinois Press, 1990), 116–120; Douglas Gomery, "Failed Opportunities: The Integration of the U.S. Motion Picture and Television Industries," *Quarterly Review of Film Studies* (Summer 1984): 219–227; and Christopher Anderson, *Hollywood TV* (Austin: University of Texas Press, 1994), 40–45.

4. Quoted in Ken Auletta, *Three Blind Mice* (New York: Random House, 1991), 38.

5. Ibid., 32.

6. Robert Britt Horwitz, *The Irony of Regulatory Reform* (New York: Oxford University Press, 1989), 278.

7. Alex Ben Block and Lucy Autrey Wilson, eds., *George Lucas's Blockbusting* (New York: HarperCollins, 2010), 607.

8. For an excellent account of this period in broadcasting, see Auletta, *Three Blind Mice*.

9. James Walker and Douglas Ferguson, *The Broadcast Television Industry* (Boston: Allyn & Bacon, 1998), 35.

10. James F. Peltz, "General Electric Agrees to Buy RCA for $6.28 Billion," *The Associated Press*, December 12, 1985, accessed December 28, 2009 via Lexis-Nexis.

11. The purpose of these guidelines is to describe the general principles and specific standards normally used by the Justice Department in analyzing mergers. They also served as an update to the 1982 Guidelines. Revisions in the Merger Guidelines are written from time to time to reflect any significant changes in enforcement policy or to clarify aspects of existing policy. (*1984 Merger Guidelines*, U.S. Department of Justice.) The 1984 Guidelines were revised and updated eight years and two presidential administrations later by the 1992 Merger Guidelines under President Clinton.

12. William F. Shughart, "Antitrust Policy in the Reagan Administration: Pyrrhic Victories?" in *Regulation and the Reagan Era*, ed. by Roger E. Meiners and Bruce Yandle (New York: Homes & Meier, 1989), 93.

13. Parsons and Frieden, *The Cable and Satellite Television Industries*, 58.

14. Matt Stump and Harry Jessell, "Cable: The First Forty Years," *Broadcasting* 115, no. 21 (November 21, 1988): 35+.

15. Auletta, *Three Blind Mice*, 386.

16. Thomas Streeter, *Selling the Air* (Chicago: University of Chicago Press, 1996), 179.

17. Ibid.

18. See Federal Communications Commission Cable Television Report and Order, 36 FCC 2d 143, 166 (1972).

19. Ken Auletta, "The Lost Tycoon," *The New Yorker*, April 23–30, 2001, 149.

20. "Ted Turner and CNN," *The Pop History Dig*, http://www.pophistorydig.com/?tag=ted-turner-cable-tv.

21. Auletta, *Three Blind Mice*, 283.

22. H. W. Brands, *Masters of Enterprise* (New York: The Free Press, 1999), 279.

23. Auletta, "The Lost Tycoon," 147.

24. Eric Guthey, "Ted Turner's Media Legend and the Transformation of Corporate Liberalism," *Business and Economic History* 26, no. 1 (1997): 192.

25. Robert Goldberg and Gerald Jay Goldberg, *Citizen Turner: The Wild Rise of an American Tycoon* (New York: Harcourt Brace & Company, 1995), 166.

26. Ibid., 194.

27. Brands, *Masters of Enterprise* (New York: The Free Press, 1999), 279.

28. Auletta, "The Lost Tycoon," 147.

29. Jimmie L. Reeves and Michael M. Epstein, "The Changing Face of Television," in *The Columbia History of American Television*, ed. Gary R. Edgerton (New York: Columbia University Press, 2007), 327–328.

30. Jeff Denberg, "Turner Assesses His Liabilities: Wife, Kids and Atlanta Hawks," *Variety*, March 2, 1983, 4, 358.

31. Subrata N. Chakravarty, "What New Worlds to Conquer?" *Forbes* 151, no. 1 (January 4, 1993): 82–87.

32. Quoted in "Neither Broke nor Broken: The Ever-Resurgent Ted Turner," *Broadcasting*, August 17, 1987, 46+.

33. Auletta, "The Lost Tycoon," 149.

34. Correspondence between Ed Turner, VP CNN/Washington, and Larry Speakes, Deputy Press Secretary, January 5, 1982, and White House memo for Fred Fielding from Larry Speakes, January 15, 1982, accessed at David H. Waller Collection, OA 12685, Box 9, Folder: CNN—Documents for Possible Supplementation to Document Production, Reagan Presidential Library.

35. USDC for Northern District of GA, Summons in Civil Action, May 11, 1981, Civil Action File No. C81–871A, pages 8–9. Accessed at David H. Waller Collection, OA 12684–12685, Box 7, Folder: CNN Pleadings [1 OF 4] OA 12685, Reagan Presidential Library.

36. Note to David R. Gergen, Assistant to the President for Communications, from Ed Turner, Sr. VP, CNN, January 27, 1983, accessed at David H. Waller Collection, Box 10, Folder: CNN-General [1 of 6], Reagan Presidential Library.

37. Goldberg, *Citizen Turner*, 277.

38. "Ted Turner Becomes King of Cable News," *Newsweek*, October 24, 1983, 108.

39. "Sole Survivor," *Time*, October 24, 1983, http://www.time.com/time/magazine/article/0,9171,926295,00.html.

40. Ted Turner, *Call Me Ted* (New York: Grand Central Publishing, 2008), 200.

41. "Ted Turner's Quantum Leap," *Broadcasting* 110 (March 31, 1986): 40+.

42. See Turner, *Call Me Ted*, 226.

43. Goldberg, *Citizen Turner*, 338.

44. Turner, *Call Me Ted*, 230.

45. Adam Paul Weisman, "As Ted Turns: Odyssey of the Cable Mogul," *The New Republic*, December 29, 1986, 16+.

46. Goldberg, *Citizen Turner*, 344.

47. Weisman, "As Ted Turns," 16; and Patrick Sheridan, "Turner's Turn on CBS and MGM," *Broadcasting*, November 4, 1991, 48.

48. "Neither Broke nor Broken: The Ever-Resurgent Ted Turner," 46.

49. *Variety*, April 10, 1985, 3.

50. Hilmes, *Hollywood and Broadcasting: From Radio to Cable*, 194–195.

51. Bill Powell, Vern E. Smith, and Peter McAlevey, "Turner's Windless Sails," *Newsweek* February 9, 1987, 46.

52. Jane Galbraith, "Turner Keeps Pics, Drops Rest of MGM," *Variety*, June 11, 1986, 3.

53. Scott Ticer, et al., "Captain Comeback," *Business Week*, July 17, 1989, 98.

54. Brands, *Masters of Enterprise*, 287.

55. Auletta, "The Lost Tycoon," 151.

56. Stump and Jessell, "Cable: The First Forty Years," 35+.

57. "Neither Broke nor Broken: The Ever-Resurgent Ted Turner," 46.

58. Goldberg, *Citizen Turner*, 393.

59. Richard Zoglin, "Heady Days Again for Cable," *Time*, May 30, 1988, 52.

60. Ticer, "Captain Comeback," 98.

61. Ibid.

62. Jim McConville, et al., "The Insider," *Electronic Media*, November 22, 1999, 8.

63. Douglas Gomery, "Vertical Integration, Horizontal Regulation: The Growth of Rupert Murdoch's US Media Empire," *Screen* 27, nos. 3–4 (May–August 1986): 79.

64. Thomas Moore, "Citizen Murdoch Presses for More," *Fortune*, July 6, 1987, 90+.

65. Prince, *A New Pot of Gold*, 47.

66. Tino Balio, "Introduction to Part II," *Hollywood in the Age of Television* (Boston: Unwin Hyman, 1990), 276.

67. Prince, *A New Pot of Gold*, 48.

68. Once Davis realized how entrenched Murdoch was in the deal for Metromedia and how far he would go to achieve his goals, the price for the remaining "half" of Fox went up $75 million. See Gomery, "Vertical Integration, Horizontal Regulation: The Growth of Rupert Murdoch's US Media Empire," 82.

69. Ibid., 80.

70. Chenoweth, *Virtual Murdoch*, 41. Also see Section 310(b)(4) of the 1934 Communications Act.

71. "The End of the Warner-Murdoch War," *Broadcasting*, March 26, 1984, 59+.

72. Greenmail is a type of blackmail (with "greenbacks") that forces a company to buy shares of its own stock back at a premium price when it is being threatened with a hostile takeover by a major shareholder.

73. Laurie Thomas and Barry R. Litman, "Fox Broadcasting Company, Why Now?" *Journal of Broadcasting and Electronic Media* 35, no. 2 (Spring 1991): 140.

74. Mark N. Vamost et al., "Rupert Murdoch's Big Move," *Business Week*, May 20, 1985, 104+.

75. "Charting the Future: The Prospects for a Fourth Network," *Broadcasting*, February 10, 1986, 36+.

76. Thomas and Litman, "Fox Broadcasting Company, Why Now?" 146.

77. Ibid., 141.

78. Michael Schrage and David A. Vise, "Murdoch, Turner Launch Era of Global Television," *Washington Post*, August 31, 1986, H1.

79. Moore, "Citizen Murdoch," 90+.

80. Quoted in Thomas and Litman, "Fox Broadcasting Company, Why Now?" 148.

81. Auletta, *Three Blind Mice*, 197.

82. John Caldwell, *Televisuality* (New Brunswick, NJ: Rutgers University Press, 1995), 257–258.

83. William Shawcross, *Murdoch* (New York: Simon and Schuster, 1992), 216.

84. Over forty properties were grandfathered in when the rules were adopted. The rules have been under some review, court-ordered stay, or deliberation since FCC Chair Michael Powell's attempt to change them in 2003. See John Eggerton, "Third Circuit Lifts Stay on Media-Ownership Rules," *Multichannel News*, March 23, 2010. http://www.multichannel.com/article/450642-Third_Circuit_Lifts_Stay_On_Media_Ownership_Rules_.php. Accessed June 25, 2010.

85. See Kim I. Mills, "Murdoch Gains Time from Court, Support from Reagan," *Associated Press*, January 26, 1988, www.lexisnexis.com (accessed August 4, 2009).

86. "Fox Wins 18.5 Hour, One Year Fin-Syn Waiver," *Broadcasting*, May 7, 1990, 28.

87. "Matsushita Takeover of MCA Could Make WWOR-TV Attractive Target," *Communications Daily*, September 28, 1990, 1.

88. Geraldine Fabrikant, "Paramount to Buy Option for Control of TV Stations," *New York Times*, January 18, 1989, D1.

89. The network's status as a bona-fide success was solidified after adding twelve more affiliates in 1994, mostly defectors from CBS after Fox acquired the rights to NFL football.

90. Marc Gunther, "Will Fox Ever Grow Up?" *Fortune*, March 4, 2002, 137+.

91. Albert Moran, ed., *Film Policy: International, National and Regional Perspectives* (New York: Routledge, 1996), 13.

92. For one of the best analyses of Murdoch's challenges in expanding his global empire, particularly in relation to his ventures in East Asia, see Michael Curtin, "Murdoch's Dilemma, or 'What's the Price of TV in China?'" *Media, Culture & Society* 27, no. 2 (2005): 155–175.

CHAPTER 4   1986-1988: GOLDEN ERA REDUX

1. These theaters were divorced from Paramount and became United Paramount Theaters (UPT). The new UPT, led by Leonard Goldenson, merged with ABC in 1953. This decision was a contested one that took the FCC nearly two years to approve. In addition to representing an early, if limited, combination of film and television interests, historian Timothy White has also noted in his study of this merger that "each of the two major companies involved had been created to remedy restraints of trade—UPT was the result of Paramount Inc.'s divorce of exhibition from production and distribution, and ABC was the former Blue network, sold by RCA in response to the FCC's *1941 Report on Chain Broadcasting*" (22). For more on the UPT-ABC merger and the fascinating hearings surrounding the FCC decision, see Timothy White, "Hollywood on (Re)Trial: The American Broadcasting–United Paramount Merger Hearing," *Cinema Journal* 31, no. 3 (Spring 1992): 19–36.

2. *United States v. Loew's Inc. et al.*, Memorandum of Warner and Universal in Opposition to Motions to Vacate Paramount Decrees, 87–273 (S.D.N.Y. May 15, 1979), 3.

3. Because the case was actually litigated, the judgments are not consent decrees in the traditional sense. Only the details of relief were negotiated and entered into by consent.

4. Justice Edmund L. Palmieri, Memorandum Opinion, *United States v. Paramount Pictures, Inc., et al.*, August 28, 1980, p. 4–5.

5. See *United States v. Loew's Inc.*, 1969 Trade Cas. p. 72, 767 (S.D.N.Y. 1969).

6. Michael Conant, "The Paramount Decrees Reconsidered," in *The American Film Industry*, ed. Tino Balio (Madison: University of Wisconsin Press, 1985), 557, see n. 169.

7. National General, Corp. is also referred to as National Theaters Corp. or National Theaters, Inc. The name of National Theaters was changed several times and by 1973, the name was National General Theaters, Inc.

8. *United States v. Loew's Inc.*, 1969 Trade Cas. p. 72, 767 (S.D.N.Y. 1969).

9. Conant, "The Paramount Decrees Reconsidered," 557.

10. Ultimately, National General Corp. would sell all of its theater assets—including 240 theaters—to the Mann Theatre Corp. in California for an estimated $67.5 million in 1973 (Conant, "The Paramount Decrees Reconsidered," 567). The name of the theater company would subsequently be changed to Mann Theatres. The deal held that Mann Theatres would not be subject to the decree obligations of National General because the acquisition was an "asset transaction" only.

11. *United States v. Loew's Inc.*, 1969 Trade Cas. p. 72, 767 (S.D.N.Y. 1969).

12. Thomas Schatz, "The Return of the Hollywood Studio System," in *Conglomerates and the Media* (New York: The New Press, 1997), 83.

13. *Variety*, August 4, 1982, 28.

14. *United States v. Loew's Inc.*, Memorandum in Support of Motion to Vacate Decree, 87–273 (S.D.N.Y. February 26, 1979).

15. Ibid., 18.

16. Gerald F. Phillips, "The Recent Acquisition of Theatre Circuits by Major Distributors," *The Entertainment and Sports Lawyer* 5, no. 3 (Winter 1987): 13.

17. *United States v. Loew's Inc.*, Memorandum of Warner and Universal in Opposition to Motions to Vacate Paramount Decrees, 87–273 (S.D.N.Y. May 15, 1979), 2.

18. This was customary; since many consent decrees did not contain a built-in expiration date, they were required to be revisited in order to ascertain whether their objectives have been accomplished. Also, there is some measure of potential obsolescence in any decree, as market structure, technology and industries are constantly changing. Now, it is more standard for consent decrees to run ten years or less.

19. Bernard M. Hollander, "Fifty-eight Years in the Antitrust Division, Oral History," Washington D.C., American Antitrust Institute, 2008: 199.

20. "Vertical Restraints Guidelines," U.S. Department of Justice, Antitrust Division, January 23, 1985.

21. Thomas J. Maier, "Judge vs. Justice Dept," *Newsday*, December 16, 1988, 61.

22. Department of Justice Press Release, February 6, 1985, 2.

23. *Variety*, January 8, 1986, 13.

24. "Gotham Screen Power Shift in the Air," *Variety*, May 15, 1985, 3, 44.

25. *Variety*, March 13, 1985, 3.

26. Ibid.

27. See H.R. 4247, 99th Cong., 2d Sess. (1986).

28. Joseph F. Brodley, "Current Topics in Antitrust," *Hastings Law Journal* 38, no. 547 (March 1987): 11.

29. Ibid., 2.

30. *U.S. v. Loew's Inc. et al.* (S.D.N.Y., Order. August 27, 1986).

31. Kathryn Harris, "Tri-Star Looks for Hits on Road to Big Time," *Los Angeles Times*, July 5, 1987, D1.

32. Paul J. Tagliabue, "Developments 1986–87: Antitrust Developments in Sports and Entertainment," *Antitrust Law Journal* 56 (August 10/12, 1987): 4.

33. One of the conditions of the temporary order for interim relief was that Loew's and/or Tri-Star would have to file a motion for permanent relief no later than March 31, 1987. (See Phillips, "Recent Acquisition," 13.)

34. Tagliabue, "Developments," 4.

35. Ibid.

36. Will Tusher, "Gov't Vows to Uphold Consent Decrees," *Variety*, June 10, 1987, 3.

37. Ibid, 23.

38. Ibid.

39. See Herbert Hovenkamp, "Antitrust Policy after Chicago," Michigan Law Review 84 (1985): 213–284; and Keith Conrad, "Media Mergers: First Step in a New Shift of Antitrust Analysis?" *Federal Communications Law Journal* 49, no. 675 (April 1997): 11.

40. *Variety*, January 14, 1987, 3.

41. Ibid., 1.

42. Ibid., 3.

43. Thomas Guback, "The Evolution of the Motion Picture Theater Business in the 1980s," *Journal of Communication* 37, no. 2 (Spring 1987): 74.

44. In March 1987 Coca-Cola turned around and resold Reade theaters to Cineplex Odeon for $32.5 million, capitalizing on the exhibition craze and making a tidy profit. See *Variety*, March 25, 1987, 3.

45. Tom Girard, "MCA Buys a Half Interest in Cineplex Odeon," *Variety*, May 14, 1986, 14.

46. Will Tusher, "Distribution's Theater Buys Near Peak," *Variety*, January 7, 1987, 24.

47. Jaime Hubbard, *Public Screening: The Battle for Cineplex Odeon* (Toronto: Lester & Orpen Dennys Ltd., 1990), 38.

48. Tusher, "Distribution's Theater Buys Near Peak," 7.

49. All information from *Variety* and Phillips, "Recent Acquisition," n.1, 20–21.

50. Coke and Columbia experienced a difficult year in 1987, resulting in the sale of the Reade circuit to Cineplex Odeon in June.

51. *Variety*, December 30, 1987, 3.

52. Stephen Prince, *A New Pot of Gold: Hollywood Under the Electronic Rainbow, 1980–1987* (Berkeley: University of California Press, 2002), 88.

53. A. D. Murphy, "Par Repeats as King of B.O.," *Variety*, January 6, 1988, 1. Buena Vista (Disney) was second with 14 percent and Warner Brothers came in third with 13 percent.

54. *Variety*, November 25 1987, 6.

55. Paul Farhi, "Columbia to Buy Most of Roth's Local Theaters," *Washington Post*, August 2, 1988, CI.

56. Palmieri Opinion, *US v. Loew's Inc., et al.*, 705 F.Supp. 878 (S.D.N.Y. 1988).

57. Ronald Grover, "Suddenly Wall Street Stops Going to the Movies," *Business Week*, June 1, 1987, 112.

58. *U.S. v. Loew's Inc., et al.*, S.D.N.Y. 705 F.Supp. 878; 1988–2 Trade Cas. (CCH).

59. *U.S. v. Loew's Inc., et al.*, S.D.N.Y., 882 F.2d 29 (2nd Cir. 1989), 33.

60. Will Tusher, "Gov't Official Says WCI's Buy-In of Theaters Won't Hinder Trade," *Variety*, December 30, 1987, 17. However, this is incorrect, since, as noted above, Paramount was never barred from owning theaters.

61. *U.S. v. Loew's Inc., et al.*, 705 F.Supp. 878 (S.D.N.Y. 1988).

62. Ibid.

63. *U.S. v. Loew's Inc., et al.*, 882 F.2d 29 (S.D.N.Y. 1989), 31.

64. *U.S. v. Loew's Inc., et al.*, 705 F.Supp. 878 (S.D.N.Y. 1988).

65. Ibid.

66. Ibid.

67. Ibid.

68. Ibid.

69. Aljean Harmetz, "Hollywood Seeks Control of Outlets," *New York Times*, March 3, 1986, DI.

70. Tom Girard, "MCA Buys A Half Interest in Cineplex," *Variety*, May 14, 1986, 28.

71. *Variety*, November 5, 1986, 7.

72. Howard S. Abramson, "Garth Drabinsky's Coming Attractions," *Washington Post*, March 9, 1987, FI; and Hubbard, *Public Screening*, 37.

73. Hubbard, *Public Screening*, 63; and Barry Litman, *The Motion Picture Mega-Industry* (Boston: Allyn & Bacon, 1998), 116.

74. Will Tusher, "NATO Wants Distribs Out of Exhibition," *Variety*, March 19, 1986, 3.

75. "NATO Embraces Chain-Owning Distribs," *Variety*, August 14, 1986, 5.

76. *Variety*, November 5, 1986, 7.

77. Tusher, "Gov't Official Says WCI's Buy-In of Theaters Won't Hinder Trade," 17.

78. Hubbard, *Public Screening*, 89.

79. Kathryn Harris, "General Cinema More Wall St. than Hollywood," *Los Angeles Times*, August 11, 1985, G6.

80. Benjamin Compaine and Douglas Gomery, *Who Owns the Media?*, 3rd ed. (Hillsdale, NJ: Lawrence Erlbaum Associates, 2000), 387.

81. *Variety*, October 29, 1986, 46. This is often attributed, or blamed on, Cineplex Odeon and Garth Drabinsky's strategy to lock up market share regardless of prices. The 1985 purchase of the Plitt circuit sparked a dramatic increase in the price of theaters and Drabinsky/Cineplex would be denounced for years because of their role in driving up costs.

82. *Variety*, June 18, 1986, 3.

83. *Variety*, February 26, 1986, 3; and November 27, 1985, 3.

84. *Variety*, October 29, 1986, 46.

85. MPAA, *1996 U.S. Economic Review.*

86. Ibid.

87. Tusher, "Distribution's Theater Buys Near Peak," 24.

88. *Variety*, January 14, 1987, 7.

89. Tusher, "Distribution's Theater Buys Near Peak," 24.

90. Aljean Harmetz, "Hollywood Seeks Control of Outlets," *New York Times*, March 3, 1986, D1.

91. See *United States v. Loew's Incorporated, et al.*, 882 F.2d 29 (2nd Cir. 1989).

92. Ibid.

93. See *United States v. Loew's Incorporated, et al.*, 783 F.Supp. 211 (S.D.N.Y. 1992).

94. Hollander, "Fifty-eight Years in the Antitrust Division, Oral History," 234.

95. "War Continues; NCTA Reloads and Fires More Antitrust Claims at Hollywood," *Communications Daily*, April 8, 1987, 4.

96. *Variety*, February 25, 1987, 1. It should also be noted that there was a concurrent decline in drive-in, porn, and repertory theaters that added to the woes of the independent exhibitors at this time.

97. Aljean Harmetz, "Now Showing, Survival of the Fittest," *New York Times*, October 22, 1989, B1.

98. Charles Acland, "Theatrical Exhibition: Accelerated Cinema," in *The Contemporary Hollywood Film Industry*, ed. Paul McDonald and Janet Wasko (Malden, MA: Blackwell, 2008), 85.

99. *United States v. Loew's Inc.*, Memorandum in Support of Motion to Vacate Consent Decree, 87–273 (S.D.N.Y. February 26 1979), 8–9.

CHAPTER 5   1989-1992: BIG MEDIA WITHOUT FRONTIERS

1. Michael Schrage and David A. Vise, "Murdoch, Turner Launch Era of Global Television," *Washington Post*, August 31, 1986, H1.

2. "1991: Ted Turner," *Time*, January 6, 1992, http://www.time.com/time/subscriber/person-oftheyear/archive/stories/1991.html (accessed December 16, 2008).

3. Ibid.

4. National Cable & Telecommunications Association, Statistics: Basic Cable Subscribers, http://www.ncta.com/Statistic/Statistic/BasicSubs.aspx (accessed August 3, 2008).

5. Benjamin Compaine and Douglas Gomery, *Who Owns the Media?*, 3rd ed. (London: Lawrence Erlbaum Associates, 2000), 208.

6. Bill Carter, "With America Well Wired, Cable Industry Is Changing," *New York Times*, July 9, 1989, http://query.nytimes.com/gst/fullpage.html?res=950DE2D7113AF93A A35754C0A96F948260&sec=&spon=&pagewanted=all (accessed August 8, 2008). See also National Cable & Telecommunications Association, "Statistics: Basic Cable Subscribers" and "Statistics: Revenue from Customers," http://www.ncta.com/Statistic/Statistic/BasicSubs.aspx and http://www.ncta.com/Statistic/Statistic/RevenuefromCustomers.aspx (accessed August 3, 2008).

7. National Telecommunications and Information Administration (NTIA), *Video Program Distribution and Cable Television: Current Policy Issues and Recommendations*, 14 and National Cable & Telecommunications Association, "Statistics: Revenue from Customers and Total Advertising Revenue," http://www.ncta.com/Statistic/Statistic/RevenuefromCustomers.aspx and http://www.ncta.com/Statistic/Statistic/CableAdvertisingRevenue.aspx (accessed August 8, 2008).

8. National Telecommunications and Information Administration (NTIA), *Video Program Distribution and Cable Television: Current Policy Issues and Recommendations*, 11.

9. Compaine and Gomery, *Who Owns the Media?*, 221.

10. Patrick R. Parsons, *Blue Skies: A History of Cable Television* (Philadelphia: Temple University Press, 2008), 521.

11. For a more detailed look at these developments, see chapter 6 in Megan Mullen, *The Rise of Cable Programming in the United States* (Austin: University of Texas Press, 2003).

12. *Broadcasting*, November 23, 1987, 41–42.

13. Barbara Esbin and Adam Thierer, "Where Is the FCC's Annual Video Competition Report?" *Progress Snapshot,* The Progress and Freedom Foundation, Release 4.11, May 2008, http://www.pff.org/issues-pubs/ps/2008/ps4.11whereisFCCvidcompreport.html#ftn6 (accessed December 15, 2008).

14. The OTP (Office of Telecommunications Policy), which was established under President Nixon, was streamlined under President Carter, moved to the Department of Commerce and reborn in 1977 as the NTIA.

15. National Telecommunications and Information Administration, *Video Program Distribution and Cable Television: Current Policy Issues and Recommendations*, 3.

16. Ibid., 85.

17. Ibid., 63.

18. In the FCC's first formal regulations for cable television issued in 1966, cable was initially regulated in order to prevent any "adverse impact" on broadcasting, and the technology was defined as being supplementary to the existing broadcast system. See the FCC Second Report and Order, 2 FCC 2d 725 (1966).

19. See Applications of Tel. Companies for Section 214 Certificates for Channel Facilities, 21 F.C.C.2d 307, 325 (1970).

20. These rules were progressively chipped away at by various legal decisions, mergers, and shifting regulatory policies. Ultimately, the 1996 Telecommunications Act would allow telcos to be involved in cable ownership. For more on this, see Robert Britt Horwitz, *The Irony of Regulatory Reform* (New York: Oxford University Press, 1989).

21. These particular hearings took place before the Subcommittee on Communications, Committee on Commerce, Science, and Transportation on June 14, 21, and 22, 1989.

22. Senate Committee on Commerce, Science, and Transportation, *Media Ownership: Diversity and Concentration*, 101st Cong., June 14, 1989, S. Hearing, 101–357.

23. Mark Robichaux, *Cable Cowboy: John Malone and the Rise of the Modern Cable Business* (Hoboken, NJ: John Wiley & Sons, 2002), 85.

24. John Malone Interview, Cable Center Oral History Archive, http://www.cablecenter. org/education/library/oralHistoryDetails.cfm?id=142 (accessed December 26, 2008).

25. Testimony of Gene Kimmelman, Senate Committee on Commerce, Science, and Transportation, *Oversight of Cable TV*, 101st Cong., November 16, 1989, S. Hearing, 101–464, 301.

26. Testimony of John Malone, Senate Committee on Commerce, Science, and Transportation, *Oversight of Cable TV*, 163.

27. Testimony of John Malone, Senate Committee on Commerce, Science, and Transportation, *Oversight of Cable TV*, 152.

28. Tasneem Chipty, "Vertical Integration, Market Foreclosure, and Consumer Welfare in the Cable Television Industry," *American Economic Review* 91, no. 3 (June 2001): 428–453, http://www.jstor.org/stable/2677872 (accessed January 8, 2009).

29. For the most detailed look at the events surrounding the Time-Warner merger, see Connie Bruck, *Master of the Game* (New York: Simon & Schuster, 1994).

30. For an insightful discussion on the corporate holdings of Time-Warner and their relationship to *Batman*, refer to Eileen Meehan, "'Holy Commodity Fetish, Batman!': The Political Economy of a Commercial Intertext," in *The Many Lives of the Batman*, ed. Roberta Pearson and William Uricchio (New York: Routledge, 1991), 47–65.

31. For more on this aspect of the merger, see Thomas Schatz, "The Return of the Hollywood Studio System," in *Conglomerates and the Media*, ed. Erik Barnouw, et al.(New York: The New Press, 1997), 73–106.

32. The companies had actually been bitter enemies competing in the cable landscape during the late 1970s; the two were often going after the same local franchises and Warner repeatedly outmaneuvered Time to win the contracts.

33. See Mullen, *The Rise of Cable Programming in the United States*,106–107; and Gary Edgerton, "A Brief History of HBO," in *The Essential HBO Reader*, ed. Gary Richard Edgerton and Jeffrey P. Jones (Lexington: University Press of Kentucky, 2008), 1–2.

34. At the time of the merger, they also owned Warner Bros. studios, Warner Bros. Television, Warner Bros. International, and Warner Home Video (essentially 100 percent of their distribution), the most successful record company in America (with the Warner Brothers, Atlantic, Elektra labels, and their many subsidiaries), music publishing, movie theaters, and broadcasting interests.

35. Information on holdings taken from Annual Reports.

36. See Bruck, *Master of the Game*, 236, 246–248.

37. John Dempsey, "Warners' TV Revs Leave Par's in the Dust," *Variety*, June 14–20, 1989, 4.

38. Meehan, "'Holy Commodity Fetish, Batman!,'" 51.

39. Lester Bernstein, "Time Inc. Means Business," *New York Times*, February 26, 1989, Section 6, 22.

40. Statement of Steven J. Ross, House Committee on the Judiciary, *Time Warner Merger:*

Competitive Implications, House of Representatives, 101st Cong., First Session, March 14, 1989, 7.

41. Richard Gold, "No Bigness Like Show Bigness," *Variety*, June 14–20, 1989, 1+.

42. For a more detailed discussion of Paramount's transformation, see Stephen Prince, *A New Pot of Gold: Hollywood Under the Electronic Rainbow* (Berkeley: University of California Press, 2002), 60–64.

43. George Lucas, "The Paramount Import of Becoming Time-Warner—World Market Is the Last Crusade," *Wall Street Journal*, July 13, 1989, 1, www.wallstreetjournal.com (accessed November 23, 2008).

44. Richard Gold, "Time Inc. Rebuffs Par's Sweetened Bid; Remains Intent on Warner Acquisition," *Variety*, June 28–July 4, 1989, 5.

45. See Bruck, pp. 272–276.

46. Richard Gold, "Par's Block Looks Like a Bust as Court Backs Time Directors' Stand," *Variety*, July 19–25, 1989, 1.

47. Testimony of Steven J. Ross, *Time Warner Merger: Competitive Implications*, 42.

48. Time Warner Annual Report 1990, 12–13.

49. Prince, *New Pot of Gold*, 46.

50. Elizabeth Guider, "Alien Invasion of Hollywood more like 'Lost in Space,'" *Variety*, November 8, 1989, 1.

51. Bill Powell, "What Japan Will Buy Next," *Newsweek*, November 11, 1991, http://www.newsweek.com/id/127322 (accessed August 8, 2009).

52. Arnold S. Wolfe and Suraj Kapoor, "The Matsushita Takeover of MCA: A Critical, Materialist, Historical, and First Amendment View," *Journal of Media Economics* 9, no. 4 (1996): 3.

53. Rod Carveth, "The Reconstruction of the Global Media Marketplace," *Communication Research* (December 1992): 712.

54. Geraldine Fabrikant, "Movie Companies Hot on Wall St.," *New York Times*, October 27, 1988, D8.

55. Madelon DeVoe Talle, "Investors Confront a New Europe," *New York Times*, September 24, 1989, Section 6, 21; and Steven Greenhouse, "The Television Europeans Love, and Love to Hate," *New York Times*, August 13, 1989, Section 4, 24.

56. Carveth, "Global Media Marketplace," 712.

57. Testimony of Jack Valenti, House Committee on Energy and Commerce, Subcommittee on Telecommunications and Finance, *Television Broadcasting and the European Community*, 101st Cong., First Session, July 26, 1989, 34.

58. Opening Remarks by Edward J. Markey, House Committee on Energy and Commerce, Subcommittee on Telecommunications and Finance, *Television Broadcasting and the European Community*, 101st Cong., 1st sess., July 26, 1989, 1.

59. Ibid., 2.

60. Testimony of Jack Valenti, *Television Broadcasting and the European Community*, 35.

61. Jack Valenti, "Television with Manacles," *Washington Post*, December 1, 1989, A27.

62. For an excellent discussion of the dispute between the United States and the EC over this matter, see Duncan H. Brown, "Citizens or Consumers: U.S. Reactions to the European Community's Directive on Television," *Critical Studies in Media Communication* 8 (1991):1–12.

63. Testimony of Robert Maxwell, House Committee on Energy and Commerce, Subcommittee on Telecommunications and Finance, *Television Broadcasting and the European Community*, 101st Cong., First Session, July 26, 1989, 48–49.

64. Charles Acland, *Screen Traffic: Movies, Multiplexes, and Global Culture* (Durham, NC: Duke University Press, 2003): 135.

65. Jim Robbins, "And What about Cinamerica, WB/Par Joint Circuit?" *Variety*, June 14–20, 1989, 5.

66. Robert Marich, "Foreign Profits Buoyed Industry," *The Hollywood Reporter*, March 18, 1992, www.lexisnexis.com (accessed August 4, 2009).

67. Testimony of J. Richard Munro, Chairman and CEO, Time, Inc., House Committee on the Judiciary, *Time Warner Merger: Competitive Implications*, 101st Cong., First Session, March 14, 1989, 9.

68. Richard W. Stevenson, "Lights! Camera! Europe!" *New York Times*, February 6, 1994, Section 3, 1.

69. Quoted in Steven Greenhouse, "The Television Europeans Love, and Love to Hate," *New York Times*, August 13, 1989, Section 4, 24.

70. Testimony of Robert Maxwell, *Television Broadcasting and the European Community*, 86.

71. Daniel Pedersen, "A 'Grenade' Aimed at Hollywood," *Variety*, October 16, 1989, 58.

72. The park was renamed Disneyland Paris in October 1994.

73. Richard Stevenson, "In Hollywood, Big Just Gets Bigger," *New York Times*, October 14, 1990, F 12, www.lexisnexis.com (accessed November 7, 2008).

74. See Timothy Havens, *Global Television Marketplace* (London: BFI, 2006), 28.

75. David Kissinger, "MCA Deal May Seal Finsyn Fate," *Variety*, December 3, 1990, 98.

76. Stephen J. Cannell et al., "Lifting Restraints on TV Networks Would Kill Competition," *New York Times*, May 6, 1990, Section 4, 22, http://www.nytimes.com/1990/05/06/opinion/1-lifting-restraints-on-tv-networks-would-kill-competition-016590.html (accessed August 16, 2009).

77. Testimony of Robert C. Wright, President and CEO, NBC, Inc., Senate Committee on Commerce, Science, and Transportation, *Media Ownership: Diversity and Concentration*, 101st Cong., June 22, 1989, 426.

78. Ibid., 427.

79. The networks were now allowed to acquire financial interest in prime-time programming, but there was a somewhat cumbersome thirty-day, two-step process. Networks could negotiate license agreements for a pilot but were then forced to wait thirty days before bidding on the show's syndication rights. For an extraordinarily detailed and original account of the entire lifespan of fin-syn, see Mara Einstein, *Media Diversity: Economics, Ownership, and the FCC* (Hillsdale, NJ: Lawrence Erlbaum Associates, 2004).

80. *United States Court of Appeals for the Seventh Circuit, Schurz Communications, Inc., et al. v. Federal Communications Commission and United States of America*, 982 F.2d 1043 (7th Cir. 1992).

81. Dennis Wharton, "FCC Chairman Sikes Psyches Out," *Variety*, December 14, 1992, 26.

82. See FCC Second Report and Order, 23 FCC 2d 816 (1970).

83. David Kelly, "White House: Cross Owner Ban Should Go," *Hollywood Reporter*, May 15, 1992, www.lexisnexis.com (accessed August 19, 2009).

84. Paul Farhi, "FCC Takes First Step Toward Letting Broadcast Networks Buy Cable Systems," *Washington Post*, August 5, 1988, F1.

85. According to the new rules, the networks could own cable systems when the network–cable combination did not exceed 10 percent of homes passed by cable nationwide and 50 percent of cable homes in a local market. The local restrictions did not apply, however, if there was competition in the local market.

86. For an excellent history of retransmission consent, see Charles Lubinsky, "Reconsidering Retransmission Consent: An Examination of the Retransmission Consent Provision (47 U.S.C. § 325(b)) of the 1992 Cable Act," *Federal Communications Law Journal* 49, no. 1 (November 1996), http://www.law.indiana.edu/fclj/pubs/v49/no1/lubinsky.html.

87. Parsons, *Blue Skies*, 599–600.

88. William M. Kunz, *Culture Conglomerates* (Lanham, MD: Rowman & Littlefield Publishers, Inc., 2007), 170, 174.

89. "FCC Caps MSO Channel Ownership," *Variety*, October 4, 1993, 32.

90. Patrick R. Parsons, "Horizontal Integration in the Cable Television Industry: History and Context," *Journal of Media Economics* 16, no. 1 (2003): 26.

91. John Huey and Andrew Kupfer, "What that Merger Means for You," *Fortune*, November 15, 1993, http://money.cnn.com/magazines/fortune/fortune_archive/1993/11/15/78609/index.htm (accessed October 25, 2008).

92. Edmund L. Andrews, "The Media Business; A Cable Vision (Or Nightmare): 500 Channels," *New York Times*, December 2, 1992, http://query.nytimes.com/gst/fullpage.html?res=9E0CE3DA133AF930A35751C1A964958260&ec=&spon=&pagewanted=all (accessed July 27, 2008).

93. Quoted in Richard Gold, "Intense Propaganda Fight Marks Par vs. WCI War," *Variety*, June 28–July 4, 1989, 4.

CHAPTER 6   1993–1995: THE LAST MILE

1. The "last mile" is a term that refers to the final stage of delivery from the telecommunications or cable service provider to the paying customer at home.

2. Brooks Boliek, "FCC prophet Duggan Says Cable 'Holy War' Must End," *Hollywood Reporter*, March 23, 1993, www.lexisnexis.com (accessed September 16, 2009).

3. National Telecommunications and Information Administration (NTIA), *Globalization of the Mass Media*, Executive Summary, Special Publication 93–290, Washington, D.C., 1993.

4. Linda Keslar, "Fed Study: Showbiz is Global-est," *Variety*, January 18, 1993, 91.

5. The Uruguay Round of GATT was a seven-and-a-half-year multilateral trade negotiation involving 123 countries and issues ranging from agriculture to banking to intellectual property. It began in September 1986 and concluded in April 1994. GATT had been an umbrella organization overseeing world trade since 1948, and 1994 marked the final year before its duties were formally overtaken by the WTO (World Trade Organization).

6. Michael Williams and Chris Fuller, "France Adamant on GATT," *Variety*, October 18, 1993, 41.

7. Chris Fuller, "GATT Sez Scat to H'Wood," *Daily Variety*, December 1, 1993, 1.

8. Leonard Klady, "Scorsese, Spielberg in Euro GATT Spat," *Variety*, November 8, 1993, 7.

9. Ibid.

10. Ibid.

11. Information on TCI and Disney from Richard W. Stevenson, "Lights! Camera! Europe!," *New York Times*, February 6, 1994, sec. 3, 1.

12. Statistics about Warner Bros., NBC, and HBO from Christian Moerk and Michael Williams, "Moguls Swat GATT-Flies," *Variety*, November 8, 1993, 62; and Louise McElvogue, "HBO Takes a More Global View of TV," *Los Angeles Times*, May 2, 1995, http://articles.latimes.com/1995–05–02/business/fi-61471_1_pay-television (accessed October 8, 2009).

13. Mark Schapiro, "The Cable Guise: When Communism Crashed, HBO Rewrote the Rules," *The Nation*, November 29, 1999, 20.

14. Financial services, telecommunications, and shipping were also either left out or included in a very limited manner.

15. Michael Williams, et al., "GATT Spat Wake-Up on Yank Market Muscle," *Variety*, December 27, 1993–January 2, 1994, 45.

16. The original Baby Bells were Ameritech, Bell Atlantic, BellSouth, NYNEX, Pacific Telesis, Southwestern Bell, and U S West. All have since been acquired by other companies.

17. See *United States v. American Tel. and Tel. Co.*, 552 F. Supp. 131 (D.D.C. 1982).

18. See Applications of Tel. Companies for Section 214 Certificates for Channel Facilities, 21 F.C.C.2d 307, 325 (1970).

19. Dennis Wharton, "FCC Gives Bell Atlantic OK to go Hollywood," *Variety*, January 16–22, 1995, 33.

20. Patrick R. Parsons, *Blue Skies: A History of Cable Television* (Philadelphia: Temple University Press, 2008), 601.

21. National Telecommunications and Information Administration (NTIA), *Globalization of the Mass Media*, 124, n. 390.

22. Parsons, *Blue Skies*, 572.

23. See Telephone Company–Cable Television Cross-Ownership Rules, 7 FCC Rcd 5781 (1992) (Second Report and Order, Recommendation to Congress, and Second Further Notice of Proposed Rulemaking).

24. Kathryn Harris, "Reordering the Cable Universe," *Los Angeles Times*, July 25, 1993, D1.

25. Quoted in Christopher H. Sterling, Phyllis W. Bernt, and Martin B. H. Weiss, *Shaping American Telecommunications* (Hillsdale, NJ: Lawrence Erlbaum Associates, 2006), 242.

26. Paul Noglows and John Dempsey, "The Big Fish Are Biting," *Variety*, October 25, 1993, 1.

27. John Huey and Andrew Kupfer, "What that Merger Means for You," *Fortune*, November 15, 1993, http://money.cnn.com/magazines/fortune/fortune_archive/1993/11/15/78609/index.htm (accessed October 25, 2008).

28. John Dempsey, "Cloud Over Cable May Rain Networks," *Variety*, February 28–March 6, 1994, 1.

29. Ibid.

30. Other than Fox, of course, which had a waiver due to the FCC's desire to spur competition with a fourth broadcast network in 1986. For more on this exception, see chapter 3.

31. United States Court of Appeals for the Seventh Circuit, *Schurz Communications, Inc., et al. v. Federal Communications Commission and United States of America*, 982 F.2d 1043 (7th Cir. 1992).

32. Dennis Wharton, "Webs Revive War over Finsyn," *Variety*, February 19, 1993, 30.

33. Mara Einstein, *Media Diversity: Economics, Ownership, and the FCC* (Hillsdale, NJ: Lawrence Erlbaum Associates, 2004), 169–170.

34. See "Evaluation of the Syndication and Financial Interest Rules," Federal Communications Commission Second Report and Order, 8 FCC Rcd 3282 (1993).

35. Dennis Wharton, "Fin-Syn Voted Out," *Variety*, July 18–24, 1994, 22.

36. See *United States v. National Broadcasting Co., Inc.*, 449 F. Supp. 1127 (C.D. Cal. 1978). See also *United States v. American Broadcasting Co., Inc.*, 45 Fed. Reg. (1980); *United States v. CBS, Inc.*, 45 Fed. Reg. (1980).

37. *United States of America v. National Broadcasting Company, Inc.*, 842 F. Supp. 402; 1993.

38. "Department of Justice Will Not Change Position on 'Fin-Syn,'" Press Release 93–285, Anti-Trust Division, United States Department of Justice, September 23, 1993.

39. See Joe Flint, "Cable Webs' Future Muddled," *Variety*, February 21–27, 1994, 179.

40. *Capital Cities/ABC, Inc. v. FCC*, 29 F.3d 309 (7th Cir. 1994). *Capital Cities/ABC, Inc. et al., v. Federal Communications Commission and United States of America*, 29 F.3d 309; (U.S. App. July 12, 1994 Decided.) www.lexisnexis.com (accessed October 24, 2009).

41. Dennis Wharton, "Fin-Syn Rules Prepared for Burial," *Variety*, March 6–12, 1995, 45.

42. Steve McClellan, "Fin Syn," *Broadcasting and Cable* (January 24, 2000): 30+.

43. Michael Schneider and Josef Adalian, "Nets Get It Together," *Variety*, May 22–28, 2000, 15.

44. Maria Elena Fernandez, "TV New Series Report Card," *Los Angeles Times*, May 22, 2009, http://latimesblogs.latimes.com/showtracker/2009/05/tv-new-series-report-card.html (accessed November 2, 2009).

45. Jay Greene, "Sumner's Star Rises," *Variety*, February 21–27, 1994, 1.

46. Paul Noglows, "It's Official: Viacom Inc." *Variety*, July 11–17, 1994, 11.

47. See Paul C. Wieler, *Entertainment, Media, and the Law: Text, Cases, Problems* (St. Paul: West Group, 2002), 919.

48. Ken Auletta, *The Highwaymen* (New York: Harcourt Brace, 1998), 118.

49. Ibid., 131.

50. Frederick Wasser, *Veni, Vidi, Video* (Austin: University of Texas Press, 2001), 1.

51. Spelling had a significant library of its own, including *Little House on the Prairie*, *Dallas*, *Basic Instinct*, *Total Recall*, *Platoon*, and the *Rambo* trilogy.

52. See "Viacom-Par Merger: What's in It," *Variety*, February 21–27, 1994, 185.

53. Auletta, *The Highwaymen*, 61.

54. UPN was a joint venture between Paramount and Chris-Craft Industries.

55. MPAA, "U.S. Entertainment Industry: 2003 MPAA Market Statistics," 41 and MPAA, "U.S. Entertainment Industry: 2006 Market Statistics," 37.

56. For an excellent discussion of this aspect of the WB and UPN beginnings, see page 13 in Larry Collette and Barry R. Litman, "The Peculiar Economics of New Broadcast Network Entry: The Case of United Paramount and Warner Bros," *Journal of Media Economics* 10, no. 4 (2009): 3–22.

57. Joe Flint and Jim Benson, "WB, Par Weblets Square Off," *Variety*, January 2–8, 1995, 37.

58. The network had since moved on from their original audience, surprising many by outbidding CBS for the NFL rights in December 1993 and taking the NFL tradition away from the broadcast network that had hosted it for the last thirty-eight years straight. This completely stunned the television industry and signaled a new era for Fox, major league sports, and the broadcast industry as a whole. There were officially four major networks after this deal.

59. Bill Carter, "2 Would-Be Networks Get Set for Prime Time," *New York Times*, January 9, 1995, D6.

60. Time-Warner Annual Reports, 1990 and 1996.

61. Flint and Benson, "WB, Par Weblets Square Off," 37.

62. Collette and Litman, "Peculiar Economics," 8.

63. Steve McClellan, "Fin Syn," *Broadcasting and Cable*, January 24, 2000, 30+.

64. Gary Levin, "Weblets Worth Swim in Red Sea for Par, WB," *Variety*, November 18–24, 1996, 27.

65. Douglas Gomery, "Disney's Business History: A Reinterpretation," in *The Disney Discourse*, ed. Eric Smoodin (New York: Routledge, 1994), 80.

66. Tom Schatz, "The Return of the Studio System," in *Conglomerates and the Media*, ed. Erik Barnouw (New York: The New Press, 1997), 87–88.

67. See Alisa Perren, *Indie, Inc.* (Austin: University of Texas Press, forthcoming 2011). chap. 5.

68. Robert W. McChesney, "The Global Media Giants," *Extra!* (November/December 1997), http://www.fair.org/index.php?page=1402 (accessed November 24, 2009).

69. Roger Smith. "It's Only Money," *Daily Variety*, October 13, 1999, 15.

70. For extended discussion and analysis of this partnership, see Christopher Anderson, *Hollywood TV* (Austin: University of Texas Press, 1994).

71. Steve Lohr, "Steady Gains by New Media Pose a Threat," *New York Times*, August 2, 1995, D5.

72. Quoted in Janine Jaquet, "The Wages of Synergy," *The Nation*, December 20, 2001, http://www.thenation.com/doc/20020107/jaquet (accessed December 7, 2009).

73. Diane Mermigas, "Eisner Justifies ABC Purchase," *Electronic Media*, January 12, 1998, 46.

74. Ronald Grover, *The Disney Touch* (Chicago: Irwin, 1997), 287–288.

75. Even after selling KCAL for over $60 million in profit, Disney still retained a financial interest in it, as CapCities/ABC owned 14 percent of Young Broadcasting, the station group that bought KCAL. This did not trouble regulators. See Jim Benson, "KCAL's Young At Heart," *Daily Variety*, May 14, 1996, 1.

76. John Dempsey and Joe Flint, "Amid Dereg Anxiety, Cablers Talk Tall, Tilt Toward Tech," *Variety*, December 4–10, 1995, 27.

77. Joe Flint, "One Month that Shook the World," *Variety*, September 4–10, 1995, 33.

78. See Geraldine Fabrikant, "Turner Buying New Line and Castle Rock Film Companies," *New York Times*, August 18, 1993, http://www.nytimes.com/1993/08/18/business/turner-buying-new-line-and-castle-rock-film-companies.html (accessed November 28, 2009) and Alan Citron, "Turner Gets Nod to Buy New Line and Castle Rock Entertainment," *Los Angeles Times,* August 18, 1993, http://articles.latimes.com/1993-08-18/business/fi-25054_1_castle-rock-production (accessed November 28, 2009).

79. That purchase of the MGM library included many old Warner Bros. cartoons.

80. Peter Bart, "Time for a Ted Offensive," *Variety*, August 16, 1993, 1; and Martin Peersj et al., "Merger Puts Many Chiefs Under One Roof," *Variety*, September 25–October 1, 1995, 1.

81. John Greenwald and John Moody, "Hands Across the Cable," *Time*, October 2, 1995, 34.

82. FTC Press Release, "FTC Requires Restructuring of Time Warner/Turner Deal: Settlement Resolves Charges That Deal Would Reduce Cable Industry Competition," FTC File No. 961–0004, September 12, 1996, http://www.ftc.gov/opa/1996/09/timewarn.shtm (accessed November 29, 2009).

83. See Stanley M. Besen et al., "Vertical and Horizontal Ownership in Cable TV: Time Warner-Turner (1996)," in *The Antitrust Revolution*, 3rd ed., ed. John E. Kwoka and Lawrence J. White (New York: Oxford University Press, 1998), 452–475.

84. Separate Statement of Federal Trade Commission Chairman Pitofsky, and Commissioners Steiger and Varney In the Matter of Time Warner Inc., File No. 961–0004, http://www.ftc.gov/os/1996/09/twother.htm (accessed November 29, 2009).

85. Eric Pooley and John Moody, "The Third Man: John Malone," *Time*, October 2, 1995, 37.

86. While Time-Warner chose MSNBC, Fox filed a lawsuit to require the company to carry Fox News as well, and after messy dealings that included New York City Mayor Rudy Giuliani getting involved on behalf of Fox, the two parties eventually settled on terms that included Fox News being carried on Time Warner Cable. Information about the settlement comes from FTC Press Release, "FTC Requires Restructuring of Time Warner/Turner Deal: Settlement Resolves Charges That Deal Would Reduce Cable Industry Competition," FTC File No. 961–0004, September 12, 1996, http://www.ftc. gov/opa/1996/09/timewarn.shtm (accessed November 29, 2009).

87. See "Time Warner Widens," *Variety*, July 22–28, 1996, 67.

88. Michael Fleming and Timothy M. Gray, "Follies of '95," *Variety*, January 1–7, 1996, 4.

89. Dan Cox, "Studio on Steroids," *Variety*, October 2–8, 1995, 1.

90. See Anderson, *Hollywood TV*. Of course, many cinephiles would rightfully take issue with the notion of Turner's preserving cinema history, given Turner's position on colorizing classic black-and-white films. My point is more about visibility, and the fact that the strategic manner in which he exploited his holdings ultimately devoted countless cable hours to the exhibition of feature films.

91. Martin Peersj et al., "Merger Puts Many Chiefs Under One Roof," *Variety*, September 25–October 1, 1995, 1.

92. They were replaced by Thomas Bailey (R-VA), Jack Fields (R-TX), and Senator Larry Pressler (R-SD).

93. Dennis Wharton, "Telco Dereg May Hasten Consolidation," *Variety*, January 15–21, 1996, N1.

CONCLUSION   1996 AND BEYOND–THE POLITICAL ECONOMY
OF TRANSFORMATION

1. Reed E. Hundt, "The Hard Road Ahead: An Agenda for the FCC in 1997," Speech delivered December 26, 1996, excerpted in Patricia Aufderheide, *Communications Policy and the Public Interest* (New York: Guilford Press, 1999), 284.

2. Martin Peers and Dennis Wharton, "D.C. Greenlights Goliaths," *Variety*, February 5, 1996–February 11, 1996, 1.

3. For more extensive scholarly exploration of the Telecommunications Act and its ramifications, see Aufderheide, *Communications Policy and the Public Interest*; Nina B. Huntemann, "Policy and Culture in the Digital Age: A Cultural Policy Analysis of the US Commercial Radio Industry" (Ph.D. diss., University of Massachusetts, Amherst, 2005); Thomas G. Krattenmaker, "The Telecommunications Act of 1996," *Connecticut Law Review* 29, no. 1 (1996): 123–173; and Robert McChesney, *Rich Media, Poor Democracy* (New York: New Press, 1999).

4. Jon M. Garon, "Media & Monopoly in the Information Age: Slowing the Convergence at the Marketplace of Ideas," *Cardozo Arts & Entertainment Law Journal* 17, no. 491 (1999): 60–77.

5. There were many other deregulatory provisions in the Act related to content, licensing, rates, equipment, and other aspects of broadcast and telecommunications service, but those discussed here are the ones germane to the study of media ownership and convergence.

6. Brian L. Roberts, "The Greatest Story Never Told: How the 1996 Telecommunications Act Helped to Transform Cable's Future," *Federal Comm Law Journal* 58, no. 3 (June 2006): 571.

7. *Fox Television Stations, Inc. v. FCC*, 280 F.3d 1027, 1044 (D.C. Cir. 2002).

8. Other modified rules proposed included allowing cross-media ownership (newspapers and broadcasters) in the same local market, and allowing one company to own a daily newspaper plus three television and eight radio stations in the same market.

9. FCC Press Release, "Divided FCC Votes to Roll Back Media Merger Protections," June 2, 2003, http://fjallfoss.fcc.gov/edocs_public/attachmatch/DOC-235047A6.pdf.

10. For the most thorough and historically accurate accounting of the events around the proposed 2003 rule changes, see Robert McChesney, "Media Policy Goes to Main Street: The Uprising of 2003," *The Communication Review* 7, no. 3 (July 2004): 223–258.

11. Michael K. Powell, "The Public Interest Standard: A New Regulator's Search for Enlightenment," Speech before the American Bar Association, 17th Annual Legal Forum on Communications Law, Las Vegas, NV, April 5, 1998, http://www.fcc.gov/Speeches/Powell/spmkp806.html (accessed December 15, 2009).

12. S. Sutel, "Redstone: Age of the Media Conglomerate Is Over," *Associated Press*, July 8, 2005, http://www.forbes.com/associatedpress/feeds/ap/2005/07/08/ap2130170.html (accessed September 3, 2005).

13. Declan McCullagh, "AOL, Time Warner to Merge," *Wired*, January 10, 2000, http://www.wired.com/techbiz/media/news/2000/01/33531 (accessed December 19, 2009).

14. Other companies looking to distance themselves from corporate scandal followed suit, such as WorldCom changing its name in April of that same year to MCI (the name of its long-distance carrier), and cigarette maker Philip Morris changed its name to Altria Group.

15. "After the Divorce, AOL Faces Challenges," *New York Times,* December 10, 2009, http://www.nytimes.com/2009/12/11/business/11views.html (accessed December 14, 2009).

16. P. McClintock, "Merger Mystery," *Variety*, November 18, 2003, A1; and J. Consoli, "Dick Wolf Castigates TV Critics," July 26, 2005, http://www.mediaweek.com/mw/search/article_display.jsp?vnu_content_id=1000992089 (accessed September 3, 2005).

17. The proposed deal was for Comcast to own 51 percent of NBC Universal and GE to retain

49 percent of the company. As of this writing, the merger is undergoing extensive regulatory review. The new company is not expected to have any problems clearing that hurdle.

18. Meg James, "Comcast to Buy Control of NBC Universal in $30-billion Transaction," *Los Angeles Times*, December 4, 2009, http://articles.latimes.com/2009/dec/04/business/la-fi-ct-comcast4–2009dec04 (accessed June 28, 2010).

19. Georg Szalai, "Zucker Mum on Comcast Deal," *The Hollywood Reporter*, November 19, 2009, https://secure.vnuemedia.com/hr/content_display/television/news/e3if9obc 32271c417b821f33a93444f4525 (accessed December 20, 2009).

20. Claire Atkinson, "Comcast, G.E. Announce Deal on NBCU," *Broadcasting and Cable*, December 3, 2009, http://www.broadcastingcable.com/article/406948-Comcast_G_E_Announce_Deal_on_NBCU.php (accessed December 5, 2009).

21. For an original take on the tentpole concept, see Charles Acland, "*Avatar* as Technological Tentpole," *Flow*, January 22, 2010, http://flowtv.org/?p=4724.

22. Information in this section, including figures that were used to generate all charts, comes from numerous Annual Reports and SEC filings for Time (1988–1989), Time-Warner (1987–1997, 2008), Disney (1987–1995, 2008), News Corp. (1988, 1991–1996, 2008), Viacom (1987–1996, 2008) and GE (2008–2009).

23. Tim Arango, "Better-Than-Expected Profit is Reported by News Corp," *New York Times*, November 4, 2009, http://www.nytimes.com/2009/11/05/business/media/05news.html (accessed November 12, 2009).

24. Sam Schechner, Jeffrey McCracken, and Max Colchester, "Comcast, GE Set to Unwrap NBC Universal Pact," *Wall Street Journal*, December 3, 2009, B1.

25. Ithiel de Sola Pool, *Technologies of Freedom* (Cambridge, MA: Harvard University Press, 1983), 7.

26. Ibid., 8.

27. H. Peter Nesvold, "Communication Breakdown: Developing an Antitrust Model for Multimedia Mergers and Acquisitions," *Fordham Intellectual Property, Media & Entertainment Law Journal* 6, no. 781 (Spring 1996): 14.

28. Oliver Wendell Holmes, "The Profession of the Law," in *Collected Legal Papers* (New York: Harcourt, Brace and Howe, 1920), 29.

BIBLIOGRAPHY

In addition to these materials, I have also consulted and cited a significant number of corporate annual reports and SEC filings, as well as trade journal and popular press stories from publications including *Variety*, *Daily Variety*, *Hollywood Reporter*, *Broadcasting and Cable*, *New York Times*, *Washington Post*, and *Los Angeles Times*.

BOOKS AND ARTICLES

Acland, Charles. *Screen Traffic: Movies, Multiplexes, and Global Culture.* Durham, NC: Duke University Press, 2003.

———. "Theatrical Exhibition: Accelerated Cinema." In *The Contemporary Hollywood Film Industry*, ed. Paul McDonald and Janet Wasko, 83–105. Malden, MA: Blackwell, 2008.

Anderson, Christopher. *Hollywood TV.* Austin: University of Texas Press, 1994.

Aufderheide, Patricia. *Communications Policy and the Public Interest.* New York: Guilford Press, 1999.

Auletta, Ken. *The Highwaymen.* New York: Harcourt Brace, 1998.

———. *Media Man.* New York: W. W. Norton, 2004.

———. *Three Blind Mice.* New York: Random House, 1991.

Bagdikian, Ben. *The Media Monopoly.* 5th ed. Boston: Beacon Press, 1997.

Balio, Tino. "Adjusting to the New Global Economy: Hollywood in the 1990s." In *Film Policy: International, National and Regional Perspectives*, ed. Albert Moran, 23–38. New York: Routledge, 1996.

Barnes, David W. "Revolutionary Antitrust: Efficiency, Ideology, and Democracy." *University of Cincinnati Law Review* 58, no. 59 (1989), www.lexisnexis.com.

Besen, Stanley M., E. Jane Murdoch, Daniel P. O'Brien, Steven C. Salop, John Woodbury. "Vertical and Horizontal Ownership in Cable TV: Time Warner-Turner (1996)." In *The Antitrust Revolution*, 3rd ed., ed. John E. Kwoka and Lawrence J. White, 452–475. New York: Oxford University Press, 1998.

Block, Alex Ben. *Outfoxed.* New York: St. Martin's Press, 1990.

Block, Alex Ben, and Lucy Autrey Wilson, eds. *George Lucas's Blockbusting.* New York: HarperCollins, 2010.

Bork, Robert. *The Antitrust Paradox.* New York: The Free Press, 1993.

Brands, H. W. *Masters of Enterprise.* New York: The Free Press, 1999.

Brodley, Joseph F. "Current Topics in Antitrust." *Hastings Law Journal* 38, no. 547 (March 1987), http://www.lexisnexis.com/.

Brown, Duncan H. "Citizens or Consumers: U.S. Reactions to the European Community's Directive on Television." *Critical Studies in Media Communication* 8 (1991): 1–12.

Bruck, Connie. *Master of the Game.* New York: Simon & Schuster, 1994.

Cabinet Committee on Cable Communications. *Cable: Report to the President.* Washington, D.C., 1974.

Caldwell, John. *Televisuality.* New Brunswick, NJ: Rutgers University Press, 1995.

Carveth, Rod. "The Reconstruction of the Global Media Marketplace." *Communication Research* 9, no. 6 (December 1992): 705–723.

Chenoweth, Neil. *Virtual Murdoch: Reality Wars on the Information Superhighway.* London: Secker & Warburg, 2001.

Chipty, Tasneem. "Vertical Integration, Market Foreclosure, and Consumer Welfare in the Cable Television Industry." *American Economic Review* 91, no. 3 (June 2001): 428–453. http://www.jstor.org/stable/2677872.

Collette, Larry, and Barry R. Litman. "The Peculiar Economics of New Broadcast Network Entry: The Case of United Paramount and Warner Bros." *Journal of Media Economics* 10, no. 4 (2009): 3–22.

Compaine, Benjamin, and Douglas Gomery. *Who Owns the Media?.* 3rd ed. London: Lawrence Erlbaum Associates, 2000.

Conant, Michael. "The Paramount Decrees Reconsidered." In *The American Film Industry,* edited by Tino Balio, 537–573. Madison: University of Wisconsin Press, 1985.

Conrad, Keith. "Media Mergers: First Step in a New Shift of Antitrust Analysis?" *Federal Communications Law Journal* 49, no. 675 (April 1997), http://www.law.indiana.edu/fclj/pubs/v49no3.html.

Cook, David. *Lost Illusions: American Cinema in the Shadow of Watergate and Vietnam, 1970–1979.* Berkeley: University of California Press, 2000.

Curtin, Michael. "Murdoch's Dilemma, or 'What's the Price of TV in China?'" *Media, Culture & Society* 27, no. 2 (2005): 155–175.

De Sola Pool, Ithiel. *Technologies of Freedom.* Cambridge, MA: Harvard University Press, 1983.

Edgerton, Gary. "A Brief History of HBO." In *The Essential HBO Reader,* ed. Gary Richard Edgerton and Jeffrey P. Jones, 135–150. Lexington: University Press of Kentucky, 2008.

Einstein, Mara. *Media Diversity: Economics, Ownership, and the FCC.* Hillsdale, NJ: Lawrence Erlbaum Associates, 2004.

Fowler, Mark S. and Daniel L. Brenner. "A Marketplace Approach to Broadcast Regulation." *Texas Law Review* 60, no. 2 (1981–1982): 207–257.

Fox, Eleanor M. and Lawrence A. Sullivan. "Antitrust—Retrospective and Prospective: Where Are We Coming From? Where Are We Going?" *New York University Law Review* 62 (November 1987): 931–935.

Fox, Kraig G. "Paramount Revisited: The Resurgence of Vertical Integration in the Motion Picture Industry." *Hofstra Law Review* 21 (Winter 1992): 505–536.

Garon, Jon M. "Media & Monopoly in the Information Age: Slowing the Convergence at the Marketplace of Ideas." *Cardozo Arts & Entertainment Law Journal* 17 (1999): 491–621.

Geisst, Charles R. *Monopolies in America.* New York: Oxford University Press, 2000.

Goldberg, Robert, and Gerald Jay Goldberg. *Citizen Turner: The Wild Rise of an American Tycoon.* New York: Harcourt Brace, 1995.

Gomery, Douglas. "Corporate Ownership and Control in the Contemporary US Film Industry." *Screen* 25, nos. 4–5 (July-October 1984): 60–69.

———. "Disney's Business History: A Reinterpretation." In *The Disney Discourse,* ed. Eric Smoodin, 71–86. New York: Routledge, 1994.

———. "Failed Opportunities: The Integration of the U.S. Motion Picture and Television Industries." *Quarterly Review of Film Studies* (Summer 1984): 219–227.

——. "Vertical Integration, Horizontal Regulation: The Growth of Rupert Murdoch's US Media Empire." *Screen* 27, nos. 3–4 (May-August 1986): 78–86.

Grover, Ronald. *The Disney Touch*. Chicago: Irwin, 1997.

Guback, Thomas. "The Evolution of the Motion Picture Theater Business in the 1980s." *Journal of Communication* 37, no. 2 (Spring 1987): 60–77.

Guthey, Eric. "Ted Turner's Media Legend and the Transformation of Corporate Liberalism." *Business and Economic History* 26, no. 1 (Fall 1997): 184–199.

Harvey, David. *A Brief History of Neoliberalism*. New York: Oxford University Press, 2005.

Havens, Timothy. *Global Television Marketplace*. London: BFI, 2006.

Hertsgaard, Mark. *On Bended Knee: The Press and the Reagan Presidency*. New York: Farrar Straus Giroux, 1988.

Hilmes, Michele. *Hollywood and Broadcasting: From Radio to Cable*. Chicago: University of Illinois Press, 1990.

——. "Pay Television: Breaking the Broadcast Bottleneck." In *Hollywood in the Age of Television*, ed. Tino Balio, 297–318. Boston: Unwin-Hyman, 1990.

——. "Nailing Mercury: The Problem of Media Industry Historiography," in *Media Industries: History, Theory, Method*. Jennifer Holt and Alisa Perren, eds. Malden: Blackwell, 2009. Pp. 21–33.

Hollander, Bernard M. *Fifty-eight Years in the Antitrust Division 1949–2007, Oral History*. Edited Transcript. Washington, DC: American Antitrust Institute, 2008.

Holmes, Oliver Wendell. "The Profession of the Law." In *Collected Legal Papers*. New York: Harcourt, Brace and Howe, 1920.

Horwitz, Robert Britt. *The Irony of Regulatory Reform*. New York: Oxford University Press, 1989.

Hovenkamp, Herbert. *The Antitrust Enterprise: Principle and Execution*. Cambridge, MA: Harvard University Press, 2005.

——. "Antitrust Policy after Chicago." *Michigan Law Review* 84 (1985): 213–284.

Hubbard, Jaime. *Public Screening: The Battle for Cineplex Odeon*. Toronto: Lester & Orpen Dennys Ltd., 1990.

Huntemann, Nina B. "Policy and Culture in the Digital Age: A Cultural Policy Analysis of the US Commercial Radio Industry." Ph.D. diss., University of Massachusetts, Amherst, 2005.

Jenkins, Henry. "Convergence? I Diverge," *Technology Review* (June 2001), http://www.technologyreview.com/Biztech/12434/page1/.

Klitzman, Stephen H. "More than a Fight between the Very Rich and the Very Wealthy: The Impact of the Internet on the Media Consolidation and Ownership Debate." *CommLaw Conspectus* 15, no. 2 (2007): 615–627. http://commlaw.cua.edu/articles/v15/15_2/Book%20Review.pdf.

Krasnow, Erwin G., and Jack N. Goodman. "The 'Public Interest' Standard: The Search for the Holy Grail." *Federal Communications Law Journal* 50, no. 3 (1998): 605–635.

Krattenmaker, Thomas G. "The Telecommunications Act of 1996." *Connecticut Law Review* 29, no. 1 (1996): 123–173.

Kunz, William M. *Culture Conglomerates*. Lanham, MD: Rowman & Littlefield, 2007.

Levin, Harvey J. "Television's Second Chance: A Retrospective Look at the Sloan Cable Commission." *Bell Journal of Economics and Management* 4, no. 1 (Spring 1973): 343–365.

Litan, Robert E., and Carl Shapiro. "Antitrust Policy during the Clinton Administration." In *American Economic Policy in the 1990s*, ed. J. Frankel and P. Orszag, 435–485. Cambridge, MA: The MIT Press, 2002.

Litman, Barry. *The Motion Picture Mega-Industry.* Boston: Allyn & Bacon, 1998.

Lubinsky, Charles. "Reconsidering Retransmission Consent: An Examination of the Retransmission Consent Provision (47 U.S.C. § 325(b)) of the 1992 Cable Act." *Federal Communications Law Journal* 49, no. 1 (November 1996). http://www.law.indiana.edu/fclj/pubs/v49/no1/lubinsky.html

MacDonald, J. Fred. *One Nation Under Television.* Chicago: Nelson-Hall, 1990.

Mair, George. *Inside HBO.* New York: Dodd, Mead, 1988.

McChesney, Robert W. "The Global Media Giants." *Extra!* (November/December 1997_, http://www.fair.org/index.php?page=1402 (accessed November 24, 2009).

———. "Global Media, Neoliberalism, and Imperialism." *Monthly Review* 52, no. 10, http://www.monthlyreview.org/301rwm.htm.

———. *Rich Media, Poor Democracy.* New York: The New Press, 1999.

———. "Media Policy Goes to Main Street: The Uprising of 2003." *Communication Review* 7, no. 3 (July 2004): 223–258.

———. *The Problem of the Media.* New York: Monthly Review Press, 2004.

Meehan, Eileen. "'Holy Commodity Fetish, Batman!': The Political Economy of a Commercial Intertext." In *The Many Lives of the Batman*, ed. Roberta E. Pearson and William Uricchio, 47–65. New York: Routledge, 1991.

Motion Picture Association of America. "1999 U.S. Economic Review."

———. "U.S. Entertainment Industry: 2003 MPAA Market Statistics."

———. "U.S. Entertainment Industry: 2006 Market Statistics."

Mullen, Megan. *The Rise of Cable Programming in the United States.* Austin: University of Texas Press, 2003.

Napoli, Philip M. *Foundations of Communication Policy.* Cresskill, NJ: Hampton Press, Inc., 2001.

National Cable & Telecommunications Association. "Statistics: Revenue from Customers and Total Advertising Revenue." http://www.ncta.com/Statistic/Statistic/Revenuefrom-Customers.aspx and http://www.ncta.com/Statistic/Statistic/CableAdvertisingRevenue.aspx (accessed August 8, 2008).

———. "Statistics: Basic Cable Subscribers." http://www.ncta.com/Statistic/Statistic/BasicSubs.aspx (accessed August 3, 2008).

Nesvold, H. Peter, "Communication Breakdown: Developing an Antitrust Model for Multimedia Mergers and Acquisitions." *Fordham Intellectual Property, Media & Entertainment Law Journal* 6 (Spring 1996): 781–869.

Parsons, Patrick R. *Blue Skies: A History of Cable Television.* Philadelphia: Temple University Press, 2008.

———. "Horizontal Integration in the Cable Television Industry: History and Context." *Journal of Media Economics* 16, no. 1 (2003): 3–28.

Parsons, Patrick R., and Robert M. Frieden. *The Cable and Satellite Television Industries.* Boston: Allyn & Bacon, 1998.

Phillips, Gerald F. "The Recent Acquisition of Theatre Circuits by Major Distributors." *The Entertainment and Sports Lawyer* 5, no. 3 (Winter 1987): 1–23.

Pitofsky, Robert. "Introduction: Setting the Stage." In *How the Chicago School Overshot the Mark*, ed. Robert Pitofsky, 3–6. New York: Oxford University Press, 2008.

Powell, Michael K. "The Public Interest Standard: A New Regulator's Search for Enlightenment." Speech before the American Bar Association. 17th Annual Legal Forum on Communications Law, Las Vegas, NV. April 5, 1998 http://www.fcc.gov/Speeches/Powell/spmkp806.html (accessed December 15, 2009).

Prince, Stephen. *A New Pot of Gold: Hollywood Under the Electronic Rainbow, 1980–1987*. Berkeley: University of California Press, 2002.

Reeves, Jimmie L., and Michael M. Epstein, "The Changing Face of Television." In *The Columbia History of American Television*, ed. Gary R. Edgerton, 323–345. New York: Columbia University Press, 2007.

Roberts, Brian L. "The Greatest Story Never Told: How the 1996 Telecommunications Act Helped to Transform Cable's Future." *Federal Comm Law Journal* 58, no. 3 (June 2006): 571–580.

Robichaux, Mark. *Cable Cowboy: John Malone and the Rise of the Modern Cable Business*. Hoboken, NJ: John Wiley & Sons, 2002.

Schatz, Thomas. "The New Hollywood." In *Film Theory Goes to the Movies*, ed. Jim Collins, Hilary Radner, and Ava Preacher Collins, 8–36. New York: Routledge, 1993.

———. "The Return of the Hollywood Studio System." In *Conglomerates and the Media*, 73–106. New York: The New Press, 1997.

Shawcross, William. *Murdoch*. New York: Simon & Schuster, 1992.

Shughart, William F. "Antitrust Policy in the Reagan Administration: Pyrrhic Victories?" In *Regulation and the Reagan Era*, ed. Roger E. Meiners and Bruce Yandle, 89–103. New York: Homes & Meier, 1989.

Sloan Commission on Cable Communications. *On the Cable: The Television of Abundance*. New York: McGraw-Hill, 1971.

Sobel, Lionel S. "Justice Department Opposition to Showtime/Movie Channel Merger Raises Questions about Tri-Star Pictures and other HBO Deals." *Entertainment Law Reporter* 5, no. 2 (July 1983), www.lexisnexis.com.

Sterling, Christopher H., Phyllis W. Bernt, and Martin B. H. Weiss. *Shaping American Telecommunications*. Hillsdale, NJ: Lawrence Erlbaum Associates, 2006.

Stewart, James. *Disney War*. New York: Simon & Schuster, 2005.

Streeter, Thomas. *Selling the Air*. Chicago: University of Chicago Press, 1996.

Tagliabue, Paul J. "Developments 1986–87: Antitrust Developments in Sports and Entertainment." *Antitrust Law Journal* 56 (August 10/12, 1987): 341–359.

Thomas, Laurie, and Barry R. Litman. "Fox Broadcasting Company, Why Now?" *Journal of Broadcasting and Electronic Media* 35, no. 2 (Spring 1991): 139–157.

Turner, Ted. "My Beef with Big Media." *Washington Post*, April 7, 2004, http://www.washingtonmonthly.com/features/2004/0407.turner.html.

Turner, Ted, with Bill Burke. *Call Me Ted*. New York: Grand Central Publishing, 2008.

U.S. Department of Commerce, National Telecommunications and Information Administration (NTIA). *Globalization of the Mass Media*, Executive Summary, Special Publication 93–290. Washington, D.C., 1993.

———. *Video Program Distribution and Cable Television: Current Policy Issues and Recommendations*. NTIA Report 88–233, June 1988.

U.S. Department of Justice: Antitrust Division. Sherman Antitrust Act 15, U.S.C., http://www.usdoj.gov/atr/foia/divisionmanual/ch2.htm#a1.

———. "Merger Guidelines." June 30, 1982. 47 FR 28493.

———. "Vertical Restraints Guidelines." January 23, 1985.

United States House of Representatives, 101st Congress, First Session, Committee on Energy and Commerce, Subcommittee on Telecommunications and Finance. *Television Broadcasting and the European Community*, July 26, 1989.

United States House of Representatives. 101st Congress, First Session, Committee on the Judiciary. Hearings on *Time Warner Merger: Competitive Implications*, March 14, 1989.

United States Senate, 98th Congress, Senate Committee on Commerce, Science, and

Transportation. Hearing 98–583, Subcommittee on Communications, *Competition in Television Production Act*, November 2 and 4, 1983.

United States Senate, 101st Congress, Committee on Commerce, Science, and Transportation. Hearing 101–357, *Media Ownership: Diversity and Concentration*, June 14, 21 and 22, 1989.

United States Senate, 101st Congress, Committee on Commerce, Science, and Transportation. Hearing 101–464, *Oversight of Cable TV*, November 16, 1989.

Vogel, Harold. *Entertainment Industry Economics*. 4th Ed. New York: Cambridge University Press, 1998.

Walker, James, and Douglas Ferguson. *The Broadcast Television Industry*. Boston: Allyn & Bacon, 1998.

Wasser, Frederick. *Veni, Vidi, Video*. Austin: University of Texas Press, 2001.

Waterman, David, and Andrew A. Weiss. *Vertical Integration in Cable Television*. Cambridge, MA: The MIT Press, 1997.

White, Lawrence. "Antitrust and Video Markets: The Merger of Showtime and the Movie Channel as a Case Study." In *Video Media Competition*, ed. Eli M. Noam, 338–363. New York: Columbia University Press, 1985.

White, Timothy. "Hollywood on (Re)Trial: The American Broadcasting-United Paramount Merger Hearing." *Cinema Journal* 31, no. 3 (Spring 1992): 19–36.

Whiteside, Thomas. "Cable I." *The New Yorker*, May 20, 1985, 45–87.

———. "Cable II." *The New Yorker*, May 27, 1985, 43–73.

———. "Cable III." *The New Yorker*, May June 3, 1985, 82–105.

Wieler, Paul C. *Entertainment, Media, and the Law: Text, Cases, Problems*. St. Paul: West Group, 2002.

Wolfe, Arnold S., and Suraj Kapoor. "The Matsushita Takeover of MCA: A Critical, Materialist, Historical, and First Amendment View." *Journal of Media Economics*, 9, no. 4 (1996): 1–21.

Wyatt, Justin. *High Concept: Movies and Marketing in Hollywood*. Austin: University of Texas Press, 1994.

Zarkin, Kimberly A., and Michael J. Zarkin. *The Federal Communications Commission: Front Line in the Culture and Regulation Wars*. Westport, CT: Greenwood Press, 2006.

ARCHIVES

Cable Center Oral History Archive, "Nick Davatzes Interview." http://www.cablecenter.org/education/library/oralHistoryDetails.cfm?id=76 (accessed May 12, 2009).

———. "Raymond E. Joslin Interview." http://www.cablecenter.org/education/library/oralHistoryDetails.cfm?id=76 (accessed May 12, 2009).

———. "Paul F. Kagan Interview." http://www.cablecenter.org/education/library/oralHistoryDetails.cfm?id=128 (accessed July 27, 2008).

David H. Waller Collection, Ronald Reagan Presidential Library, Simi Valley, CA.

Ronald Reagan Presidential Library Files, Simi Valley, CA.

LEGAL AND REGULATORY COMMISSION MATERIALS

Applications of Tel. Companies for Section 214 Certificates for Channel Facilities, 21 FCC2d 307, 325 (1970).

Capital Cities/ABC, Inc. v. FCC, 29 F.3d 309 (7th Cir. 1994).

Capital Cities/ABC, Inc. et al., v. Federal Communications Commission and United States of America, 29 F.3d 309 (U.S. App. July 12, 1994 Decided.)

Comments of the Staff of the Bureau of Economics of the Federal Trade Commission before the Federal Communications Commission, in re Review of the Prime Time Access Rule, MM Docket No. 94–123, March 7, 1995. http://www.ftc.gov/be/v950003.shtm.

Evaluation of the Syndication and Financial Interest Rules, 8 FCC Rcd 3282 (1993) (Second Report and Order).

Federal Communications Commission Cable Television Report and Order, 36 FCC 2d 143, 166 (1972).

Federal Communications Commission Second Report and Order, 23 FCC 2d 816 (1970).

Federal Communications Commission Press Release. "Divided FCC Votes to Roll Back Media Merger Protections." June 2, 2003, http://fjallfoss.fcc.gov/edocs_public/attachmatch/DOC-235047A6.pdf.

Federal Trade Commission Press Release. "FTC Requires Restructuring Of Time Warner/Turner Deal: Settlement Resolves Charges That Deal Would Reduce Cable Industry Competition." FTC File No. 961–0004. September 12, 1996, http://www.ftc.gov/opa/1996/09/timewarn.shtm.

Fox Television Stations, Inc. v. FCC, 280 F.3d 1027, 1044 (D.C. Cir. 2002).

Home Box Office v. Federal Communications Commission, 567 F. 2d (D.C. Cir. 1977). Cert. denied, 434 U.S. 829 (1977).

Schurz Communications, Inc., et al. v. Federal Communications Commission and United States of America, 982 F.2d 1043 (7th Cir. 1992).

Telephone Company-Cable Television Cross-Ownership Rules, 7 FCC Rcd 5781 (1992) (Second Report and Order, Recommendation to Congress; and Second Further Notice of Proposed Rulemaking).

United States v. American Broadcasting Co., Inc., 45 Fed. Reg. (1980).

United States v. American Tel. and Tel. Co., 552 F. Supp. 131 (D.D.C. 1982).

United States v. CBS, Inc., 45 Fed. Reg. (1980).

United States v Columbia Pictures Industries, Inc.; Getty Oil Company; MCA, Inc.; Paramount Pictures Corporation; and *Twentieth Century-Fox Film Corporation* and *Premiere* 80 Civ 4438 (S.D.N.Y. 1980).

United States v. Loew's Inc., 1969 Trade Cas. p. 72, 767(S.D.N.Y. 1969).

United States v. Loew's Inc., Memorandum in Support of Motion to Vacate Decree, 87–273 (S.D.N.Y. February 26, 1979).

United States v. Loew's Inc. et al., Memorandum of Warner and Universal in Opposition to Motions to Vacate Paramount Decrees, 87–273 (S.D.N.Y. May 15, 1979).

United States v. Loew's Inc. 87–273 (S.D.N.Y. 1979).

United States v. Loew's Inc. et al. (S.D.N.Y., Order. August 27, 1986).

United States v Loew's Inc., et al., 705 F.Supp. 878. (S.D.N.Y. 1988).

United States v. Loew's Incorporated, et al., 882 F.2d 29 (2nd Cir. 1989).

United States v. Loew's Incorporated, et al., 783 F.Supp. 211 (S.D.N.Y. 1992).

United States v. National Broadcasting Co., Inc., 449 F. Supp. 1127 (C.D. Cal. 1978).

United States v. National Broadcasting Company, Inc., 842 F. Supp. 402; 1993

United States v. Paramount Pictures, Inc., et al., Justice Edmund L. Palmieri Memorandum Opinion, August 28, 1980.

INDEX

ABOUT THE AUTHOR

JENNIFER HOLT is an assistant professor of Film and Media Studies at the University of California, Santa Barbara. She is the co-editor of *Media Industries: History, Theory, and Method* (Blackwell, 2009). Her work has also appeared in journals and anthologies including *Film Quarterly*, *JumpCut*, and *Media Ownership: Research and Regulation*.

CPSIA information can be obtained at www.ICGtesting.com
264223BV00001B/55/P